Daniela Russ, James Stafford (eds.)
Competition in World Politics

Global Studies

Daniela Russ, born 1987, is a postdoctoral researcher at the University of Toronto and the University of Guelph, Canada. Trained as a historical sociologist in Berlin, New York, and Bielefeld, she is currently working on her first book, *Working Nature: Steam, Power, and the Making of the Energy Economy (1830-1980)*. Her research interests lie in historical epistemology, energy history and the critical theory of nature.

James Stafford, born 1988, is a postdoctoral researcher at the Research Training Group "World Politics" at Bielefeld University. A historian of Ireland, Britain and Europe since 1750, his first book, *The Case of Ireland: Commerce, Empire and the European Order 1776-1848*, is forthcoming with Cambridge University Press. He completed his Ph.D. in History at Cambridge University in 2016, and worked as a Lecturer in Modern History at St. Hugh's College, Oxford, before coming to Bielefeld in 2017.

Daniela Russ, James Stafford (eds.)

Competition in World Politics

Knowledge, Strategies and Institutions

[transcript]

We would like to record our thanks to Professor Mathias Albert, Dr. Mustafa Aksakal, Catharina Wessing, Kim Keller and Gaby Trompetero for their advice and assistance with the workshops and with this volume. We are also grateful for the participation and ideas supplied by other workshop attendees not represented in the volume: Jens Bartelson, Aziz Elmuradov, Sandra Holtgreve, Jutta Joachim, Marc Kidson, Iver B. Neumann, Karlson Preuss, Yasin Sunca and Gladys Vsquez.

This volume was made possible by funding from the German Federal Research Council (DFG) Research Training Group GRK 2225/1 'World Politics'. The Research Training Group hosted two workshops on 'Competition in World Politics' at Bielefeld University in 2018 and 2019, which produced the majority of the contributions included in this volume.

Bibliographic information published by the Deutsche Nationalbibliothek
The Deutsche Nationalbibliothek lists this publication in the Deutsche Nationalbibliografie; detailed bibliographic data are available in the Internet at http://dnb.d-nb.de

First published in 2021 by transcript Verlag, Bielefeld
© Daniela Russ, James Stafford (eds.)

Cover layout: Kordula Röckenhaus, Bielefeld
Cover illustration: James Gillray, 'The Plumb-pudding in danger, or, State epicures taking un petit souper' (1805), public domain.

Print-ISBN 978-3-8376-5747-0
PDF-ISBN 978-3-8394-5747-4
https://doi.org/10.14361/9783839457474
Buchreihen-ISSN: 2702-9298
Buchreihen-eISSN: 2703-0504

Contents

Competition and Emergent Technologies

Afterword

Introduction

Daniela Russ & James Stafford

Competition is a central organizing principle of modern world politics. Rankings provided by international organizations are predicated on an idea of permanent competition between states to achieve 'excellence' in a range of policy fields: from health and education to defense, inequality and business taxation. Beyond these explicitly organized forms of competition, states are often observed to be competing for less clearly defined goods: power (of the 'soft' and the 'hard' variety), wealth, attention, influence, and status. They are frequently joined (and challenged) in this by a range of other prominent global actors, such as charities, major world religions, multinational corporations, and armed insurgencies.

The relevance of competition to contemporary literatures on (among others) neoliberalism, US-China relations, trade, technological change, energy and security is largely taken for granted. Yet competition itself is rarely problematized or explored in its own right. This volume interrogates competition from an interdisciplinary perspective, combining history, sociology, legal studies and international relations. We believe that this interdisciplinary perspective is necessary to understand the multiplicity of forms and contexts in which concepts and practices of competition structure modern world politics.

In the mainstream IR literature, 'competition' or 'competitive behavior' is handled in one of three ways. Realist and neorealist scholars make competition an explicit focus of their research, counterposing 'competition' to 'cooperation' as one of two possible poles of state behavior under conditions of anarchy, insecurity and limited knowledge. Identifying the factors or situations that might lead states to emphasize 'competition' or 'cooperation' as part of their strategic posture is a primary concern for this scholarship (Glaser 2010). In Marxian and Bourdieusian approaches to IR, meanwhile, constant competition over economic, cultural, or symbolic 'capitals' is a prior assumption that is rarely interrogated in its own right (Wallerstein 2004; Bigo 2011). Liberal scholars of 'global governance' emphasize the importance of international organizations as spaces for cooperation, as well as for normative 'contestation' over underlying values (Wiener 2014).

In this volume, we seek to understand the complexes of knowledge, strategies and institutions that make it possible to conceive of world politics in terms of 'competition'. The contributions gathered here attempt to identify the concrete conditions under which competition has become a globally relevant political category. They explore the relationships between different forms of competition in past and contemporary world politics. And they analyze the responses of a range of actors to the specific forms of world-political competition generated by these shifting institutional and ideational contexts.

In the rest of this introduction, we identify and explain the main contours of this perspective on the role of competition in world politics. The next section explains the need to interrogate the concept of the competition not simply from the perspective of individual state behavior, but from that of "world politics" (Albert 2016)—understood as a historically conditioned social system—as a whole. The third section offers a short conceptual history of the term competition in European social and political theory of the eighteenth and nineteenth centuries, culminating in the classic sociological accounts of Simmel and Weber. We find that these are particularly useful for constructing a distinction—at once analytical and normative—between 'competition' and 'conflict'.

The fourth section then elaborates on this distinction by outlining a brief outline of the structural features and normative justifications for a world politics based on the idea of 'competition'. The fifth section pivots to a consideration of the uses of 'competition' within and beyond the discipline of IR, beginning with realist, neo-realist, constructivist and Bourdieuean discussions of the term before considering recent developments in international political economy and historical sociology. The sixth section takes this discussion forward to the present day, examining contemporary foreign policy discourse on the 'new strategic competition' and highlighting, in particular, the emergent paradigm of 'weaponized interdependence' as a way of understanding the strong technological and economic focus of competitive state practices in contemporary world policies. The final section then summarizes individual contributions to the volume, establishing how each helps us to construct a new understanding of 'competition' as a central category in modern world politics.

Contextualizing 'Competition'

Existing paradigms of international relations theory rarely address the question of 'competition' directly. As we discuss in further detail below, 'competition' is largely an assumed category for scholars who are primarily interested in predicting states' behavior in the international system. One recent survey of current research proposes a definition in precisely these behavioral terms:

> "Competition in the international realm involves the attempt to gain advantage, often relative to others believed to pose a challenge or threat, through the self-interested pursuit of contested goods such as power, security, wealth, influence, and status." (Mazarr et al. 2018: 5)

This definition rests on a rationalist and agent-centered account, in which competition appears as one possible strategy individual states can adopt for dealing with the innate insecurity of inter-state politics. From a more interdisciplinary perspective, however, it raises more questions than it answers. Economists, economic historians and sociologists have long investigated the *conditions* of competition in markets, culture and education (White 1981; Burt 2009; Uzzi 1997; Beckert 2009; Bürkert et. al. 2019). Markets, in particular, have increasingly been understood as a "social order", where "reciprocal expectations on the part of market actors ... have their basis in the social-structural, institutional and cultural embedding of markets" (Beckert 2009: 245). Merely focusing on individual agents and their relationship to a global balance of power forecloses, we suggest, a deeper investigation of the 'embeddedness' of competition in the socially and historically conditioned structures of "world politics" (Albert 2016; Buzan/Lawson 2015).

Despite the continued expansion of international political sociology and historical international relations as sub-fields in international studies, however, competition among actors in the international realm—whether for wealth, power, technological superiority, or prestige—has not been socially or historically contextualized to the same degree as other key ideas in international relations theory, such as anarchy (Keene 2001) or hierarchy (Zarakol 2017). To begin to address this gap, we propose two starting points for the investigation of competition in world politics.

The next section draws on the classic accounts of Georg Simmel and Max Weber to develop a sociological definition of 'competition' as a form of social interaction which can be analytically separated from conflict. We illustrate that this distinction carried a normative as well as an analytical implication by tracing its origins in a conceptual history stretching back to the European Enlightenment. In the following section, we explore the relevance of the competition/conflict distinction for a particular model of what we call 'world politics *as* competition'.

Conflict and Competition: from Hobbes to Simmel

IR-realists frequently claim an intellectual heritage going back to the seventeenth-century English philosopher Thomas Hobbes (Bull 1981; Malcolm 2002). For our purposes, however, what is most interesting about Hobbes' central political text, *Leviathan* (1651), is the prominent role enjoyed by the concept—indeed the very word—competition in his account of the "natural condition", a situation where, in the absence of coercive authority, agents must look to self-preservation as their sole legitimate imperative (Hobbes 1994: 79-88). For Hobbes, as for his subsequent interpreters, there was a simple analogy to be drawn between sovereigns in the international realm and individual subjects in the "state of nature" (Tuck 2001). Assertions about "man" were taken also to apply to "kings and person of sovereign authority" (Hobbes 1994: 78).

Both of these, he asserted, were condemned to live in a state of fundamental insecurity, defined by the constant possibility of conflict, of "war of every man against every man" (Hobbes 1994: 76). Hobbes attributed to human beings "a perpetual and restless desire of power after power, that ceaseth only in death": not because of endless greed or ambition, but because it was impossible to ensure present gains without striving to deny others their relative position. Thus "competition of riches, honour, command or other power, inclineth to contention, enmity and war; because the way of one competitor to the attaining of his desire is to kill, subdue, supplant or repel the other" (Hobbes 1994: 58). Scarcity, too, implied a short and direct road to violent conflict: "if any two men desire the same thing, which nevertheless they cannot both enjoy, they become enemies ... [and] endeavour to destroy one another" (Hobbes 1994: 75).

The Hobbesian equation of competition with conflict was based on a conception of human interaction in which material interdependence played little or no part in limiting possibilities for violence. Over the following two centuries, however, European thinkers concerned with the problem of 'sociability'—the question of how and why human beings had come to be able to live together—increasingly leaned on material interdependence as a possible explanation for how society was possible in the absence of constant divine intervention (Hont 2015; Robertson 2005). These new theories of 'commercial society'—pioneered most influentially by the Scottish philosopher and jurist Adam Smith—were intensely concerned with the balance of fellow-feeling and acquisitive behavior that was produced by market societies based on wage labor and notionally egalitarian social relations (Phillipson 2010).

It is well-known that this line of thinking gave rise to classical political economy, with its fundamental commitment to competition on price—Richard Cobden's "divine law of cheapness"—as the guarantor of both material abundance and social and international peace (Trentmann 2008). According to this line of thinking, material interdependence could ultimately become a complete solvent of political conflict, rendering much of the apparatus of the modern state—especially standing armies and professional diplomacy—surplus to requirements (Howe 1997). What is less appreciated, however, is that Smith, David Hume, and a range of lesser-known Enlightenment figures had their own interpretations of the relevance of 'commercial society' to international politics, generating novel accounts of what we might think of as 'competitive co-existence' among the rival empires of eighteenth-century Europe.

This perspective on the problem of competition had originated in France, where theories of political economy were profoundly influenced by the failure of Louis XIV's campaign of military conquest at the close of the eighteenth-century. They argued that, at least within Europe, inter-state competition should no longer take the form of deliberate wars of conquest and destruction. It would instead be mediated through the arts of economic and technological "emulation": mutual observation of economic capacity and governing innovations that would enable a balance of commercial power to be maintained (Reinert 2011). Smith and Hume took a similar perspective on the problems of Britain's overstretched colonial empire in the last quarter of the eighteenth century. The challenge this faced, they argued, was the need to build an effective fiscal state and a productive manufacturing base capable of paying for an effective navy, rather than to hold onto distant territories that cost more to govern than they brought in revenue (Hont 2005).

The normative ideal that underpinned this Enlightened critique of violent conflict was not that of cosmopolitanism—in contemporary language, "universal benevolence". Instead, it urged the positive benefits of peaceful forms of international competition, motivated by the mutual desire of "improvement" and "emulation", over the vices of envy and "jealousy" (Hume 1994).

Where, for Hobbes, the psychological foundations of competition were such that they could *only* lead to violence, eighteenth-century thinkers saw far more potential for varieties of competition that could be held within normative and institutional boundaries. This not only made market competition possible at the domestic or global level: it also made it possible to think of an international politics in which national units, conceived in primarily economic terms, could compete with one another on productivity and state capacity without engaging in direct military conflict. The stage was set by a nineteenth century in which the European powers engaged in constant practices of "competitive comparisons" (Steinmetz 2019), before an increasingly internationalized public (Werron 2015).

The eighteenth-century imagination of 'improvement' through competition remained associated with the idea of a dynamic balance which was restored by competing forces. Migrating easily between natural philosophy, political theory and political economy, the metaphor of balancing forces implied an endless movement around a perfect state (Wise/Smith 1989a). In the words of a British geologist and member of parliament George Scrope,

> "Competition is, indeed, the soul of industry, the animating spirit" of production, the ever-present, all-pervading elastic principle, which, like the power of gravitation on the atmosphere and ocean, fills every vacuum in the market of exchanges—equalizes the quantity of every commodity to the necessity for it—and preserves their relative values at the mean level of their comparative estimation in the regard of the great body of consumers" (Scrope 1833: 200).

The massive economic changes of the nineteenth century, however, dispelled the belief in harmony through competition. The economy could no longer be symbolized by "the balance with its natural limits but the steam engine with its capacity for change." The economy meant evolution, not balance (Wise/Smith 1989b: 382), transforming the future into an open, insecure, and changeable horizon (Koselleck 2010).

In face of rapid technological changes, states began to compete for the *capacity* to compete in the form of a maximization of labor power—an early form of competitiveness. Since the French physiocrats, work—understood as human self-reproduction—depended on both the riches of nature and its realization among the free competition of producers. This implied a possible inability to compete and sustain oneself through work, which became the blunt reality of factory workers in the nineteenth century. Nineteenth century political economists highlight work, not soil, as the ultimate source of wealth: Capital, labor, and soil are productive only insofar as they are put to work (Frambach 2002; Rabinbach 1990). With international trade and conditions of production changing rapidly, there was now a constant risk of labor, soil and capital lying idle because they could not realize themselves in the competition with production in other places. As William Whewell explained in 1843, "the productive power of nations must be compared by comparing the moving forces plus the whole quantity of working mechanism" (Wise/Smith 1989b: 419). In competing for productive power—be it human, animal, or mechanical—states compete for agents of change.

Nineteenth century thinkers increasingly challenged the idea and practice of a civil society between citizens or states in which material interdependence and the competition of private interests foster the common good. For Georg Friedrich Hegel writing in the early nineteenth century, bourgeois society was not the transcendence, but the realization of the Hobbesian state of nature, an arena for the struggle of private interests *omnium contra omnes* (Hegel 1821: §289). Where liberal political economists had envisioned an international civilized society based on free trade among equal nations, the German 'national economist' Friedrich List pointed to the devastating consequences this had for the economically "weaker" nations (List 1841).

Later in the nineteenth century, the rise of powerful monopolies, trusts, and combinations whose financial power could exceed that of states, posed the question of whether private capitalist competition could be straightforwardly transmuted into a political competition between states. The British liberal John A. Hobson put forth an economic explanation of the cycle of imperial expansion that took place in the final decades of the nineteenth century: "Overproduction (…) and access capital which could not find sound investments within the country, forced [countries] to place larger and larger portions of their economic resources outside the area of their present political domain, and then stimulate a policy of political expansion so as to take in the new areas" (Hobson 1902: 80).

While Hobson based his argument on a concrete study of (mainly) British and American imperialism, Lenin and Rosa Luxemburg transformed it into an argument describing imperialism as the latest stage of capitalism (Lenin 2010; Luxemburg 1951; Brewer 1990). The ability of large corporations to avoid competition—already acknowledged by Smith in his *Wealth of Nations*—gave rise to the idea that, as Marx put it, "the sole defense against capitalists is competition." (Marx/Engels 2009: 41) This tension between the critique of competition, and the demand for the overthrow of monopolies, is echoed in the anti-imperialist writings of the end of the nineteenth century (Cain 2002: 166).

Sociological accounts of competition of the early twentieth century similarly reflect this ambivalence. In their endeavour to establish sociology as an independent discipline, sociologists abstracted competition from its nineteenth-century contexts in political economy. Georg Simmel and Max Weber wrote at a time in which finance, trusts and imperial wars made headlines; their abstractions—competition as "social form" (Simmel) or "type of social action" (Weber)—sought to transcend these historical conditions. As a social form or type of social action, competition could be distinguished from rivalry or conflict, and compared across different social fields. The *Nationalökonom* Weber conceived of competition as a peaceful struggle (*Kampf*) "insofar as it consists in a formally peaceful attempt to attain control over opportunities and advantages which are also desired by others" (Weber 1956: §8). As such, he argued, competition for power and capital has long been part of the interaction between states (Weber 1956: §31). Simmel also discusses competition in relation to conflict, and, more specifically, to jealousy—"that social phenomenon in which the construction of antagonism by way of unity achieves its [...] most radical form" (Simmel 2009: 258). He conceived of competition as a triadic constellation, in which two actors are opposed to each other and at the same time united in their relation to the third object or person they compete for. For both Weber and Simmel, competition is a specific kind of struggle, which is "formally peaceful".

'World Politics as Competition': Norms and Structures

This short conceptual history of competition as both a normative ideal and an analytical category shows that there is a much richer tradition of thinking about competition than the conventional IR literature assumes. Drawing on this brief account, we now turn to a more extended definition of what we understand to be a configuration of world politics in which competition is central. This, we argue, will possess both normative and structural features.

A configuration of world politics in which competition is viewed to be central is in the first instance a world of *notionally equal, sovereign states*—even if, in practice, the key participants in international competition are a select group of "great powers" (Müller 2020). These share a *common set of cultural expectations*, and means of communication, that enable mutual observation and comparison according to a shared goal on a sustained basis (Heintz/Werron 2011). As Simmel pointed out, competition is the manifestation of an *antagonism* not despite but *through* this mutual recognition and unity deriving from a shared object of desire. This structure of communications and expectation compels them to engage in an *open-ended, dynamic competition* for power, wealth and status: there is no stable state to be reached, but the continuing need to adapt to changing forms of competition—a capacity that comes to be discussed under the term 'competitiveness'. This also implies a change in the objects states compete for, or rather, a change of what constitutes power, wealth, and status *as scarce objects* at different times.

A strong sense of mutual recognition among a group of competing states is necessary in order to set limits to the possibilities for violence. All who compete are recognized as legitimate 'players' in the international arena. This legitimacy can be additionally conferred through diplomatic practices, or membership of international organizations. As our historical discussion of ideas of competition in eighteenth and nineteenth century Europe indicates, the idea of international competition is also strongly bound up with the history of European colonialism. It was the binding glue of an idea of European 'civilization', culturally and racially superior to non-European societies, that enabled eighteenth and nineteenth-century Europeans to conceive of one another as legitimate participants in the international.

A conception of world politics based on competition is likely to assign a greater weight to the economic, cultural and technological attributes of states than it will to their raw military capacity. Because these 'softer' attributes are often validated by expert opinion, international media systems and (in the modern era) international organisations may become central arenas for competitive behavior. These "rationalized third-parties" (Werron 2013: 66; 2015) supply and collate the information—whether on military expenditure, public health preparedness, or cultural achievement—that makes "competitive comparisons" (Steinmetz 2019) possible.

Yet competition is only 'formally peaceful': when world politics are organized in this way, existential threats and violent conflict is not eliminated. The modernization race of the mid-twentieth century and the neoliberal reforms of competitiveness since the 1980s had devastating consequences for significant parts of the global population. What is more, violence has frequently been visited on racialized others who are not viewed as legitimate participants in "the international" (Pitts 2018), through the competitive acquisition of colonies that characterized both the European imperialisms of the eighteenth and nineteenth centuries, and the 'proxy wars' that shaped US-Soviet confrontation of the twentieth (Westad 2005).

The usefulness of this outline of 'world politics as competition' is twofold. It allows us to see, firstly, that competition is not simply to be viewed as a problem for international order. It is also an idea that is normatively attractive to many participants, past and present, in world politics; an alternative to violent conflict that is actively designed into central institutions of international order. Secondly—as Heidi Tworek argues forcefully in her contribution—it allows us to identify and problematize the blind spots and exclusions of a conception of world politics as based on competition between nation states. Thirdly, it allows us to analytically separate competition from conflict; not from any deep conviction that these are always separable in practice, but in line with a pragmatic determination to study competition in world politics as an open-ended phenomenon, that is not predetermined to produce a descent into warfare. This, we argue in the following section, is a perspective that is missing from established schools of international relations, although it is present in the fields of international political economy and the emergent sociology of competition.

Competition and International Relations Theory

'Competition' became a central concept in international theory in the late 1940s, when Hans Morgenthau distinguished two constellations of the balance of power —the "pattern of direct opposition" and the "pattern of competition"—in his first version of *Politics Among Nations* (Morgenthau 1948: 131-133). The Simmel-style "pattern of competition" describes a triadic structure, in which two imperialist powers compete in their domination of a third, smaller power. In the face of the Korean war, Morgenthau dedicated in subsequent editions an entire subsection to it, thus enhancing its status as a theoretical concept (Morgenthau 1954: 162-165) From this point on, students of international relations could relate the balance of power to competition by merely glimpsing at a classic's table of contents. However, Morgenthau's concept of competition and opposition are not as structuralist as his famous metaphor of billiard balls suggest. In fact, the "patterns" are a way to systemize the ways in which the balance of power can be sustained or disturbed; within these constellations, there can as well *not* be competition (Wendt 1992: 395-396; Little 2007: 93).

Only the neorealists turn competition into a structure underlying all international politics. Likening the anarchical system of self-help to the coordination on a market, Kenneth Waltz conceives of the international system as a "competitive realm". Competition is the order that emerges between uncoordinated units emulating each other and socializing themselves to their system (Waltz 1979: 127-128). Just like in an oligopolistic market, competition does not necessarily serve the greater good: "states compete, but not by contributing their individual efforts to the joint production of goods for their mutual benefit" (Waltz 1979: 107). Waltz's structural reformulation of realism not only understates the possibility of cooperation (for which it has often been attacked) but eclipses the distinction between conflict and competition which Morgenthau had articulated.

The constructivist critique leveled against neorealism argues that anarchy should not be treated as structure, but the absence of it. In the absence of structure, international politics fundamentally depends on "what states make of it" (Wendt 1992). While not explicitly targeting the concept of competition, constructivism does enable us to start to think of competition as a historically developed institution within world politics. What is more, the argument that the identity and interests of states both emerge in and shape the institutions of international politics has opened up a new way to think across the lines of neorealism and neoliberalism. This is most notable when Wendt points out that "institutions may be cooperative or conflictual, a point sometimes lost in scholarship on international regimes, which tends to equate institutions with cooperation" (Wendt 1992: 399). Despite this observation, Wendt's work has sparked critical analyses of the concept of power (Guzzini 2005) and of how states even know their interests (Haas 1992) within IR—but not of competitive institutions.

In his later works, Wendt articulates an agent-structure-problem in IR by drawing on social theory (Wendt 1999). Over the last two decades, some IR scholars have begun to reconceptualize the realm of international politics in line with Bourdieu's field theory, in order to overcome the opposition of structure and agency.[1] Like constructivism the Bourdieusian approach pays

---

1   Bourdieu emphasizes that there is no "field theory" apart from empirical studies of concrete fields. While Bourdieu has recently been popularized through the "relational sociology" of english-speaking scholars (Julian Go, Monika Krause, Rebecca Adler-Nissen), there has been a (mostly) french-speaking discourse on Bourdieu's value to IR since at least the 2000s (Yves Chouala, Frédéric Mérand, Vincent Pouliot).

attention to both the symbolic and material dimensions of domination and struggle within world politics (Mérand/Pouliot 2008: 609). According to Bourdieu, fields are configurations of objective relations between positions (Bourdieu/Wacquant 1992: 97). These relations are always changing: "As a space of potential and active forces, the field is also a field of struggles aimed at preserving or transforming the configuration of these forces" (ibid: 101). The field concept conceives of international politics as a "competitive realm" as Waltz had done, but without making it into an ahistorical structure: the positions, borders, capitals and rules of the field are subject to the field's struggle (ibid: 99-100).

Political scientists and sociologists began to diagnose "competition states" in the globalized world economy of the 1990s. In contrast to the early Marxist theories which treated the state as a vehicle for economic interests, this scholarship develops a theory of both the state and international relations. Since the 1980s, there has been a discussion about the crisis of the welfare states and their growing inability to enable and limit the domestic capitalist economy (Offe 1983). The new state form forged by international economic competition—the "competition state"—"prioritizes the pursuit of strategies intended to create, restructure, or reinforce (...) the competitive advantages of its territory, population, built environment, social institutions and economic agents" (Jessop 2002: 86; cf. Cerny 1997: 297; Hirsch 1995). According to Jessop, competitive advantage no longer refers to a Ricardian static comparative (e.g. lower costs of resource exploitation) but to a Schumpeterian dynamic of competitive advantages (e.g. the capacity to succeed in competition) (Jessop 2002: 119-122). Spurred by international organizations such as the WTO, the IMF and the World Bank, competition states reduce taxes on capital, increase the flexibility of their labor markets, and cut welfare spending. This change is accompanied by a "new spirit of capitalism", which tenders the "possibilities of self-realization and room for freedom of action" to anyone adopting the competitive logic as their own (Boltanski/Chiapello 2005: 16; Davies 2015).

Apart from critical theorists studying the neoliberal mode of governance, there is a more recent research strand in sociology, which follows Simmel's classical account of competition as a triadic social form. Tobias Werron has recently revived this tradition and elaborated on the social form of competition with regard to the role of the object of competition, the construction of its scarcity and its evaluation by a third party (Werron 2014; Werron 2019: 31-36). While critical theorists and sociologists of the social form differ in the status they assign to competition—a universal social form or a symptom of

a historically specific form of capitalism—they come together in their studies of contemporary management methods, such as rankings, indices, and
performance-based measures (Jessop 2015; Werron 2015).

In recent years, attention has shifted to the role of third parties—such
as international law, the global media system, or non-governmental organizations—in mediating state competition. Distinguishing between 'legal' and
'illegal' competition, rules-based international institutions such as the World
Trade Organization can both limit and prescribe state competition (Davies
2013; Slobodian 2018). Scholarship on a "global public" has pointed out how
the global media system is a source of legitimation and attention, for which
states compete to make their interests heard. Not only states but think tanks,
NGOs and epistemic communities compete for the authority "to define what
is to be governed, how, and why" (Sending 2015: 4). In doing this, these actors
in world politics seek to change the policies states pursue, and the purposes
they compete for.

New Challenges: 'Great Power Competition'
and 'Weaponized Independence'

Even if these new approaches to the sociology and political economy of competition disagree about its distinctive importance in an era of neoliberalism,
they share a common interest in its uses as an ordering device in distinct and
identifiable institutional settings, in which rankings and metrics can exercise
a disciplinary function. Where states are subject to these disciplines by international organizations and other 'universalized third parties', it is primarily
to compare them against a common and notionally objective standard, within
relatively discrete areas of policy.

In recent years, however, world politics has witnessed the return of traditional 'great power' rivalry between a range of global and regional powers,
including the US, China, Iran, the EU, and Russia. Institutionalized competition, mediated by identifiable third parties and productive of metrics and
rankings, now co-exists uneasily with a less clearly structured competition between nation-states for power and prestige in an increasingly unstable global
order.

The growing instability of contemporary world politics creates problems
for both the neo-realist and sociological accounts of international competition discussed in the previous section. The role and significance of rankings,

metrics and international organization is likely to change where states are engaged in sustained strategic competition with one another. The return of this form of competition, however, cannot be abstracted from the underlying institutional and economic architecture of a complex and heavily interdependent global political economy and media system. In the new era of inter-state competition, the "dominant measure of standing" is not "military", but "economic, informational, and geopolitical" (Mazarr et. al. 2018).

Over the course of the 2010s, the 'return of great power competition' has become a constant refrain of the US foreign policy community, with growing hostility to China a rare area of bipartisan consensus between Republicans and Democrats (Small 2018). The Trump administration stated bluntly in its 2017 national security strategy that "we face an era of increased strategic competition, global challenges, and erosion of the U.S. comparative military advantage" (White House 2017). The European Union similarly took the uncharacteristic step of describing China both as an "economic competitor in the pursuit of technological leadership, and a systemic rival promoting alternative models of governance" (European Commission 2019).

The highly organized and interconnected character of modern world politics was once held to be a solvent of this kind of direct power competition. According to varieties of 'neoliberal' international relations theory prominent in the 1990s and 2000s, the proliferation of multilateral organizations covering trade, the environment and human rights—could act to contain competition to distinct "issue areas".[2] On this understanding, conflict and disagreement over economic, social, health or environmental policy would not be subsumed into broader conflicts between states or alliance systems. In a world of "complex interdependence", the "structure of the issue area, rather than the global balance of traditional military or economic power", was said to shape "who the main actors are and what kinds of resources they can use to realize their goals" (Milner 2009: 25).

This conception of world order was always challenged by IR theorists in realist and Marxian traditions (Mearsheimer 1990; Gowan 2003). These focused on the ultimate dominance of the United States in liberal institutions of global governance, whether by virtue of its military power or its centrality to global (financialized) capitalism. The latter was amply demonstrated during

---

2   "Neoliberalism" as a position in the discipline of International Relations (IR) will be referred to as "IR-neoliberalism", to distinguish it from "neoliberalism" as a broader political ideology.

the Global Financial Crisis of 2007-8, when the US Federal Reserve unilaterally acted to backstop large parts of the global financial system through the provision of dollar financing to chosen allies (Tooze 2018). The Federal Reserve acted with similar decisiveness during the 'Covid Crash' of 2020 (Tooze 2020).

The current intensification of competition in world politics has taken a form, however, that is specific to an era in which capitalist globalization has advanced further and deeper than ever before (Milanovic 2019). In a 2016 essay collection, the European Council on Foreign Relations argued that, in a globalized world, interdependence "has turned into a currency of power, as countries try to exploit the asymmetries in their relations". Here, migration, energy, technical regulation and investment controls are listed as new battlegrounds for a multipolar world, in which enhanced geopolitical competition takes place in a context of unprecedented economic openness (Leonard 2016).

The emergent scholarship on 'weaponized interdependence' suggests that economic interdependence is not a recipe for international stability. Interstate rivalries—far from dissolving into the structural logics of discrete 'issue areas'—overlay interaction across a whole range of policy areas. Across all of these, the vital issue is the control of 'central nodes in the international networked structures through which money, goods and information travel' (Farrell/Newman 2019: 45). States are powerful actors, but they are one among many. Corporate actors—especially in the tech, finance and security sectors—are themselves significant players in this 'geo-economic' form of competition, characterized by 'securitization of economic policy and economization of strategic policy' (Roberts et al. 2019).

In this new configuration of competition, different major powers enjoy contrasting abilities to influence world politics. While the United States enjoys an outsized ability to use a global reserve currency to achieve its geopolitical goals, the European regulatory state (Bradford 2020), Russian energy politics (Siddi 2019), and Chinese overseas investment initiatives (Nordin/Weissmann 2018) offer comparable examples of the increasingly close relationship between economics, technology and power-politics in the 21st century.

Lineages and Varieties of Competition

The new literature on 'weaponized interdependence' is a powerful provocation to rethink the nature of world politics and world society in the 21st century, beyond the easy 'realist-idealist', 'competition versus cooperation' opposition that still structures much public and popular commentary on the world political situation (Ashworth 2002). Contemporary world politics are often said to be departing from a 'liberal international order' based on a combination of US hegemony and robust international institutions (Ikenberry 2018). Yet international organizations remain vital political arenas, and world politics is to a large extent 'performed' before a global public and an integrated media system based on the internet. Economic interdependence remains significant, and (some) non-state actors remain geopolitically relevant. Indeed, in the age of "financialization" (Thomson/Dutta 2018) and "platform capitalism" (Srnicek 2017; Zuboff 2019), the relative autonomy of globally relevant financial and technology firms is arguably greater than ever before.

The complex and intensely mediated character of competition in contemporary world politics calls for a more sophisticated and varied approach to analyzing its origins and character. The chapters gathered here open a new interdisciplinary perspective on the emergence and persistence of 'competition' as a central organizing category in modern world politics. They share an interest in the ways in which competition is observed and mediated, recognizing that, while there are structural reasons for states and other actors to compete over 'scarce goods' like power, wealth or prestige, the form and nature of international competition is highly sensitive to institutional contexts, the generation of relevant knowledge, and the identity of political actors. They also bring new research on emergent policy fields to the table, examining dynamics of competition within the formally 'cooperative' spaces created by international organizations. Finally, they place competition in a historical perspective, identifying the close linkages between evolving concepts of competition and the historical emergence of 'world politics' itself.

The volume is separated into three sections, each of which explores a distinct thematic focus that grows out of this overall approach to the problem of competition in world politics. The first section analyses the dynamics of status competition within international organizations. Ramy Youssef's comparison of early modern ceremonial rankings and modern nation-state rankings invites a radical historicization of competition as a 'social form'. Far from being a transhistorical condition of human interaction, status competition is a distinctively modern phenomenon, qualitatively different from the fixed status hierarchies that defined early modern diplomacy. Thomas Müller and Katja Freistein offer a Bourdieusian analysis of the politics of "capital conversion", focusing on the efforts of Brazil, Russia, India and China to convert their economic clout into greater political influence and status. They argue for the continued importance of international organizations as arenas for status competition, and the contested nature of status in itself under a configuration of world politics that "is today much more institutionalized and polycentric than it was in previous phases of world history." As Anatoly Boyashov argues in his analysis of the European Union's participation in "network competition" at the UN Human Rights Council (UNHRC), navigating this institutionalized and polycentric environment requires political actors to compete for dominant structural positions in complex networks constituted by states, international organizations, and civil society organizations. As an international organization confined to a formal "observer" role at the UNHCR, the EU is nonetheless able to play a significant role as a coordinator of nation-state coalitions behind its preferred human rights initiatives.

The second section of the volume considers the historical evolution of ideologies of competition, and of the forms of knowledge that have enabled and advanced them. The focus here is on political economy, and on the complicated relationships between ideas of national power and cosmopolitan progress that run through its modern intellectual history. James Stafford's examination of British trade policy in the later eighteenth century re-examines the 'rise of free trade' as a mutation, rather than a rejection, of a mercantilist logic of national power competition. Examining the writings of the Anglo-Dutch merchant Matthew Decker alongside those of the better-known Scottish philosopher Adam Smith, Stafford's chapter identifies a switch from a competition over trade balances in precious metals, to an all-pervasive struggle for labor discipline and productivity, applying not just to princes and rulers but entire 'nations'. While Stafford's contribution emphasizes the nationalist potentialities of liberal political economy, Tobias Werron and Johannes Nagel's chapter moves in the opposite direction, highlighting the cosmopolitan *telos* of US-American ideologies of economic nationalism and naval power in the nineteenth century. US-American theorists, Werron and Nagel argue, were able to simultaneously stake a place for the United States as entitled to struggle for a share of the 'scarce goods' of wealth and power, while "also claiming for the US the role of a standard-bearer of cosmopolitan values and global progress"—albeit at an undefined point in the future.

As Daniela Russ and Thomas Turnbull's chapter demonstrates, this kind of conjoined nationalist-cosmopolitan reasoning was also in evidence in the new form of "materialist" and "energetic" economics pioneered by Edwardian "technocrats" and Soviet energy planners in the early decades of the twentieth century. What Russ and Turnbull term "energetic productivism" created a

new form of competition over the expansion of energetic resources and productivity, mediated through a new body of official statistics dedicated to the
measurement of "energetic capacities". Dieter Plehwe's chapter offers a contrasting examination of the politics of measurement and its relevance to state
competition, recounting the intellectual and organizational origins of neoliberal measures of "economic freedom" designed to encourage states to compete against one another in providing a "business-friendly" environment for
international capital. Against accounts that identify ranking and economic
measurement with a general logic of Eurocentric, capitalist modernity, Plehwe urges us to consider the concrete agents and intellectual agendas behind
the specific forms of knowledge that have informed competing paradigms of
political economy.

The third section of the book extends Russ, Turnbull and Plehwe's interest
in the emergence of new technological arenas and new standards of comparison, offering a series of case studies exploring how artificial intelligence and
cybersecurity are opening new vistas of global political competition, in the
2020s and beyond. Didzis Kļaviņš examines the promise and peril of artificial intelligence for traditional understandings of diplomacy. Particularly in
smaller countries such as Latvia and other Baltic states, ministries of foreign
affairs are being pressured to draw on new forms of expertise, and new public-
private partnerships, to equip themselves with the tools necessary to secure
positions of autonomy—and even leadership—in a global AI landscape shaped
by the power ambitions of China and the United States. Madeleine Myatt's
contribution explores how the new terrain of cybersecurity offers opportunities for small states to exercise new forms of power on the world stage, assuming agenda-setting positions in international organizations such as NATO
and positioning themselves as model hosts for new institutions of cyberwarfare. Yuliya Miadyvetskaya's chapter considers emergent efforts to regulate
this new landscape of cyberwarfare, arguing for the potential of the European Union's new cyber-sanctions regime to initiate a global dialogue about
the need to extend principles of international law governing state behavior in
other domains to the new terrain of cyberspace. Cyber-sanctions emerge as
simultaneously a strategy pursued by a major actor in global power competition; *and* a potential means of establishing new norms, and new standards of
comparison, that will structure and mediate this new terrain of competition
as it develops in the 21st century.

Competition in the Age of Covid-19

All intellectual production is the product of its historical moment, alongside its social and its natural environment. The present volume is no exception. Conceived during face-to-face workshops at Bielefeld University in 2018 and 2019 and completed under the conditions of lockdown in the spring and autumn of 2020, the present introduction was written with one eye on the unfolding drama of a new international competition in both public health and macroeconomic policy. Daily statistics brought home the relative successes (and failures) of different states in containing the spread of the novel coronavirus; alongside measures of the size and duration of the collapses in national Gross Domestic Products (GDP) brought on by regional and national lockdowns.

It was with new vista of global public health competition in mind—at once familiar and totally novel—that we decided to approach Professor Heidi Tworek, a historian of both global competition and public health policy, to offer some closing reflections on how the Covid-19 crisis should affect our understandings of the role of competition in world politics. Tworek's afterword to this collection joins a brief historical survey of the origins of modern health statistics in the League of Nations Health Office of the 1920s to a pointed critique of the uses and abuses of national rankings and comparisons in the current crisis. She powerfully reminds us that historicizing, relativizing and questioning the assumption that world politics should be understood as competition between nation states is not merely an analytical or academic exercise. The distorting imaginaries of competition and rankings, Tworek argues, have handicapped governments in their response to the Covid-19 epidemic, obscuring the importance of social and racial equity to public health, and rendering invisible the sufferings of the countless individuals who make up blunt, and often incommensurable, bodies of national case statistics. At least in some instances, it seems, competition is an imaginary that has been chosen and manipulated for political ends. Only with this awareness can we begin to transcend its more damaging consequences for contemporary world politics.

References

Albert, Mathias (2016): A Theory of World Politics, Cambridge: Cambridge University Press.

Ashworth, Lucian M. (2002): "Did the Realist-Idealist Great Debate Really Happen? A Revisionist History of International Relations." In: International Relations 16/1, pp. 33-51.

Beckert, Jens (2009): "The Social Order of Markets." In: Theory and Society 38/3, pp. 245-269.

Bigo, D. (2011): "Pierre Bourdieu and International Relations: Power of Practices, Practices of Power." In: International Political Sociology 5/3, pp. 225-258.

Boltanski, Luc/Chiapello, Eve (2005): The New Spirit of Capitalism, London: Verso.

Bourdieu, Pierre/Wacquant, Loïc (1992): An Invitation to Reflexive Sociology, Cambridge: Polity Press.

Bradford, Anu (2020): The Brussels Effect: How the European Union Rules the World, Oxford: Oxford University Press.

Brewer, Anthony (1990): Marxist Theories of Imperialism: A Critical Survey, London: Routledge.

Bürkert, Katrin/Engel, Alexander/Heimerdinger, Timo/Tauschek, Markus/Werron, Tobias (eds.) (2019): Auf den Spuren der Konkurrenz: Kultur- und sozialwissenschaftliche Perspektiven, Freiburger Studien zur Kulturanthropologie, Münster: Waxmann.

Bull, Hedley (1981): "Hobbes and the International Anarchy." In: Social Research 48/4, pp. 717-738.

Burt, Ronald S. (2009): Structural Holes: The Social Structure of Competition, Cambridge, MA: Harvard University Press.

Buzan, Barry/Lawson, George (2015): The Global Transformation, Cambridge: Cambridge University Press.

Cain, P. J. (2002): Hobson and Imperialism: Radicalism, New Liberalism, and Finance 1887-1938, Oxford: Oxford University Press.

Cerny, Philip G. (1997): "Paradoxes of the Competition State: The Dynamics of Political Globalization." In: Government and Opposition 32/2, pp. 251-274.

Davies, William (2013): "When Is a Market Not a Market?: 'Exemption', 'Externality' and 'Exception' in the Case of European State Aid Rules." In: Theory, Culture & Society 30/2, pp. 32-59.

Davies, William (2015): The Limits of Neoliberalism: Authority, Sovereignty and the Logic of Competition, London: SAGE.

European Commission (2019): EU-China—A Strategic Outlook, Brussels: European Commission.

Farrell, Henry/Newman, Abraham L. (2019): "Weaponized Independence: How Global Economic Networks Shape State Coercion." In: International Security 44/1, pp. 42-79.

Frambach, Hans A. (2002): "Zum Verständnis von Arbeit im historischen Wandel: Eine Untersuchung aus nationalökonomischer Perspektive." In: Arbeit 11/3, pp. 226-243.

Glaser, Charles L. (2010): Rational Theory of International Politics: The Logic of Competition and Cooperation, Princeton: Princeton University Press.

Gowan, Peter (2003): "US: UN." In: New Left Review 24, unpaginated.

Guzzini, Stefano (2005): "The Concept of Power: A Constructivist Analysis." In: Millennium 33/3, pp. 495-521.

Haas, Peter M. (1992): "Epistemic Communities and International Policy Coordination." In: International Organization 46/1, pp. 1-35.

Hegel, Georg Wilhelm Friedrich (1821): Grundlinien der Philosophie des Rechts, Berlin: Nicolaische Buchhandlung.

Heintz, Bettina/Werron. Tobias (2011): "Wie ist Globalisierung möglich? Zur Entstehung globaler Vergleichshorizonte am Beispiel von Wissenschaft und Sport." In: KZfSS Kölner Zeitschrift für Soziologie und Sozialpsychologie 63/3, pp. 359-394.

Hirsch, Joachim (1995): Der nationale Wettbewerbsstaat: Staat, Demokratie und Politik im globalen Kapitalismus, Berlin: Edition ID-Archiv.

Hobbes, Thomas (1994 [1651]): Leviathan: With Selected Variants from the Latin Edition of 1668, Indianapolis: Hackett.

Hobson, J. A. (1902): Imperialism: A Study, London: James Nisbet & co.

Hont, Istvan (2005): Jealousy of Trade: International Competition and the Nation-State in Historical Perspective, Cambridge, MA: Harvard University Press.

Hont, Istvan (2015): Politics in Commercial Society: Jean-Jacques Rousseau and Adam Smith, Cambridge, MA: Harvard University Press.

Howe, Anthony (1997): Free Trade and Liberal England, 1846-1946, Oxford: Clarendon Press.

Hume, David (1994 [1752]): "Of the Jealousy of Trade." In: Knud Haakonssen (ed.), Hume: Political Essays, Cambridge: Cambridge University Press, pp. 150-153.

Ikenberry, G. John. (2018): "The End of Liberal International Order?" In: International Affairs 94/1, pp. 7-23.

Jessop, Bob (2002): The Future of the Capitalist State, Cambridge: Polity Press.

Jessop, Bob (2015): "The Course, Contradictions, and Consequences of Extending Competition as a Mode of (Meta-)Governance: Towards a Sociology of Competition and Its Limits." In: Distinktion: Journal of Social Theory 16/2, pp. 167-185.

Keene, Edward (2001): Beyond the Anarchical Society, Cambridge: Cambridge University Press

Koselleck, Reinhart (2010): "'Fortschritt' und 'Niedergang'—Nachtrag zur Geschichte zweier Begriffe." In: Begriffsgeschichten: Studien zur Semantik und Pragmatik der politischen und sozialen Sprache, Berlin: Suhrkamp, pp. 159-182.

Lenin, Vladimir Ilich (2010 [1917]): Imperialism: The Highest Stage of Capitalism: A Popular Outline, London: Penguin Books.

Leonard, Mark (ed.) (2016) Connectivity Wars: Why Migration, Finance and Trade are the Geo-Economic Battlegrounds Of The Future, London: European Council on Foreign Relations.

Link, Stefan (2018): "How Might 21st-Century De-Globalization Unfold? Some Historical Reflections." In: New Global Studies 12/3, pp. 343-365.

List, Friedrich (1841): Das nationale System der politischen Oekonomie, Stuttgart: J.G. Cotta.

Little, Richard (2007): The Balance of Power in International Relations: Metaphors, Myths and Models, Cambridge: Cambridge University Press.

Luxemburg, Rosa (1951): The Accumulation of Capital, London: Routledge & Kegan Paul.

Malcolm, Noel (2002): Aspects of Hobbes, Oxford: Clarendon Press.

Marx, Karl/Engels, Friedrich (2009): The Economic and Philosophic Manuscripts of 1844 and the Communist Manifesto, New York: Prometheus Books.

Mazarr, Michael J./Blake, Jonathan S./Casey, Abigail/McDonald, Tim/Pezard, Stephanie/Spirtas, Michael (2018): Understanding the Emerging Era of International Competition: Theoretical and Historical Perspectives, Washington, DC: RAND Institute

Mearsheimer, John J. (1990): "Back to the Future: Instability in Europe after the Cold War." In: International Security 15/1, pp. 5-56.

Mérand, Frédéric/Pouliot,Vincent (2008): "Le Monde de Pierre Bourdieu: Éléments pour une théorie sociale des relations internationales." In: Canadian Journal of Political Science/Revue canadienne de science politique 41/3, pp. 603-625.

Milanovic, Branko (2019): Capitalism, Alone: The Future of the System That Rules the World, Cambridge, MA: Harvard University Press.

Milner, Helen V. (2009): "Power, Interdependence and Nonstate Actors in World Politics: Research Frontiers." In: Andrew Moravcsik/Helen V. Milner (eds.), Power, Interdependence, and Nonstate Actors in World Politics, Princeton: Princeton University Press.

Morgenthau, Hans J. (1948): Politics among Nations: The Struggle for Power and Peace, New York: Knopf.

Morgenthau, Hans J. (1954): Politics among Nations: The Struggle for Power and Peace, 2nd ed., New York: Knopf.

Müller, Thomas (2020): "Institutional Reforms and the Politics of Inequality Reproduction: The Case of the League of Nations' Council Crisis in 1926." In: Global Society 34/3: pp. 304-317.

Nordin, Astrid H. M./Weissmann. Mikael (2018): "Will Trump Make China Great Again? The Belt and Road Initiative and International Order." In: International Affairs 94/2, pp. 231-249.

Offe, Claus (1983): Contradictions of the Welfare State, Cambridge, MA: MIT Press.

Phillipson, Nicholas (2010): Adam Smith: An Enlightened Life, London: Penguin.

Pitts, Jennifer (2018): Boundaries of the International: Law and Empire, Cambridge, MA: Harvard University Press.

Rabinbach, Anson (1990): The Human Motor: Energy, Fatigue, and the Origins of Modernity, Berkeley: University of California Press.

Reinert, Sophus A. (2011): Translating Empire, Cambridge, MA: Harvard University Press.

Roberts, Anthea/Choer Moraes, Henrique /Ferguson, Victor (2019): "Toward a Geoeconomic Order in International Trade and Investment." In: Journal of International Economic Law 22/4, pp. 655-676.

Robertson, John (2005): The Case for The Enlightenment: Scotland and Naples 1680-1760, Cambridge: Cambridge University Press.

Scrope, George Poulett (1833): Principles of Political Economy, deduced from the Natural Laws of Social Welfare, applied to the Present State of Britain, London: Longman.

Sending, Ole Jacob (2015): The Politics of Expertise: Competing for Authority in Global Governance, Ann Arbor: University of Michigan Press.

Siddi, Marco (2019): "Theorising Conflict and Cooperation in EU-Russia Energy Relations: Ideas, Identities and Material Factors in the Nord Stream 2 Debate." In: East European Politics 36/4, pp. 544-563.

Simmel, Georg (2009): Sociology: Inquiries into the Construction of Social Forms, Leiden, Boston: Brill.

Slobodian, Quinn (2018): Globalists: The End of Empire and the Birth of Neoliberalism, Cambridge, MA: Harvard University Press.

Small, Andrew (2018): "Turning Against China." In: Renewal: A Journal of Social Democracy 26/3.

Srnicek, Nick (2017): Platform Capitalism, Cambridge: John Wiley & Sons.

Steinmetz, Willibald (2019): "Introduction: Concepts and Practices of Comparison in Modern History." In: The Force of Comparison: A New Perspective on Modern European History and the Contemporary World, New York: Berghahn Books, 1-33.

Thomson, Frances/Dutta, Sahil (2018): Financialisation: A Primer, Amsterdam: Transnational Institute.

Tooze, Adam (2018): Crashed: How a Decade of Financial Crises Changed the World, London: Penguin.

Tooze, Adam (2020): 'Crashed to Corona 3: The Fed Beyond Swap Lines', April 5 (https://adamtooze.com/2020/04/05/crashed-to-corona-3-the-fed-beyond-swap-lines/).

Trentmann, Frank (2008): Free Trade Nation: Commerce, Consumption, and Civil Society in Modern Britain, Oxford: Oxford University Press.

Tuck, Richard (2001): The Rights of War and Peace: Political Thought and the International Order from Grotius to Kant, Oxford: Oxford University Press.

Uzzi, Brian (1997): "Social Structure and Competition in Interfirm Networks: The Paradox of Embeddedness." In: Administrative Science Quarterly 42/1, pp. 35-67.

Wallerstein, Immanuel Maurice (2004): World-Systems Analysis: An Introduction, Durham: Duke University Press.

Waltz, Kenneth Neal (1979): Theory of International Politics, London: Random House.

Weber, Max (1956): Wirtschaft und Gesellschaft; Grundriss der verstehenden Soziologie. Mit einem Anhang; die rationalen und soziologischen Grundlagen der Musik, Tübingen: Mohr.

Wendt, Alexander (1992): "Anarchy Is What States Make of It: The Social Construction of Power Politics." In: International Organization 46/2, pp. 391-425.

Wendt, Alexander (1999): Social Theory of International Politics, Cambridge, Cambridge University Press.

Werron, Tobias (2014): "On Public Forms of Competition." In: Cultural Studies ↔ Critical Methodologies 14/1, pp. 62-76.

Werron, Tobias (2015): "Why Do We Believe in Competition? A Historical-Sociological View of Competition as an Institutionalized Modern Imaginary." In: Distinktion: Journal of Social Theory 16/2, pp. 186-210.

Werron, Tobias (2019): "Formen und Typen der Konkurrenz." In: Katrin Bürkert/Alexander Engel/Timo Heimerdinger/Markus Tauschek/Tobias Werron (eds.), Auf den Spuren der Konkurrenz: Kultur- und sozialwissenschaftliche Perspektiven, Freiburger Studien zur Kulturanthropologie, Münster: Waxmann.

Westad, Odd Arne (2005): The Global Cold War: Third World Interventions and the Making of Our Times, Cambridge: Cambridge University Press.

White, Harrison C. (1981): "Where Do Markets Come From?" In: J.A.C. Baum/F. Dobbin (eds.), Economics Meets Sociology in Strategic Management, Bingley: Emerald Group Publishing Limited, pp. 323-350.

White House (2017): National Security Strategy of the United States of America, Washington, DC: White House.

Wiener, Antje (2014): A Theory of Contestation, Heidelberg: Springer.

Wise, M. Norton/Smith, Crosbie (1989a): "Work and Waste: Political Economy and Natural Philosophy in Nineteenth Century Britain (I)." In: *History of Science* 27/3, pp. 263-301.

Wise, M. Norton/Smith, Crosbie (1989b): "Work and Waste: Political Economy and Natural Philosophy in Nineteenth Century Britain (II)." In: *History of Science* 27/4, pp. 391-449.

Zarakol, Ayşe (ed.) (2017): Hierarchies in World Politics, Cambridge: Cambridge University Press

Zuboff, Shoshana (2019): The Age of Surveillance Capitalism: The Fight for a Human Future at the New Frontier of Power, Cambridge, MA: Harvard University Press.

Status and International Organizations

Status in Early Modern and Modern World Politics
Competition or Conflict?

Ramy Youssef

A high status is often considered to be a desirable and scarce good. Competition for status, therefore, is regarded as a universal condition of social life and a driving force in international relations—not only in contemporary world politics, but also in Greek-Roman antiquity, in ancient China, the ancient Orient, ancient Mesoamerica and even in hunter-gatherer societies (Dafoe et al. 2014; Wohlforth 2009; Wood 2013). The following contribution questions this view. It argues instead that the very form of status competition is by no means an ahistorical or anthropological constant in international relations but is itself a historically contingent social form. It is only under specific structural and semantic conditions that competition appears as a distinct social form. Historical change in international relations has not only taken place in the sense that, for example, ceremonial status as a contested good has been replaced by quantifiable military capacities in the modern international system. This would merely mean that the same game is being played with different stakes and means. Instead, it is only under modern conditions that status competition itself appears as a genuine and distinct 'game' or social form. In European courtly society it was hardly distinguishable from status conflicts—both analytically, for us today, and for the historical actors themselves.

Drawing a clear distinction between conflict and competition is therefore a central task for this chapter. The second section argues that a mere typological distinction between conflict and competition is insufficient if social structures and self-descriptions of a field are not taken into account. In the third section, I compare ceremonial rankings of the early modern period with modern nation-state rankings in order to show whether and to what extent conflict and competition can be distinguished with respect to status issues. At first glance, rankings from the early 16th century to the middle of the 18th century seem to depict, create, and influence competitive relationships, thereby confirming an ahistorical view of competition. However, if the socio-structural and semantic context of these rankings is considered, the distinction between competition and conflict becomes blurred. In early modern courtly society, status was established performatively in face-to-face interactions. Contradictory status claims were effectively fought out mostly among princes and diplomats present, which is why it was and still is hardly possible to distinguish between direct conflict and indirect competition in this historical context. Moreover, no distinct semantics of competition can be found in relevant ceremonial treatises. Instead, the assumption prevailed that there are God-given status prerogatives and thus an ideal God-given order, which was, however, considered to be threatened by mundane conflicts.

As the fourth section outlines, the situation is quite different in modern world politics, where competition is an openly expressed motive in comparative nation-state rankings. Nation-state competition for the favor of a global public is explicitly seen as an alternative to inter-state conflicts. This is structurally facilitated by the fact that, on the one hand, status competition takes place 'virtually' in rankings produced by international (non-)governmental organizations, and no longer has to be fought out in diplomatic face-to-face situations. On the other hand, the emergence of competition is facilitated by the fact that the loss of status in one policy field does not simultaneously entail the loss of status in other fields, whereas in the early modern period the loss of rank in one interaction could well have consequences for all other interactions. In the last section, I will draw some conclusions from the finding that status competition is a distinct social form only in modern world politics, whereas in early modern courtly society it is hardly distinguishable from conflicts.

Competition: Conceptual and Methodological Issues

According to Georg Simmel (2009: 258-260), competition presupposes a scarce good to be competed for. To obtain this good, however, competitors do not have to confront each other directly, but focus their ambitions on the good itself. This distinguishes competition from conflicts in which defeating the opponent is an end in itself. Furthermore, it can be very helpful to take a closer look at how the distribution of scarce goods is constructed and legitimized in specific social contexts. There are certainly contexts or social systems in which competition may occur by pure coincidence but is otherwise excluded in principle. This applies, as Georg Simmel (2009: 266) points out, to families in which conflicts among siblings may be the rule, but not competition between them. This is because in families, the maintenance of direct personal relationships is an end in itself, which thus does not provide any structural incentive for indirect competitive relationships. A lottery represents a context in which competition is excluded or in principle pointless (ibid: 267). Certainly, a lottery is about the distribution of a scarce good that can only be obtained at the expense of others. However, the distribution is based on chance and not on the objective performance of the interested parties, which is why envy may lead to conflicts, but these do not affect the result of the lottery. In religious communities too, relationships are predominantly found to be non-competitive. There may be an atmosphere of rivalry or a competitive zeal when everybody strives for God's favor. But the latter is not a scarce good, because the divine blessing bestowed on one person does not exclude the blessing for others. Furthermore, "[a]t least according to the Christian concept there is room in God's house for all. When, nevertheless, predestination withholds this place from some and preserves it for others, the immediate senselessness of any competition is thereby enunciated" (ibid: 267). Incidentally, this is also an important point to which we will have to return when analyzing early modern rankings.

As these examples suggest, Simmel did not believe that competition is a social *a priori*. His conception of competition is not about invisible forces or about a universal struggle for existence. Instead, Simmel (ibid: 260) emphasizes the objective character of competition, by which he does not mean that it can only be observed by an objective sociologist, but rather that competition itself represents an objectified structure of social fields that is comprehensible for the involved actors. The pure form of competition is not an individual or collective feeling or an unconscious and latent relationship, but an expressive relationship directed towards specific and openly declarable goals depending on structural limitations in a given social context. Only this condition enables the emergence of a social form that functions independently of the interchangeable hidden motives of the entangled actors. And only this condition allows for an analytically clear distinction between competition and conflict. In this sense, the following considerations do not intend to 'uncover' latent motives or invisible structures by sociological means. Instead, our aim is to make generalizable statements about whether competition in Simmel's sense is a manifest, explicated, and intrinsic property of a social field or whether it is in principle senseless and only occurs by coincidence.

From a methodological point of view, the mere fact that a single actor may experience or describe a relationship in terms of competition is certainly not a sufficient condition for generalizable conclusions about a social field. Even if in a given situation several actors may feel or describe their relationship to each other in this way, this does not yet give us a methodologically adequate basis, since it can be assumed that this too can depend on chance and context. Moreover, everyday language does not distinguish very clearly between conflict and competition. Instead, it can be assumed that competition and/or conflict should also be reflected in more elaborate and sophisticated semantics of a social field, if they are typical and distinctive aspects of its structure. By semantics, however, we do not refer to the theoretical avant-garde, as represented by authors such as Thomas Hobbes, John Locke or Immanuel Kant, who are usually ahead of their time and whose texts therefore offer little information about the common sense of their contemporaries. For the same reason, Norbert Elias used conduct manuals rather than high-flown philosophy as empirical material for his theory of civilization, because they "transmit not the great or the extraordinary but the typical aspects of society" and are therefore "corresponding to the structure of this society" (Elias 2000: 54). Similarly, Niklas Luhmann (1982) based his analysis on transformations of romantic love on rather mediocre love literature of the early modern period.

We are thus now in a position not only to distinguish typologically between conflict and competition, but also to indicate the manifest conditions under which competition can be expected in a given context. Competition is thus not an essence of the social *per se*. It is rather a specific social form that occurs under certain conditions in certain social systems but not in others, or if so, then only by coincidence. In summary, it can be said that a social system makes competition structurally possible:

a) by producing a scarce good that can only be obtained at the expense of others.
b) if the distribution of the goods is neither random nor prescribed but is dependent on the objective performance of competitors.
c) by providing opportunities to avoid direct confrontation.
d) if it is an explicable part of the semantics in the given system or field.

In this sense, early modern ceremonial rankings and modern nation-state rankings will now be compared here to clarify whether and under what conditions one can speak of status competition in very different world-political contexts. In the early modern context, we are essentially dealing with a courtly society in which international politics is one of many problems of an aristocratic elite and can hardly be separated from dynastic affairs. The other context is the modern system of world politics, which is differentiated and specialized for its function. In both contexts, one finds very similar rankings, which essentially depict and/or performatively produce status. Both pre-modern ceremonial rankings (Stollberg-Rilinger 2002) and modern nation-state rankings are discussed in the relevant literature against the background of an assumed competition between the ranked units (Osborne 2007; Geevers 2012; Sittig 2010; Shore/Wright 2015; Cooley/Snyder 2015). However, both kinds of rankings refer to very different semantics and worldviews, which at one point make competition for status seem plausible and at another point implausible.

Ceremonial Rankings in Early Modern Diplomacy: Competition or Conflict?

Early modern (world) politics was not differentiated as a specialized system—it was one aspect of aristocratic communication, among others. The function of the aristocracy was to engage in significant and far-reaching communication concerning all societal functions and thereby to integrate and represent the entire society (cf. Luhmann 2013b: 50-52). In contrast to the lower class, whose contacts remained locally limited, the aristocracy had far-reaching and privileged opportunities for contact. High status obtained by noble birth and origin ensured the chance of participation in exclusively aristocratic interactions, from which members of the lower class remained largely excluded. Instead, they had to turn to their aristocratic advocates and patrons if they wanted to obtain favors in political, economic, religious or other respects and had to reciprocate these favors with personal allegiance to their patrons (Eisenstadt/Roninger 1984).

The members of the aristocracy were expected to be superior and privileged in every respect. Particularly royal sovereigns were not only to be extraordinarily powerful but also wealthy and educated, and in addition, they were to have a superior taste in art that dictated the fashion of the time. It was even considered plausible that a king could heal the sick better than a doctor by the laying on of hands. Even though this may have not always been realistic in individual cases, it was important to know these expectations and to act accordingly. One particular problem with the status of a king or queen, however, was that, at least in theory, s/he was superior to her/his followers and subjects, but her/his formal relationship to other kings and queens was by no means clear (Stollberg-Rilinger 2002). This caused considerable problems for diplomatic interactions such as royal receptions of legations, meetings of envoys or direct encounters between sovereigns.

In the early modern period, world politics was an aspect of courtly communication in which face-to-face interactions played an indispensable role in decision making (Albert 2016: 98-100). Of course, there was writing and printing. But these forms of communication played a subordinate role to face-to-face interactions. Written contracts in the context of world politics were only put into effect through rituals, while a public sphere that could be reached through published writings played by no means same role as a courtly public sphere composed of aristocratic representatives present in ceremonial interactions (Schlögl 2019). Those who wanted to observe world politics "in the making" therefore had to participate in face-to-face negotiations between princes or their representatives. The presentation, assertion, and, if necessary, defense, of one's rank and status in ceremonial interactions is crucial in premodern world politics.

> "In 1661, the year in which Louis XIV came to exercise royal authority in person, a dispute over precedence between the Count of Estrades and the Baron of Batteville, the French and Spanish envoys in London, erupted into a serious clash, with the Spaniards forcing their way ahead of the coach of the French envoy at the celebration of the arrival of a new Swedish envoy. Two servants were killed. Louis at once convened an extraordinary council. It unanimously advised moderation, but Louis, instead, decided to push the issue. He expelled the Spanish envoy and obliged Philip IV of Spain, his father-in-law, to recall Batteville and to have his new envoy in France declare publicly before Louis in a formal audience that all Spanish diplomats had been instructed not to contest precedence with their French counterparts, a key expression of the use of the diplomatic world to establish status. The thirty other diplomats accredited to Louis were present at the audience and, to underline his triumph, Louis issued a medallion depicting the audience to celebrate his victory" (Black 2010: 77).

In early modern Europe, rank and precedence in interactions reflected the social strata of the wider society (Collins/Sanderson 2009: 115-117). Status differences were effective across various situations and had to be taken into account in every interaction regardless of its topics. Interactions were thus characterized by the fact that the distribution of rank and precedence did not vary (Collins 2000: 36-37): Those with a higher status have to insist, without embarrassing themselves, that their interpretation of a given situation should be given priority. They can set topics largely ruthlessly, take initiatives on their own authority, speak out to others, and occupy the most prominent place without further questions. Those who renounce their status privileges in a particular interaction run the risk of being subordinated in other interactions and relationships as well. Status issues were critical in early modern diplomatic interactions, because the loss of status in a diplomatic interaction was not limited to a "diplomatic" status alone but could affect the status of the person as a whole and thus also: in any other relationship and situation the person may be involved. It was therefore essential for diplomatic interactions that differences in status should also be made visible by symbolic means. These included the right to enter a room first, to take a certain place at a table, or to wear a hat in the presence of others. However, it was by no means the case that in these interactions status merely had to be represented. Rather, it was also a matter of establishing status in ceremonial interactions performatively and of defending it against opponents (Roosen 1980; Youssef 2020).

Once established, rank simplifies the situation for everyone. In reality, however, decisions on the distribution of rank among princes proved to be extremely difficult. It was assumed that there was a natural, God-given order of precedence, which also encompassed the relations between princes (Stollberg-Rilinger 2014b). That the hierarchical social structure was rooted in a cosmological order did not rule out corrections within this worldview. The hierarchy itself was sacrosanct but not the position of individuals within this hierarchy, who might just as well have attained their position by error or by usurpation. Changes in status were treated as if one were previously not aware that the person concerned was always meant to be in this new position. Ennoblements, the elevation of the status of a royal title or the ascent to an exclusive club of kings were therefore not attributed to human decisions or merits but had to be stylized as a correction of an erroneous interpretation of an already given and divinely determined order (Luhmann 2013b: 61). The status and title of the Holy Roman emperor, for example, were justified historically and, above all, in terms of salvation history in that the title maintains the continuity of the Roman Empire, which, according to biblical tradition, is the last of four world empires and whose demise and fall also heralds the Last Judgement (Goez 1958: 4-6). Whoever may bear this desired title may, according to the *translatio imperii*-theory, consider himself to be a successor of Roman Emperors. It was therefore the subject of both theological debates and diplomatic conflicts because it was also associated with a secular authority and a special legal status in relation to the church (ibid: 93ff.). However, if there is any sophisticated but also practice-oriented reflection on international (or inter-dynastic) status problems in the early modern period, it is in treatises dealing with the question of ceremonial precedence.

The order of precedence among European princes was as well subject of much controversy about particular status criteria and their operationalization (Stollberg-Rilinger 1997; 2002; 2014b). The seniority of a royal title was probably the most important aspect. However, one finds quite subtle arguments in this respect. James Howell (1664: 93), for example, argued that immediately after the Roman emperor the English king could claim precedence over French and Spanish kings, since it was an English king who first freed himself from the "Roman yoke" and gained sovereignty. But he also brings other criteria into play, for example the salubriousness of London's air, which according to Howell could not be compared with the air in Paris or Madrid (ibid: 87). Conversely, in his *Cosmographia*, Stefan Münster considered the Spanish precedence against England and France to be justified and underlines this in an illustration in which Spain appears as the head and crown of Europe by aligning a map of Europe to the west—a solution which must have also been appropriate, since the Holy Roman Emperor Charles V, to whom the *Cosmographia* was dedicated, then also ruled over Spain (McLean 2007: 178).[1] Against the background of an even more complex hierarchy within the Holy Roman Empire, a ceremonial discourse emerged around the idea to identify uniform criteria for the distribution of precedence (Vec 1998).

In the context of this and similar discourses on ceremonial precedence, the first ranking lists were created to help clarify and standardize ranking issues. Rankings that take the form of a list have the decisive advantage that they do not only depict status differences spatially, i.e. vertically, but are more abstract and can imply temporal sequences as well. It seems reasonable that in early modern ceremonial discourses, orders of precedence were established as lists, since it was not only the distribution of social positions in space that was important here but also temporal precedence (Stollberg-Rilinger 2014b: 206). Who is allowed to enter a room first, who is allowed to speak first or who

---

1   A digitized version of this map is accessible online: https://de.wikipedia.org/wiki/Cos
     mographia_(Sebastian_M%C3%BCnster)#/media/Datei:Europe_As_A_Queen_Sebasti
     an_Munster_1570.jpg (February 2, 2021).

is allowed to stand up or sit down first? All these are questions that imply a temporal dimension. In the early modern context of courtly diplomacy, these were important issues as soon as the presence of a diplomatic corps at a particular court had to be reckoned with (Roosen 1980). In Renaissance diplomacy it was especially the papal court in Rome where one can speak of the emergence of a pre-modern diplomatic corps (Fletcher 2015). And it is precisely in this context that perhaps the most known and widespread ceremonial ranking of European royal titles was established: The *Ordo regum christianorum*, a ranking table set up in 1504 in the ceremonial diary of the Papal master of ceremonies, Paris de Grassi (Stenzig 2013).

At first sight, it is a simple list of royal titles written down one after the other, beginning with the title of the Roman Emperor which is followed by the Roman king, the king of France, the king of Spain etc.[2] In this form, it could also be a "messy" list, itemizing things like an inventory without any visible priorities. However, the ceremonial context tells us that the list includes the most important elements of a ranking, since it illustrates "a general prestige divide from top to bottom, which is a continuous one" as well as "a correspondingly asymmetrical communication structure with precedence at the top and subordination at the bottom; and finally [...] a permanency of corresponding status [...] which enables not only an occasionally effective orientation but also an expectable one" (Luhmann 1987a: 169). The history of the creation and reception of this ranking is, however, rather complicated (Stenzig 2013). Its basic form and order were taken up again and again well into the 18th century in order to legitimise or challenge claims to precedence. Some later reproductions of this list in the early 18th century already show a difference: the listing of royal titles is supplemented by a numeration (Lünig 1719: 8-10). The numbering, however, does not actually add any further explanation for the order of the ranking but seems above all to highlight transitivity or, respectively, sequentiality. Apart from the numbering, most ceremonial rankings do not contain any further explanations for the distribution of positions, as is the case in modern rankings e.g. in the form of simple numerical indicators. Nor did contemporaries seem to have had any particular need to emphasize changes in position in a particular way. However, this is a logical consequence when a preordained and stable order of precedence is assumed, and changes are regarded as problematic. Remarks on controversial ranking

---

2   A digitized version of this list is accessible online: https://digi.vatlib.it/view/MSS_Vat.l at.4739/0014 (February 2, 2021).

positions, such as those made by Paris de Grassi indicating conflicts between Scottish and Hungarian priority claims ("inter se discordes"), should also be understood in this sense.

Only in a ranking by Johann Christian Lünig (1719: 10-11) does one fins references to earlier authors which justify a ranking that deviates in a remarkable way from the papal model: For example, the Ottoman sultan (as the "Türckische [..] Kayser") is ranked third after the Roman emperor and king—while the title of Roman king was in practice held by the designated heir to the throne of the current emperor. At the bottom of the list, i.e. in thirty-second place, there are the Asian and African powers ("puissancen") following the free imperial knights in the order of precedence. Thus, the list exceeds already the boundaries of previous rankings, which were mainly limited to Christian titles. All in all, Lünig's ranking presents itself as a compromise, as the list does not show how the contradictory positions of different authors on ceremonial precedence were weighed against each other. The titles that are ranked one after the other are not further qualified with regard to certain criteria. Indeed, Lünig (ibid: 9) even takes the trouble to summarize how earlier authors tried to identify and systematize hierarchies and weightings between certain status indicators. The main focus was on seniority, but also on reputation, power or the number of titles held by a king. But it remains totally unclear how Lünig operationalizes these indicators for his own ranking and how he finally arrives at his results. If the Ottoman Sultan ranks third, why are other African and Asian rulers at the absolute bottom of the list? One can only speculate whether it may have been due to the fact that only occasional diplomatic contacts were maintained with these regions, but this is not explicitly shown as an indicator.

In any case, the distribution of rank among European royals was a delicate issue, which was only becoming more complicated with the reformation. The delicacy of this issue is also evident from the fact that ceremonial precedence was not considered as a decision-making problem. After all, who could have made a decision on this? Rather, arguments were first made on the basis of those "naturally grown" rankings which emerged in repeated meetings of royal envoys at the papal court. Even the first systematic ranking by Paris de Grassi did not claim to make a final decision on the distribution of rank but merely tried to infer an order from previous cases (Stenzig 2013: 548-550). After the Reformation, the ceremonial practice at the papal court could hardly serve as a standard for all European princely courts. In addition, de Grassi's papal order included titles of rulers that were no longer held by anyone, while, on the other hand, new European powers were missing on it. Moreover, ceremonial practice had to take into account not only the rank of their principals but also the social status of the envoys themselves. There was also a barely codified differentiation in diplomatic status, which could depend, for instance, on the extent of an envoy's mandate (Mattingly 1988).

These structural contradictions prevented the emergence of a permanent order of precedence between European kings and their emissaries for centuries. Every diplomatic interaction was faced with the alternative of either being a conflict or suppressing conflicts, since interactions in general can hardly isolate open conflicts and let them run alongside other issues (Luhmann 2015: 24-26). Especially ceremonial and ritual interactions of courtly society were based on the premise that everyone knew his place and played his role, which is why at least a "fiction of consensus" was necessary and conflicts could not be ignored (Luebke 2010). At the same time, conflicts had to be tolerated to a certain extent in order to find out whose claims to rank were justified and what was, so to speak, the current state of world politics that was to be represented in ceremonial interactions. The dilemma seemed insoluble: Whoever renounced his prescribed status violated a God-given order. Those who defended their status with all means against challengers also put order at risk when conflicts broke out.

Initially, procedures were developed to clarify the question of precedence in particular interactions. Conflicts were sometimes settled by lot (Stollberg-Rilinger 2014a). In other cases, appearing "incognito" was an acceptable ceremonial exception (Barth 2013). Where interactions seemed impossible due to irreconcilable status conflicts, written communication was used. The dispatch of low-ranking envoys was a way to save face and rank, as a potential renunciation of precedence could be attributed to the low rank of the envoy rather than to the principal's rank (Krischer 2009). Sometimes, diplomatically negotiated compromises in preliminary stages of ceremonial interactions were an important means of settling conflicts. However, no permanent order of precedence could be established by these practical and often improvised fixes.

These procedures were not sufficient, as stable expectations could only be formed on the basis of codified norms. In order to conduct a reasonable dispute about precedence at all, both criteria and observables had to be defined in a predictable way—a problem which was also the subject of a whole discourse on ceremonial law (Vec 1998). But here again the problem arose that nobody dared to make rules for kings. Of course, legal claims to ceremonial precedence were not legitimized in the sense of positive law that could be decided and changed by human beings. Rather, the problem was seen in interpreting an always given natural or divine order and in deriving criteria for the distribution of ceremonial prerogatives based on legal reasoning and the exegesis of canonical texts (Stollberg-Rilinger 2014b).

The consequence, however, was not so much a legal solution to questions of rank as the expansion of a princely vocabulary of motives with which claims to rank could now be formulated in a legal terminology (Krischer 2009). A position in a ranking was considered not only a matter of custom, but a God-given right. In order to understand the interaction problems that arose from the participants' point of view, a somewhat daring metaphor may be helpful: One is invited to dinner by an invisible host who put place cards on the dining table for each guest—only the names on these place cards are written quite indecipherably. What happens then is not a competition for a seat in the sense of a "musical chair" game but a dispute that breaks out over what is written on the place cards and who has to sit in which chair. In this sense, there are conflicting but not competing views about what seating arrangement is in God's mind. And those for whose recognition one could have competed were themselves competitors with their own stakes in the game. There was therefore no plausible "disinterested" third party for whose favor one could compete.

Furthermore, there was no discourse on competition as a social model that could turn enemies into competitors and in this sense represent a distinct alternative to conflict. In German ceremonial treatises of that period, words like "concurriren" and "competiren" were used rather unsystematically to describe ceremonial occasions from which conflicts could arise. Whenever kings or their envoys "concurriren," this did not mean "Konkurrenz" (competition) in modern German terms but rather an encounter, a gathering or a meeting (Nehring/Friedrich 1710: 111). In a figurative sense, "competiren" also meant the collision of several claims for precedence. Furthermore, according to the legitimate vocabulary of motives in this society, it would have been selfish to compete for God's favor because one should not act to receive certain privileges (and ultimately: salvation), but on the condition that one is loved by God (Elster 1991: 282; Simmel 2009: 267). And that meant acknowledging one's place in God's order and not striving for something higher. Therefore, the struggle for higher social status was "by no means regarded as positive social norm, but on the contrary as a violation of the norm, as turbatio ordinis" (Stollberg-Rilinger 2014b: 198). Against this background, the idea of an open-ended competition for the right of precedence would have been tantamount to blasphemy. Finally, even the emulation of higher-ranking role models was not encouraged but rather limited by social structures and semantics. "[S]oci-ety supported the *interdits* that limited competition in imitation. And however much emulation of the models valid for one's own status was recommended and the corresponding 'mirrors' held up, it made an inappropriate and ludi-crous impression if one sought to overstep the applicable limits" (Luhmann 2013b: 213).

Nor can one speak of royal competition for the favor of a courtly public because favor could only be granted top-down and not in the opposite direc-tion. In principle, even friendly relations that kings and envoys maintained with foreign courts were interpreted as asymmetrical patron-client relation-ships in which favor was exchanged for allegiance. If this were to lead to some-thing like competition for loyalty (or social capital), this view would have been discouraged by the social structures and semantics of the time (Bauer 1995; Thiessen 2011): Royal patrons were not expected to compete for clients but rather required them to act according to their ascribed status as clients and to show loyalty for favors received. The client was not to be courted by com-petitors but eventually had to deal with conflicting loyalties when he owed allegiance to opposing patrons. Both patrons and clients had to reckon with semantics for the legitimation of their actions, which were hardly concerned with the idea of selection by competition but rather with normative obliga-tions that arose from generation-spanning patron-client relationships. It was not superior competitiveness but trust in seniority and historically rooted re-lationships between families that provided the rhetorical framework for these relationships, which clients could not easily compromise without jeopardiz-ing their own reputation. This applied particularly to the relationships be-tween ceremonial scholars and the aristocratic patrons on whose goodwill they were dependent at least until the end of the 18th century (Bauer 1995). Therefore, a royal competition for the favor of scholars engaging in a ceremo-nial discourse would have probably seemed quite alienating to those involved. Here too, there were no plausible "disinterested" third parties for whose fa-vor one could compete. The situation is quite different with IGOs and NGOs, whose rankings can be so influential that nation states also compete for the favor of experts.

What we can say is that competition plays almost no significant role in pre-modern rankings. Neither textual and pictorial semantics nor the social structure make it plausible to assume that kings competed for the favor of third parties in order to raise their status. One cannot even say that these rankings represent an attempt to suppress competition. In fact, competition in particular could have been a solution to the problem that rank conflicts constantly erupted in diplomatic interactions. However, a very clear motive is the attempt to contain conflicts by making a divinely ordained order visible. Even this, to be sure, was only modestly successful. Lünig's *Theatrum Ceremoniale* (1719) provides the best proof of this, for only the first ten pages are attempts to systematize a hierarchy, followed by hundreds of pages in which a myriad of individual ceremonial events are presented which all more or less contradict Lünig's systematic approach. What was actually achieved by the intellectual discourse on ceremonial rankings, however, was the explication of status criteria and an increase in the ability to initiate and endure conflict. Legal arguments made it easier to articulate and challenge claims to status and precedence, since they could not simply be attributed to the personal preferences of those affected, as long as assumedly objective rules of interpretation were observed. It was easier to distinguish legitimate from unjustified claims and, in the latter case, to reject them. What could not be prevented was that conflicts over precedence remained morally problematic. The idea of a status order depending on the outcome of human struggles seemed downright dangerous, especially since antagonistic relationships among royals had cascade-like implications for the rest of society, which could be called upon to wage war at any time when status issues were at stake (Geevers 2012).

It has been shown that pre-modern rankings have similarities with modern rankings in many respects. Nevertheless, premodern rankings neither represent, assume or induce competition. They are based on completely different understandings of a world in which modern notions of political competition between European kings must have seemed outlandish. It must have been difficult to imagine for whose favor kings could actually have competed. Neither God nor an aristocratic audience, neither masters of ceremony nor the populace would have been plausible as relevant third parties in this sense. Suggesting that competition is taking place in this context misjudges the view of historical actors and leads to anachronistic interpretations. But what conditions must be met to be able to speak of competition in the context of world politics without reifying analytical concepts? The following considerations will show that world political status became the object of competition to the extent that communication was decoupled from the logics of face-to-face interaction. Another factor is the functional differentiation of world society and the emergence of a world political system observed by mass media and a global public.

Status Rankings in Modern World Politics:
Competition beyond Interaction

In contrast to the stratified aristocratic society of early modern times, modern world society is primarily functionally differentiated. In functional systems of modern world society (politics, law, economy, art, religion, etc.), scarce goods such as power, money or knowledge are distributed according to the system's distinct logics. This makes a single transitive ranking order of society impossible (Luhmann 2013b: 87-89): wealth is expected to be acquired legitimately only through market competition, power is expected to be acquired legitimately only through legal procedures and scientific facts are expected to be acquired legitimately only through adherence to scientific standards. A high status in one field does not automatically mean a high status in other fields. This applies not only to persons occupying multiple incongruent roles but also to states, who may be strong military but weak economic powers (Meyer/Hammond 1971; Meyer/Jepperson 2000; Larson et al. 2014: 9). States hold very different and often incongruent statuses depending on the field (see Freistein/Müller in this volume).

In general, the chance of a nation state to impose its own perspectives on other states varies depending on the respective field. Given the norm of formally equal, sovereign states, it is often considered quite problematic that there is a global super-elite that can occupy superior positions in all social fields because they illegitimately take advantages from one field to another (Phillips 2018), just as it could equally seem suspicious if a state were superior in every respect, because this could suggest that, for example, economic success is not based on fair competition in a global market economy but on military power (Go 2011). The global critique of imperialism is therefore a good example of the fact that actual cases of status congruence collide with the structures and semantics of a functionally differentiated world society. What was previously considered the ideal case of perfection because a universal monarchy was the model to be aspired to (Pagden 1995), is now suspected of corruption.

The status differences of formally equal states are also negotiated in the practice of international organizations or diplomacy (see Boyashov in this volume; Pouliot 2011, Youssef 2020). In diplomatic interactions, several field-specific status orders overlap and become relevant: "a German diplomat will use the country's reputation for fiscal discipline as an asset in a budgetary negotiation in Brussels; a Brazilian delegate will build off the country's developmental success story to gain some leverage in a debate over poverty eradication; and a Japanese representative will find, in the country's anti-military policies of the last sixty years, some credibility to make the case for disarmament" (Pouliot 2016: 84). The ambivalence that comes with such different and not always clearly distributed statuses is also expressed in the fact that diplomats can hardly, on request, explain the criteria they use to ascribe status to one another. They have to rely on their implicit "sense of one's place" in their interactions because there is no longer the expectation of a clear predefined status order in society (ibid: 51-53, 72-74). Furthermore, the diplomatic protocol is now basically decoupled from the power or prestige of diplomatic principals. The rules of protocol concerning precedence in diplomatic interactions depend primarily on the rank or seniority of the diplomat and are supplemented by an alphabetical order of nation states, which, for example, structure seating arrangements (French 2010: 7-9). Interaction parameters such as seating arrangements, speaking times or precedence when entering a room are therefore largely decoupled from other international status inequalities.

Diplomatic interactions are thus largely relieved of the task of establishing world-political status, which becomes a function of an abstract global system in which nations compete for abstract goods such as power, diplomatic recognition and global attention. Competition is now facilitated under the condition that indirect social relations are made possible, which was hardly the case in early modern face-to-face encounters. In early modern times, the only way to compete would have been to win the favor of those royal peers who were themselves competitors. For various reasons, God and the members of the lower classes were not third parties for whose favor one could have reasonably competed. This has changed with the emergence of both modern mass media and a global public sphere, for whose favor it is all the easier to compete if it does not consist of potential competitors. It is part of the logic of the political system of world society to assume a 'world opinion', i.e. a public that does not directly participate in interactions but observes world politics from a distance and plays a significant role in legitimizing it (Jaeger 2004). In this sense, the global public functions as a 'rationalized other', that is the fiction of anonymous third parties 'out there' whose interpretation of international politics must be taken into account in most decisions (Meyer et al. 1997). Therefore, it is precisely the favor of this absent audience that can be constructed and experienced as a scarce good for which it is worth competing. This public, of course, is not directly addressable as in an agora, and on the level of world politics, unlike in democratic nation states, it cannot directly contribute to legitimation through elections. It is, however, on the one hand constructed by mass media and on the other hand represented by advocates who observe, interpret and comment on world political events on behalf of the global civil society. These may be international organizations as well as mass media, NGOs and professional communities of experts in specific policy areas (Meyer 1994).

Unlike early modern authors of ceremonial literature, however, the modern advocates of civil society find it easier to claim impartiality to the extent that their accounts are derived from expertise based on evidence and adherence to journalistic and scientific standards rather than personal loyalties. To a certain extent, they act as neutral referees in many policy areas and contribute to making national performance in certain policy areas objectively comparable in terms of whether they achieve universalized welfare goals (Meyer 2000). Depending on the policy field and welfare objective, the international comparison of welfare indicators can be used to justify status differences that have been achieved in an open performance-based competition. This fulfils another condition for competition that we derived from Simmel, namely that the distribution of a scarce good (in this case: status) depends on a performance-based procedure.

The status of nation states is now determined by their perceived performance in various fields, a performance that varies over time and can be observed in terms of comparable "careers" (Dorn/Tacke 2018). "The spatial metaphor of fixed positions that can be occupied and appropriated," noted Luhmann (2013b: 261) "is replaced by a time metaphor in which the danger of displacement is succeeded by the risk of landing in unfavorable positions owing to decisions." This focus on the performance of formally equal states stands in stark contrast to fixed statuses in other fields. The permanent members of the UN Security Council, for example, are still the victorious powers of World War II. Their status is to a certain extent "set in stone" by the membership rules of the United Nations, although much has changed in the meantime with decolonisation and the rise or fall of supposed great powers (Pouliot 2014). Such one-dimensional and invariable status orders are particularly prone to conflict, while open competition in different policy fields can help to ease tensions in international relations. Indeed, if there are multiple dynamic and performance-based status orders, this increases the chances of achieving a good position in at least one ranking. For these reasons, as Amitai Etzioni (1962) argues, competition can be explicitly propagated as a nonviolent alternative to open conflict that can reduce conflict potentials to the extent that it transforms status and prestige into subjects of a fair and regulated procedure with an open outcome. Furthermore, the idea often prevails that competition can lead to improved performance, innovation and rationalisation of political decisions and performances (Cerny 1997).

Under these conditions, rankings seem to have gained in importance over the past two or three decades as a virtual arena for international competition. They are not only aimed at measuring and improving nation state performance but also at providing a stage on which the distribution of status is on the one hand made more dynamic and on the other hand achieved by less conflict-prone means (Cooley/Snyder 2015; Davis et al. 2012a, 2012b; Youssef 2018). In this way, social structures and semantics of competition also become manifest and have an impact on the production and presentation of these rankings.

Rankings can be used to substantiate status claims in a policy field. States leading a ranking on the basis of their supposedly successful policies may find it easier to fend off criticism and demands for reform, whereas this is much more difficult at lower positions in a ranking (van der Vleuten/Verloo 2012). In certain policy areas they have superior chances of asserting their view of a given situation and can present their own policies as best practice.

Modern nation-state rankings are embedded in a semantics of competition. They claim to reflect a temporally and variable social status of nation-states with regard to certain policy issues (Cooley/Snyder 2015; Shore/Wright 2015). Status in general is derived less from a divinely predetermined order and is also based less on the ascription of seniority or temporally stable qualities but is considered legitimate above all when it is acquired through temporally variable and competing achievements of various kinds (Parsons 1970; Corvellec 2017). Rankings apply this general idea in the context of international relations by constructing nation states as comparable actors competing for the favor of a public, even if the compared nation states do not otherwise perceive each other as competitors and behave accordingly. They do so by means of comparing performances, by quantification, visualization, and repeated publication. They make the distribution of status and reputation appear as a zero-sum game and transform a previously given and stable status order into a dynamic one (Brankovic et al. 2018). The semantics of competition, therefore, have an immediate impact on the production and design of these rankings.

To aggregate a variety of dimensions into one ranking position, rankings translate qualities into quantities (ibid: 274-275). Formalization and quantification are among the most important means of claiming objectivity and a formally equal measurement of the listed countries. In this sense, international organizations also use rankings to make their decision-making structures more flexible and to adapt them to a constantly changing world (Youssef 2018). Typically, measurements are also repeated over and over again, and rankings are updated accordingly (Brankovic et al. 2018: 275-276). Changes in position are emphasized by symbolic markers such as up and down arrows, curve diagrams or numerical indications of the position gain.

Another important connection between rankings and competition is that there are not only several indicators that form the basis for a single ranking, but that there are also several rankings in the same policy area. Both factors increase the probability that nation states will take leading positions at least for one indicator or at least in one ranking and thus not be completely discouraged from participating in the competition (Etzioni 1962: 29-31). If, however, these ranking procedures cannot always contribute to higher mobility in a status system because certain states repeatedly occupy the last places in all the rankings, then a decision can also be made, which, despite the statistical evidence, may lead to an increase in formal status, as was the case with Angola's rise from a "least" to a "less developed country" (United Nations 2016). And, last but not least, the temporal structure of modern society makes it possible to settle for a lower ranking position under the condition that an open future offers the plausible chance to improve one's own status. This face-saving interpretation is, so to speak, the functional equivalent of the assumption that one's own status is divinely predetermined and that one has to come to terms with it. Ambition is thus not necessarily a sin under modern conditions but the precarious promise of a better future. This view gains plausibility in a world society that is not only able to establish competition but also to evaluate it positively—regardless of whether competition actually contributes to a better world or just keeps the players in the game.

Conclusion

Competition is by no means a universal, but rather a structurally quite demanding social form that differs substantially from conflict. There are social systems that make competition in certain respects possible and others that exclude it or make it appear pointless. Analyzing the semantics of a social field is a possible way to arrive at generalizable conclusions about whether status competition is a structural factor that is part of shared convictions and reflexive expectations. Rankings and the literature accompanying them are relevant sources in this case because they form a medium in which status issues are communicated in a sophisticated but not too philosophical way. However, the selected rankings only say something about status competition in the context of world politics. They say nothing about the significance of competition and conflict in societies per se or in other social contexts such as sport, love, or commerce. It cannot be ruled out, for example, that in the early modern period there was competition in the search for marriage partners—provided that it was not prescribed by legal claims, ideas of predestination or strict marriage and kinship rules in a very small upper class. Nor can it be assumed that modern rankings do play a significant role in world politics. However, they provided sufficient evidence to raise doubts about the assumption of a universality of competition. On the one hand, the similarities between premodern and modern rankings are striking and initially speak in favor of the assumption of universal status competition. On the other hand, these rankings are embedded in structural and semantic contexts that suggest a more differentiated diagnosis. The case is quite clear in modern world politics, where competition is structurally facilitated and can even be advocated as an alternative model to conflict—at least when it comes to achieving universalistic welfare goals. In contrast, there are no manifest indications of status competition in pre-modern courtly society, where, however, diplomatic interactions were notoriously characterized by status conflicts. Neither social structures nor semantics offered favorable conditions for competition in this context. This raises the question of whether and to what extent one can actually speak of international (or inter-dynastic) status competition in early modern court society.

It is in any case appropriate to speak of competition if it can be proved in specific historical situations. However, this does not necessarily say something about the structural characteristics of a system. It is also acceptable to speak of "struggles" in a more general sense if the difference between conflict and competition is unclear. However, this also means a loss of analytical clarity.

From a theoretical point of view, the question also arises of whether competition is an appropriate model for theories of social change. This particularly concerns theories of state formation, which often assume geopolitical competition to be a driving force in the evolution of international systems (Teschke 2003: 117-119). On the one hand, they predominantly analyze the dynamics of direct (military) conflicts about territories rather than indirect competition. On the other hand, every serious theory of evolution considers randomness, rather than a "survival of the fittest", as a decisive principle (Bonner 2013). As with the lottery, it would be therefore misleading in this context to speak of competition, unless in a metaphorical, but analytically insufficient sense. Rather, social evolution could be understood more generally as a differentiation of mechanisms of structural variation, selection and stabilization (Luhmann 2013a: 251-253). Such a general theory of socio-cultural evolution would enable us to understand the differentiation of conflict, competition, cooperation or reciprocity as a historical variable, which also depends on the extent to which the reproduction and structural change of a society are dependent on face-to-face interactions (Luhmann 1987b). Finally, analysts may as well simply assume competition where it is structurally possible and semantically reflected. Where this is not the case, Ludwig Wittgenstein's dictum is to be recommended: "What we cannot speak about we must pass over in silence" (Wittgenstein 2001: 89).

References

Albert, Mathias (2016): A Theory of World Politics, Cambridge: Cambridge University Press.

Barth, Volker (2013): Inkognito. Geschichte eines Zeremoniells, München: Oldenbourg.

Bauer, Volker (1995): "Zeremoniell und Ökonomie. Der Diskurs über die Hofökonomie in Zeremonialwissenschaft, Kameralismus und Hausväterliteratur in Deutschland 1700-1780." In: Jörg J. Berns/ Thomas Rahn (eds.), Zeremoniell als höfische Ästhetik in Spätmittelalter und Früher Neuzeit, Tübingen: M. Niemeyer, pp. 21-56.

Berns, Jörg J./Rahn, Thomas (eds.) (1995): Zeremoniell als höfische Ästhetik in Spätmittelalter und früher Neuzeit, Tübingen: M. Niemeyer.

Black, Jeremy (2010): A History of Diplomacy, London: Reaktion.

Bonner, John T. (2013): Randomness in Evolution, Princeton: Princeton University Press.

Brankovic, Jelena/Ringel, Leopold/Werron, Tobias (2018): "How Rankings Produce Competition: The Case of Global University Rankings." In: Zeitschrift für Soziologie 47/4, pp. 270-288.

Cerny, Philip G. (1997): "Paradoxes of the Competition State: The Dynamics of Political Globalization." In: Government and Opposition 32/2, pp. 251-274.

Collins, Randall (2000): "Situational Stratification. A Micro-Macro Theory of Inequality." In: Sociological Theory 18/1, pp. 17-43.

Collins, Randall/Sanderson, Stephen K. (2009): Conflict Sociology. A sociological classic updated, Boulder: Paradigm.

Cooley, Alexander/Snyder, Jack L. (eds.) (2015): Ranking the World. Grading States as a Tool of Global Governance, Cambridge: Cambridge University Press.

Corvellec, Hervé (2017): Stories of Achievements. Narrative Features of Organizational Performance, London: Routledge.

Dafoe, Allan/Renshon, Jonathan/Huth, Paul (2014): "Reputation and Status as Motives for War." In: Annual Review of Political Science 17/1, pp. 371-393.

Davis, Kevin E./Fisher, Angelina/Kingsbury, Benedict/Merry, Sally E. (eds.) (2012a): Governance by Indicators. Global Power through Quantification and Rankings, Oxford: Oxford University Press.

Davis, Kevin E./Kingsbury, Benedict/Merry, Sally E. (2012b): "Indicators as a Technology of Global Governance." In: Law & Society Review 46/1, pp. 71-104.

Dorn, Christopher/Tacke, Veronika (eds.) (2018): Vergleich und Leistung in der funktional differenzierten Gesellschaft, Wiesbaden: Springer VS.

Eisenstadt, S. N./Roniger, Luis (1984): Patrons, Clients, and Friends. Interpersonal Relations and the Structure of Trust in Society, Cambridge: Cambridge University Press.

Elias, Norbert (2000): The Civilizing Process. Sociogenetic and Psychogenetic Investigations, Malden: Blackwell.

Elster, Jon (1991): "Local Justice: How Institutions Allocate Scarce Goods and Necessary Burdens." In: European Economic Review 35/2-3, pp. 273-291.

Etzioni, Amitai (1962): "International Prestige, Competition and Peaceful Coexistence." In: European Journal of Sociology 3/1, pp. 21-41.

Fletcher, Catherine (2015): Diplomacy in Renaissance Rome. The Rise of the Resident Ambassador, Cambridge: Cambridge University Press.

French, Mary (2010): United States Protocol. The Guide to Official Diplomatic Etiquette, Lanham: Rowman & Littlefield.

Geevers, Liesbeth (2012): "The Conquistador and the Phoenix: the Franco-Spanish Precedence Dispute (1564–1610) as a Battle of Kingship." In: The International History Review 35/1, pp. 23-41.

Go, Julian (2011): Patterns of Empire. The British and American Empires, 1688 to the Present, Cambridge: Cambridge University Press.

Goez, Werner (1958): Translatio imperii. Ein Beitrag zur Geschichte des Geschichtsdenkens und der politischen Theorien im Mittelalter und in der frühen Neuzeit, Tübingen: Mohr.

Howell, James (1664): Proedria-Basilike: A Discourse Concerning the Precedency of Kings, London: Ja. Cottrel.

Jaeger, Hans-Martin (2004): "'World Opinion' and the Turn to Post-Sovereign International Governance." In: Mathias Albert/Lena Hilkermeier (eds.), Observing International Relations. Niklas Luhmann and World Politics, London: Routledge, pp. 142-156.

Krischer, André (2009): "Souveränität als sozialer Status: Zur Funktion des diplomatischen Zeremoniells in der Frühen Neuzeit." In: Ralph Kauz/Giorgio Rota/Jan P. Niederkorn (eds.), Diplomatisches Zeremoniell in Europa und im Mittleren Osten in der Frühen Neuzeit, Wien: Verlag der Österreichischen Akademie der Wissenschaften, pp. 1-32.

Luebke, David M. (2010): "Ceremony and Dissent: Religion, Procedural Conflicts, and the 'Fiction of Consensus' in Seventeenth-Century Germany." In: Benjamin Marschke/David W. Sabean/Jason P. Coy (eds.), The Holy Roman Empire, reconsidered, New York: Berghahn Books, pp. 145-161.

Luhmann, Niklas (1982): Liebe als Passion. Zur Codierung von Intimität, Frankfurt/Main: Suhrkamp.

Luhmann, Niklas (1987a): Rechtssoziologie, Opladen: Westdeutscher Verlag.

Luhmann, Niklas (1987b): "The Evolutionary Differentiation between Society and Interaction." In: Jeffrey C. Alexander/Bernhard Giesen/Richard Münch et al. (eds.), The Micro-Macro Link, Berkeley: University of California Press, pp. 112-131.

Luhmann, Niklas (2013a): Theory of Society, Vol. I, Stanford: Stanford University Press.

Luhmann, Niklas (2013b): Theory of Society, Vol. II, Stanford: Stanford University Press.

Luhmann, Niklas (2015): "Ebenen der Systembildung—Ebenendifferenzierung." In: Bettina Heintz/Hartmann Tyrell (eds.), Interaktion—Organisation—Gesellschaft revisited. Anwendungen, Erweiterungen, Alternativen, Stuttgart: Lucius & Lucius, pp. 6-39.

Lünig, Johann C. (1719): Theatrum Ceremoniale Historico-Politicum, Leipzig: Weidmann.

Mattingly, Garrett (1988): Renaissance diplomacy, New York: Dover Publications.

McLean, Matthew A. (2007): The Cosmographia of Sebastian Münster. Describing the World in the Reformation, Aldershot: Ashgate.

Meyer, John W. (1994): "Rationalized Environments." In: W. R. Scott/John W. Meyer (eds.), Institutional Environments and Organizations. Structural Complexity and Individualism, Thousand Oaks: Sage, pp. 28-54.

Meyer, John W. (2000): "Globalization: Sources and Effects on National States and Societies." In: International Sociology 15/2, pp. 233-248.

Meyer, John W./Boli, John/Thomas, George M. et al. (1997): "World Society and the Nation-State." In: American Journal of Sociology 103/1, pp. 144-181.

Meyer, John W./Hammond, P. E. (1971): "Forms of Status Inconsistency", in: Social Forces 50, pp. 91-101.

Meyer, John W./Jepperson, Ronald L. (2000): "The 'Actors' of Modern Society. The Cultural Construction of Social Agency." In: Sociological Theory 18/1, pp. 100-120.

Nehring, Johann C. (1710): Joh. Christoph Nehrings Historisch-Politisch-Juristisches Lexicon, Gotha: Mevius.

Osborne, Toby (2007): "The Surrogate War between the Savoys and the Medici: Sovereignty and Precedence in Early Modern Italy." In: The International History Review 29/1, pp. 1-21.

Pagden, Anthony (1995): Lords of all the World. Ideologies of Empire in Spain, Britain and France c.1500-c.1800, New Haven: Yale University Press.

Parsons, Talcott (1970): "Equality and Inequality in Modern Society, or Social Stratification Revisited." In: Sociological Inquiry 40/2, pp. 13-72.

Paul, T. V./Larson, Deborah W./Wohlforth, William C. (eds.) (2014): Status in World Politics, New York: Cambridge University Press.

Phillips, Peter (2018): Giants. The Global Power Elite, New York: Seven Stories Press.

Pouliot, Vincent (2011): "Diplomats as Permanent Representatives: The Practical Logics of the Multilateral Pecking Order." In: International Journal: Canada's Journal of Global Policy Analysis 66/3, pp. 543-561.

Pouliot, Vincent (2014): "Setting Status in Stone: The Negotiation of International Institutional Privileges." In: Paul, T. V./Larson, Deborah W./Wohlforth, William C. (eds.), Status in World Politics, pp. 192-215.

Pouliot, Vincent (2016): International Pecking Orders, Cambridge: Cambridge University Press.

Roosen, Williams (1980): "Early Modern Diplomatic Ceremonial: A Systems Approach." In: The Journal of Modern History 52/3, pp. 452-476.

Schlögl, Rudolf (2019): "Public Sphere in the Making in Early Modern Europe", in: Annali dell'Istituto storico italo-germanico in Trento 45/2, pp. 23-40.

Shore, Cris/Wright, Susan (2015): "Governing by Numbers: Audit Culture, Rankings and the New World Order." In: Social Anthropology 23/1, pp. 22-28.

Simmel, Georg (2009): Sociology. Inquiries into the Construction of Social Forms, Leiden and Boston: Brill.

Sittig, Claudius (2010): Kulturelle Konkurrenzen. Studien zur Semiotik und Ästhetik adeligen Wetteifers um 1600, Berlin: de Gruyter.

Stenzig, Philipp (2013): Botschafterzeremoniell am Papsthof der Renaissance. Der Tractatus de oratoribus des Paris de Grassi — Edition und Kommentar, Frankfurt/Main: Peter Lang.

Stollberg-Rilinger, Barbara (1997): "Zeremoniell als politisches Verfahren. Rangordnung und Rangstreit als Strukturmerkmale des frühneuzeitlichen Reichstags." In: Johannes Kunisch (ed.), Neue Studien zur frühneuzeitlichen Reichsgeschichte, Berlin: Duncker & Humblot, pp. 91-132.

Stollberg-Rilinger, Barbara (2002): "Die Wissenschaft der feinen Unterschiede. Das Präzedenzrecht und die europäischen Monarchien vom 16. bis zum 18. Jahrhundert." In: Majestas 10, pp. 125-150.

Stollberg-Rilinger, Barbara (2014a): "Entscheidung durch das Los. Vom praktischen Umgang mit Unverfügbarkeit in der Frühen Neuzeit." In: André Brodocz/Dietrich Herrmann/Rainer Schmidt et al. (eds.), Die Verfassung des Politischen, Wiesbaden: Springer, pp. 63-83.

Stollberg-Rilinger, Barbara (2014b): "Logik und Semantik des Ranges in der Frühen Neuzeit." In: Ralph Jessen (ed.), Konkurrenz in der Geschichte. Praktiken—Werte—Institutionalisierungen, Frankfurt/Main: Campus, pp. 197-227.

Stollberg-Rilinger, Barbara (2016): "Symbolik und Technik des Wählens in der Vormoderne." In: Hedwig Richter/Hubertus Buchstein (eds.), Kultur und Praxis der Wahlen: Eine Geschichte der modernen Demokratie, Wiesbaden: Springer VS, pp. 31-62.

Teschke, Benno (2003): The Myth of 1648. Class, Geopolitics, and the Making of Modern International Relations, London: Verso.

Thiessen, Hillard von (2011): "Vertrauen aus Vergangenheit. Anciennität in grenzüberschreitender Patronage am Beispiel der Beziehungen von Adelshäusern des Kirchenstaats zur spanischen Krone im 16. und 17. Jahrhundert." In: Frank Bezner/Kirsten Mahlke (eds.), Zwischen Wissen und Politik. Archäologie und Genealogie frühneuzeitlicher Vergangenheitskonstruktionen, Heidelberg: Winter, pp. 21-39.

United Nations (2016): Graduation of Angola from the least developed country category, General Assembly Report, A/RES/70/253.

van der Vleuten, Anna/Verloo, Mieke (2012): "Ranking and Benchmarking: The political logic of new regulatory instruments in the fields of gender equality and anti-corruption." In: Policy & Politics 40/1, pp. 71-86.

Vec, Miloš (1998): Zeremonialwissenschaft im Fürstenstaat. Studien zur juristischen und politischen Theorie absolutistischer Herrschaftsrepräsentation, Frankfurt/Main: Klostermann.

Wittgenstein, Ludwig (2001): Tractatus Logico-Philosophicus, London: Taylor and Francis.

Wohlforth, William C. (2009): "Unipolarity, Status Competition, and Great Power War." In: World Politics 61/1, pp. 28-57.

Wood, Steve (2013): "Prestige in World Politics: History, Theory, Expression." In: International Politics 50/3, pp. 387-411.

Youssef, Ramy (2018): "Rankings statt Stellenordnungen? Funktionen und Folgen von Leistungsvergleichen in internationalen Organisationen", in: Christopher Dorn/Veronika Tacke (eds.), Vergleich und Leistung in der funktional differenzierten Gesellschaft, Wiesbaden: Springer VS, pp. 41-71.

Youssef, Ramy (2020): Die Anerkennung von Grenzen. Eine Soziologie der Diplomatie, Frankfurt/Main: Campus.

Network Power Europe and Competition at the UN Human Rights Council

Anatoly Boyashov

This contribution discusses the networked character of competition in world politics. While it follows the theoretical argument of competition for scarce objects in world politics (Werron 2014, 2015), the chapter engages with the question of what a scarce object in international organizations could be. Based on network theory, this chapter suggests that actors in international organizations significantly contribute to their competitiveness through the enhancement of their structural positions in networks relative to other actors. Actors establish and sustain networks to exert influence via control over communication flow within a network. In the case of networks within international organizations, the degree of centrality of an actor in the network determines their final access to the scarce objects of power, wealth, or status. The main structural positions in networks that actors compete for have tended to be largely associated with the terms of 'a network leader' and 'a network broker'. These positions enable actors to exert their influence in international organizations and, on a larger scale, in world politics.

Studies of the EU's actorness in competition have tended to concentrate around the question of what kind of power the EU is or should be. Two suggestions have framed this debate: 'normative power Europe' and 'market power Europe'. This debate continues to resonate in recent research focused on the EU capacities to set world regulatory standards and exert influence over global corporations (Bradford 2020). 'Normative power Europe' presupposes that the EU sets world regulatory standards because of its normative basis (competition for status) (Manners 2002). 'Market power Europe' argues that the EU's market is a strong impetus to compete for wealth (Damro 2012). The chapter returns to the methodological framework of EU regulatory networks, applying it to the EU external action at international organizations. The core of the EU's networks has comprised EU institutions that bridge all relevant stakeholders, thus uniting them to achieve the EU's priorities (cf. Dehousse 1997; Mathieu 2016). On that basis, the hypothesis is that the increasing complexity of international organizations pushes the EU to act as 'network power Europe' and compete for the structural position of a 'bridge' in complex networks. To test the hypothesis, this chapter poses the question of how the EU's attempts to build networks behind human rights promotion improve the EU's position relative to other actors and stakeholders at the UN Human Rights Council (UN HRC).

The subsequent sections of this chapter deal with the following objectives. The first section examines competition in world politics from the perspective of network theory. It highlights the deficiencies of a 'one-level' focus in studies of world politics, and more specifically, in research on international organizations. This tendency regards competition in world politics as exclusively competition among states and, rarely, among international legal subjects, where states constitute the international political system and all other stakeholders are considered as the system's environment. Even if the role of non-state stakeholders in world politics has been persistently highlighted by liberal institutionalists and scholars of global governance, the restricted 'one-level' focus has remained, with states and non-state stakeholders constituting their respective levels of governance or systems. At the same time, the complexity of actors and stakeholders that compete in world politics has been increasing, leading to the establishment of complex ties both within levels of governance and across them. The theoretical argument developed in this chapter pinpoints the complexity of these ties, which determines the network character of competition in world politics. It asks what 'scarcity' could mean in this context, and explores how varied actors in world politics gain advantage in network competition within international organizations.

The second section of the chapter investigates the case of network competition at the UN Human Rights Council. The section describes the institutional setting of the UN HRC and elaborates on the types of networks that have emerged at this intergovernmental body of the UN system. I argue that actors and stakeholders at international organizations, and particularly at the UN HRC, sustain complex network across three main 'levels' of governance: intergovernmental, interinstitutional, and interorganizational.

The final section of the chapter deals with the 'actorness' of the EU as one of the formal diplomatic networks at the UN HRC. Existing research on this matter points to EU attempts to compete for status or wealth, to exert external pressure through norms and regulations or through market-related benefits.

To gain advantage, the EU competes with external actors as 'normative power Europe' and 'market power Europe', the two concepts that have framed the academic debate on the EU's influence in world politics. In terms of competition for scarce goods, as 'normative power Europe', the EU competes for status, as 'market power Europe'—for wealth. Following the methodology of network theory, I argue that the EU acts as 'network power Europe' at the UN HRC, establishing complex ties with actors and stakeholders, and gaining relative advantage through network brokerage. The complex institutional setting of the EU's external action improves the EU's capacity to establish and sustain complex ties at the intergovernmental, interinstitutional (among international institutions), and interorganizational levels (among private enterprises and NGOs).

Network Competition in International Organizations

Despite its centrality in many theories of international relations, the definition of competition in international organizations has never attained scholarly consensus (see introduction to this volume). A recent general definition of competition involves "... the attempt to gain advantage, often relative to others believed to pose a challenge or threat, through the self-interested pursuit of contested goods such as power, security, wealth, influence, and status" (Mazarr et al. 2018: 5). A more sophisticated understanding of competition relates to the 'scarce goods' in world politics. From this perspective, actors and stakeholders in world politics compete for the attention of a third party while third parties frame the scarcity of attention, legitimacy, and prestige (Werron 2014). In the complex networks of international organizations, the management of the scarce goods is run by the 'brokers' that bridge all relevant nodes in a network (Kwon et al. 2020). Based on such understanding, this subsection aims to exploit how the EU ensures the position of a 'broker' within complex networks of the UN Human Rights Council.

In the nineteenth century, the Concert of Europe preserved the aspirations of 'great powers' to control the balance of power in world politics. While international organizations often follow this structural pattern today, a few of them—especially, the principal organs of the UN—maintain the principle of equal sovereignty based on the UN Charter. This principle presupposes that every state member of the UN has one vote in the UN intergovernmental bodies. The principle of equal sovereignty was a novelty introduced by the UN and changed the understanding of what a scarce good in world politics could be. Since the UN Charter entered into force on 24 October 1945, the 'great powers' have been in need for votes from 'medium' and 'small' states (Klein 1974).

At least according to their founding documents, international organizations formally function to ensure international cooperation rather than competition. Still, the formal umbrellas of international treaties have never prevented international actors and stakeholders from entering antagonistic relations with others and seeking advantages in international relations. The predominant focus on international legal treaties in theories of international relations has resulted in the view of international organizations as institutionalized forms of cooperation and competition among states. International relations scholars explain international organizations as instruments of states or arenas for state competition and cooperation that mandate international organizations to function (Koch 2009, 2015). According to the neorealist school of thought, meanwhile, an international organization is "a set of rules in which states should cooperate and compete with each other" (Mearsheimer 1994: 8). The other characteristic of competition in the realist and neorealist schools of international relations have referred to enhancement of hierarchies among 'great powers' and their environment. Competition is an intense form of international conflict embracing struggles for power, influence, and hegemony, which is an exclusive prerogative of a few states regarded as 'legitimate players' in the international arena.

This preoccupation with hierarchical intergovernmental competition in international organizations has avoided a consistent analysis of transnational and domestic stakeholders, who are also involved in world politics. Besides domestic stakeholders presenting diverging views within states, the UN system and particularly the UN Secretary-General have become more influential in peaceful settlements of conflicts (Zacher 1966). The realist assumption that the UN simply reflects the interests of the 'great powers' has been confronted by the process of autonomization of the UN and its augmenting interdependence with transnational actors, including networked cities, parliaments, commercial enterprises, and non-governmental organizations (Castells 1999).

The improved capacities of networks of transnational stakeholders in international organizations should widen our understanding of scarcity or a contested good at international organizations. According to the leading theorists of liberal institutionalism, increasing interdependence among actors and stakeholders in world politics has moved the focus of competition from absolute security gains and the struggle for power to economic growth and status (Keohane/Nye 1972; Grieco 1988). If earlier studies in realist thought promoted the view of competition as an intense form of conflict, liberal institutionalism mainstreamed the network component of competition, insisting that international organizations play a significant role in world politics due to complex interdependence. Relative advantages in attaining attention, legitimacy, and prestige can also, therefore, be a scarce good in complex networks of international organizations (Werron 2014; 2015).

Sociological studies of world politics suggest that not only the distribution of power in the world system but also the mode of power distribution have become a scarce good in world competition. The 'global transformation' of the 'long nineteenth century' has changed firstly, the distribution of power in world politics, and secondly, the mode of power (Buzan/Lawson 2015). The modern distribution of power stems through increasingly complex network relations (Buzan/Albert 2010: 22, 131). These complex network relations frame the power of actors and stakeholders in world politics, making ties and connections a 'new' scarce good in world politics. Even if the 'great powers' aim at security, wealth, and power, the activities of 'big players' are constrained by a multiplicity of non-state actors, groups of activists, and advocacy networks. These stakeholders, being interconnected with states, may not only constrain, but also enhance the states' capacity for action at international organizations.

Do all ties or specific sets of ties represent scarce goods in complex network in world politics? How do actors and stakeholders compete for a scarce good in networks? Network studies at international organizations are often combined with international relations and organizational theories, which efficiently explore cases of international organizations and governance but do not fully exploit the added value offered by network theory.

According to Hafner-Burton et al., networks at international organizations are commonly understood as sets of relations among all nodes that form a structure enabling or constraining its individual nodes (2009: 560). As Kahler finds, two approaches to networks at international organizations have emerged: networks as actors and networks as structures (Kahler 2009). In the actor-oriented approach, a network is an acting force complemented by various international legal actors and organizations. In the structure-oriented approach, a network is a form of permanent communication: a flow-forming structure, enabling or constraining its node or agents.

Scarce goods in networks at international organizations reflect varying centralization patterns among its constitutive agents or nodes (Hafner-Burton et al. 2009: 582). Networks comprise of nodes and the ties among them; and their characteristics derive from the position of a node in a network. Numerous patterns of hierarchical structuring (centralization) can therefore be observed. Some depend on the number of ties, others on the capacity to bridge isolated parts of networks or to connect to nodes that are themselves better connected (Cudworth/Hobden 2010: 403; Bovaird 2008; Bousquet/Curtis 2011: 47).

In network theory, these patterns of centralization are called 'centralities'. Centrality is the main scarce good in networks at international organizations. Centrality shows a family of properties related to the structural importance or prominence of a node in a network (Borgatti et al. 2009; Freeman 2004). With high centrality measurements a node—an actor at an international organization—has better access to resources and information flow among the other nodes. From such a standpoint, the more central an actor is, the better opportunities an actor has to expect support in a conflict, to withhold the benefits of recognition, and to coerce other actors. As argued by Beckfield, structural inequality is based on the unequal centralization of networks at international organizations, which in its turn opens room for states and societies with privileged positions to set the agenda, implement policies, and frame instruments of international regulation and cooperation (Beckfield 2008).

Measurements of centrality may be computed via a set of techniques (Gloor 2017). Two main scarce structural positions correspond to high centrality measurements. The first is that of a leader, connected to the highest number of nodes in the network. The second is that of a broker: a position that enables the actor to form a bridge between isolated clusters of a network (Hafner-Burton et al. 2009: 571).

Due to the increased complexity of international organizations, a large and varied number of actors and stakeholders are involved in networks at international organizations. These include states, NGOs, institutions, private enterprises, and transnational corporations. According to rational choice theory, each actor or stakeholder would have its own motivation to compete, seeking a scarce good of security, wealth, or status (Glaser 2010). In network competition at international organizations, actors and stakeholders would exert their influence and reach their objectives through complex network relationships and competition for structural positions of the core leaders or brokers.

Network Competition in the UN HRC

Together with relevant stakeholders, the institutional mechanisms of the Human Rights Council constitute a complex system of governance, where actors, such as the European Union, compete for brokerage across governmental, institutional, and organizational levels of governance. These networks include various types of actors and stakeholders falling into categories identified by Kaasch and Martens (2015): public and private actors, epistemic communities, states, NGOs and national human rights institutions, transnational corporations and large enterprises.[1]

The promotion of human rights at the UN Human rights Council is ensured via a multi-actor approach. Actors seek to improve their network brokerage in order to set international standards in human rights, draft international treaties, promote a particular view on the international system, or establish financial instruments to support civil society and create relative advantages in international negotiations. In doing so, actors and stakeholders establish and sustain ties across three main levels of governance at the UN HRC: interstate (among governments), interorganizational (among non-governmental organizations), and interinstitutional (among international organizations as self-sufficient actors).

At first, competition for brokerage occurs at the intergovernmental level. State diplomatic networks have been a longstanding structural characteristic of the UN system, since states hold the principal position at the UN under the sovereignty principle stipulated by the UN Charter. It is states who are members of the UN and parties to international human rights agreements. It is states, too, who take formal decisions at the UN and contribute to the UN's regular budget.

Since the UN Human Rights Council was established as an intergovernmental body, states have borne the responsibility for decision-making at HRC sessions, producing resolutions, summaries, recommendations, and conclusions. The HRC sessions are held three times per year: in March (four weeks),

---

1   The term 'relevant stakeholders' has been widely used at the UN. The UN HRC rules of procedure include states and 'other relevant stakeholders including NGOs and NHRIs'. To keep the existing lines at the UN, this contribution refers to actors in case of entities with international legal personality, and to 'relevant stakeholders' in case of entities without international legal personality, cf. Shaw 2008.

June (three weeks), and September (three weeks). The Council may hold a special session upon a request of one-third of the Council's member's request. By 2020, almost all 30 special sessions have focused on situations in a country or a region. The sessions include numerous discussions, side events, presentation of reports from the OHCHR, and the HRC subsidiary bodies.

Though the decisions at the UN HRC are taken on the intergovernmental level, the transnational access of the UN for other relevant stakeholders forces the diplomatic actors to compete for brokerage not only at the intergovernmental but also at institutional and organizational level—for the attention of NGOs, groups of people, and non-state actors, in general (Tallberg et al. 2013; Tallberg et al. 2018). How do the EU's diplomatic networks operate within this institutional context?

To address this question, we must understand clearly the nature of the diplomatic networks that act within the UN HRC. Firstly, diplomatic networks involve coalitions that exist within the UN system as well as those outside the UN. Secondly, the network perspective on diplomacy reflects the complexity of situational coalition making—networks are dynamic and may adapt to changes of environment. These networks may reconfigure themselves based on a thematic issue and exist in three main forms. The first are regional diplomatic networks—state coalitions based on five regional UN Charter groupings. The second are formal diplomatic networks—state coalitions based on formal international organizations. The third are informal diplomatic networks—informal political coalitions of 'like-minded' states.

Table 1. UN HRC Diplomatic networks

Regional diplomatic networks	Formal diplomatic networks	Informal diplomatic networks
African states (African group), Asia-Pacific States (Asian-Pacific group), Latin American and Caribbean States (GRULAC), Western European and other States (WEOG), Eastern European States (EEG)	*European Union, African Union, Eurasian Economic Union, Union State, MERCOSUR, CARICOM, Organization of Islamic Cooperation, ASEAN, Non-Aligned Movement (NAM), G77 (or G77+China), Arab League, Commonwealth, Francophonie*	*Like-Minded Group of largely developing and ex-communist countries (LMG), JUSCANZ group of US allies in the Pacific, various 'Groups of Friends', and contact groups, such as the Contact Group on the Council membership, Group of Friends on Responsibility to Protect, Group of Friends of the Syrian People, Group of Friends of the Small Island Developing States, Group of Friends on national mechanisms for implementation, reporting and follow-up (NMIRFs), Lima Group*

Even though the process of human rights promotion should in theory be based on cooperation, actors and stakeholders get actively involved in competition for structural positions in complex networks of the Human Rights Council through coalition formation. It is widely acknowledged in research on the UN Human Rights Council that the main actors in this competition are coalitions of states. The UN system has been subject to bloc politics since its establishment. Coalition formation at the UN, as claimed by Chané and Sharma (2016), allows states to increase lobbying capacities and bargaining power by maximizing their total number of votes; and reduce 'time' costs through 'burden-sharing' mechanisms. As argued by Smith, Wouters and Chané, the UN HRC is an illustrative case of the regional and political concurring blocs that have emerged since 2006 (Wouters/Chané 2016; Smith 2017; 2015). At the same time, openness to stakeholders also ensures that the UN HRC exhibits a strong degree of stratification, both among states and stakeholders. The latter has not yet received significant consideration, nor have interlinkages across the interstate, interinstitutional, or interorganizational levels.

The wealth of academic research on respective coalition formation through voting procedures or resolution co-sponsorship has yet to be reinforced with network research that extends beyond interstate coalition formation. Yet the process of human rights promotion at the UN HRC involves more than states' coalitions. It is not only state blocs who engage constructively in communication or competition but also networks of states, NGOs, private enterprises, and international institutions. Since the process of communication involves all of these, states operate within a field constituted by a range of non-state actors. It is this reality that leads to the emergence of complex networks at international organizations.

The EU represents a formal diplomatic network that has emerged at the HRC on the basis of a coordination process among states. Regional and alliance organizations usually enjoy the status of an observer to the General Assembly and are thus observers at the Human Rights Council as a subsidiary body of the General Assembly (with the exception of the EU with the status of an enhanced observer, due to the organizational changes to the Union after the Lisbon Treaty). Formal diplomatic networks have been regarded as a consistent pattern of UN politics as these networks allow the states to build sustainable coalitions and coordinate their actions at the UN regularly (Chané/Sharma 2016; Wouters/Chané 2016).

Formal diplomatic networks are based on the coordinated priorities of groups of states and regional institutional mechanisms. Coordination within these networks allows the states to increase the effectiveness of negotiations and reach their priorities through 'burden-sharing' actions, in other words, through the distribution of roles in negotiations. On the one hand, these networks may sometimes prioritize political solidarity against universal promotion of human rights, which can serve as a cause of politicization of the Human Rights Council and a decrease in consensus (Freedman/Houghton 2017). On the other hand, such political solidarity, though it may constrain the space for international dialogue, still establishes a system of checks and balances, which can foster international cooperation. The necessary condition for such enhancement of international cooperation is the bridging of various subgroups in complex networks.

To compete effectively at the UN HRC, formal diplomatic networks have to consistently augment their brokerage power: between other diplomatic networks and coalitions as well as between non-governmental stakeholders. Diplomatic networks operate through coordination and burden-sharing practices: diplomatic networks do not speak with 'one voice' but via 'multiple voices' (Smith 2010).

At the same time, these networks are no longer 'blocs' as they may have divergent thematic priorities on certain issues (Smith 2017). For example, EU human rights promotion of at the UN Human Rights Council takes three main forms. The first is the adoption of respective HRC resolutions submitted 'on behalf of the EU' as a whole. The other share of priorities is reached through HRC resolutions submitted on behalf of EU member states. The second option is usually taken in case the EU is not completely unanimous on the operationalization of a priority. The third formula is the submission of EU priorities not by the EU member states but instead by the members of the EU+ network. This includes states that are to become the EU members, closely cooperate with the EU, or are beneficiaries of the EU financial instruments. Finally, the priorities of diplomatic networks are implemented not only though coordination among states but also through regional institutional mechanisms, i.e. through the EU financial instruments of the European Instrument for Democracy and Human rights and the European Neighborhood Instrument operated by the European Commission.

Table 2. EU Resolutions of the UN HRC in 2020 (43rd and 44th sessions)

On be-half of the EU	**Situation of human rights in Myanmar** **Situation of human rights in the Democratic People's Republic of Korea** **Mandate of the Special Rapporteur on the sale and sexual exploitation of children, including child prostitution, child pornography and other child sexual abuse material** **Freedom of religion or belief**
On be-half of the EU member states	Situation of human rights in the Syrian Arab Republic Freedom of opinion and expression: mandate of the Special Rapporteur on the promotion and protection of the right to freedom of opinion and expression Situation of human rights in the Islamic Republic of Iran Rights of persons belonging to national or ethnic, religious and linguistic minorities: mandate of the Special Rapporteur on minority issues Mental health and human rights Adequate housing as a component of the right to an adequate standard of living, and the right to non-discrimination in this context Regional arrangements for the promotion and protection of human rights Promotion and protection of human rights and the implementation of the 2030 Agenda for Sustainable Development Torture and other cruel, inhuman or degrading treatment or punishment: mandate of the Special Rapporteur The right to education Trafficking in persons, especially women and children: strengthening human rights through enhanced protection, support and empowerment of victims of trafficking, especially women and children Mandate of the Special Rapporteur on extrajudicial, summary or arbitrary executions Elimination of discrimination against persons affected by leprosy and their family members Independence and impartiality of the judiciary, jurors and assessors, and the independence of lawyers Situation of human rights in Eritrea Situation of human rights in Belarus Fifteenth anniversary of the responsibility to protect populations from genocide, war crimes, ethnic cleansing and crimes against humanity, as enshrined in the World Summit Outcome of 2005 Business and human rights: Working Group on the issue of human rights and transnational corporations and other business enterprises and improving accountability and access to remedy Freedom of opinion and expression Extreme poverty and human rights

On behalf of the non-EU states (EU+ network)	Mandate of the Special Rapporteur on the situation of human rights defenders
	Cooperation with Georgia
	Promotion and protection of human rights in Nicaragua
	Awareness raising on the rights of persons with disabilities, and habilitation and rehabilitation
	The promotion and protection of human rights in the context of peaceful protests
	Special Rapporteur on the rights of persons with disabilities

Compiled by the author. Data from the UN HRC extranet. URL: https://extranet.ohchr.org/sites/hrc/ (accessed 17.09.2020)

Table 2 illustrates the variety of formats to build the EU networks at the Human Rights Council. The notable EU+ network includes states from the other formal diplomatic networks that are part of other regional organizations. While these regional organizations have their own priorities and sometimes even contest those of the EU, on some thematic matters a few states from other diplomatic networks join the EU. The HRC institutional structure reflects that formal diplomatic networks are simultaneously cooperating with and contesting the other formal networks at the HRC dependent on the particular thematic scope of an initiative (Laatikainen/Smith 2017).

The overall capacities, cohesiveness, and visibility of these networks vary. For example, the Non-Aligned Movement (NAM) comprises 120 states; the G77 networks consists of 134 states; the formal diplomatic network of the Commonwealth, 53 states; the EU network, 28 states; the African Union, 55 states; the Organization for Islamic Cooperation—57 states, and so on. These networks are often based on regional economic integration organizations—like the EU or the Eurasian Economic Union—or intergovernmental regional political organizations—like the Organization of Islamic Cooperation. These networks depend on the structural cohesiveness of the respective international organizations; they decompose once an organization ceases to exist (as in the case of the Warsaw Pact network).

While there are a variety of international organizations outside the UN with coordinating functions, not all of them visibly set and coordinate their objectives at the HRC. Only some of them can be regarded as consistent formal diplomatic networks as they coordinate their activities permanently before the HRC meetings and at the UN Office in Geneva. Among those networks, the most sustainable are those that present their statements and resolutions on behalf of their respective group and coordinate their activities at the HRC during sessions every day. In this regard, the most visible networks are the networks of the European Union, the League of Arab States, the Organization of Islamic Cooperation, the African Union, and the Organization of American States. 42% of all resolutions of the Council, submitted from 2006 to 2015, were sponsored or co-sponsored from these five formal diplomatic networks (Chané/Sharma 2016). The other sustainable formal diplomatic networks are those of the Non-Aligned Movement, the G77, and the Commonwealth of Independent States. These networks are dynamic—the G77 network has shown a high degree of cooperation with China in the coordination of priorities and has started to make statements on behalf of the G77+China network, especially, in promotion of the UN Charter and the principle of state sovereignty (Okano-Heijmans et. al 2019). Besides declaratory statements, the G77 together with China started to strengthen the UN human rights machinery by contributing extra funds to the budget of the Office of the High Commissioner for Human Rights (Lock 2006).

Network Power Europe at the UN HRC

The European Union is one of the exemplary international actors involved in network competition at international organizations. Its simultaneous operation as an intergovernmental and supranational organization has produced the complex institutional setting of the EU machinery across levels of governance in world politics, and particularly at the UN. What is the scarce good the EU competes for, however, remains a question that raises intriguing disputes. One of the earlier layers of these disputes differentiates between the civilian and military attitudes of the EU developed by Duchêne and Bull (Manners 2002; Orbie 2008). A more recent discussion follows the deepening of the European integration and suggests that the EU is able to act as 'normative power Europe' and thus competes for the definition of what is 'normal' in world politics; and also that the EU operates as 'market power Europe' hence competing on the basis of market and for power and wealth (Damro 2012). Both normative and market dimensions integrate in the sense of the general attitude of the EU to export regional standards on the global level, however, these dimensions vary in the understanding of what is the EU identity that drives the capacities of this regional economic integration organization: norms or market.

The debate on what kind of identity the EU has—'normative power Europe' or 'market power Europe'—refers respectively to the political and market-related bases of the history of the European integration. For example, since the EU has been founded on the core value of liberty, the EU competes for the promotion of this value externally. At the same time, having a significant single market, thorough institutional legislation, and interconnection with interest groups, the EU externalizes its internal economic activities to compete for economic power in the world. These bases of the EU integration, as argued by Damro, predispose the EU to act as market power Europe and compete for economic power (2012: 689).

From the perspective of network theory, EU external action is based on sustaining complex networks during the internal decision-making and externalization of the EU internal policies. The EU acts as 'network power Europe' due to the great scope of institutions and stakeholders involved in the EU external action. EU external action at international organizations involves actions of the EU member states and the EU institutions as well as all other relevant stakeholders represented by consultative institutional bodies, institutions, NGOs, and enterprises from the European region. A great variety of intergovernmental and non-governmental stakeholders represent the EU network at an international organizations and compete for the EU's structural position of a broker in world politics. Network power Europe is exercised through what Delreux and Keukeleire call the "informal division of labor" (2017). The emergence of network power Europe has a political background. The EU has given strategic priority to the HRC in both action plans on human rights and democracy in 2012-2014 and 2015-2019 (European Union 2012, 2015). The internal process of adoption priorities for the HRC involves a great variety of mechanisms. Besides the adoption of the priorities by the Council of the EU, the EU diplomatic network coordinates its actions at the HRC with the Guidelines that are developed by the European External Action Service (EEAS) after discussions at the European Council's Working Party on Human Rights (COHOM) and the European Commission. The coordination may also involve meetings of the UN Working Party (CONUN) and geographical working groups.

How does the EU compete for structural brokerage at the UN HRC? The EU has been one of the most complex actors at the HRC. Firstly, the EU aims at being a broker on the diplomatic level, among states. The diplomatic network of the EU comprises more than its 27 member states, and is often referred to as the EU+ network. It is often the case that the EU network augments its capabilities with the other countries aligning their positions with the EU one: the candidate countries to the EU (Albania, North Macedonia, Montenegro, Serbia, Turkey, plus, Bosnia and Herzegovina as a potential candidate, the members of the European Single Market); together with Iceland, Liechtenstein, Norway and Switzerland; and the states participating in the European Neighbourhood Policy, including Morocco, Israel, Mauritania, Tunisia, Ukraine, Georgia and Moldova (Weber 1995; Blauberger/van Hüllen 2020). Notwithstanding the national capacities and priorities in the EU diplomatic network, it is the 'big two'—France and Germany—that constitute the core of the network and are capable of mobilizing the entire network (Krotz/Maher 2016).

The complexity of the EU network is reflected in the variety of thematic priorities initiated at the HRC on behalf of the EU, on behalf of the EU member states. In the first case, the thematic scope of the EU as a formal organization remains allegedly limited and focuses on country-specific resolutions (on situations in Belarus, Burundi, Myanmar, or the Democratic People's Republic of Korea), plus, rights of the child and freedom of religion or belief. Still, the thematic scope of the EU diplomatic network is much wider in terms of its thematic coverage as it comprises the national priorities of the EU member states, such as the independence of the Office of the High Commissioner for Human Rights (OHCHR), the provision of safe spaces for civil society and human rights defenders, and the centrality of prevention to the work of the HRC.

Secondly, the EU has been effective in performing brokerage in connecting intergovernmental level with institutional (international organizations) and organizational (NGOs and businesses) stakeholders. As suggested by Zaru and Geurts (2012), the EU's ability to stimulate networks at the UN is provided by the complexity of the EU external representation. Even if the HRC is an intergovernmental body and the promotion of human rights at the HRC relates to the intergovernmental EU Common Foreign and Security Policy matters, the EU network extends beyond its intergovernmental nature.

First of all, EU brokerage is supported by the functioning of the EU Delegation—in case of the UN HRC, the EU Delegation in Geneva. The EU Delegation represents the EU together with the Rotating Presidency at the Council of the EU. The EU Delegation to the HRC is responsible for the coordination of the network and, sometimes, for informal negotiations that involve non-governmental stakeholders (Biedenkopf/Petri 2019; Tawhida/de Jesús Butler 2006; Maurer/Morgenstern-Pomorski 2018). The European Commission also has its own additional representation, especially in matters related to the voluntary budget of the Office of the High Commissioner on Human Rights, which in the end enables the EU institutions to be directly connected to the HRC Secretariat and subsidiary mechanisms (Willa 2017). The EU High Representative for Foreign Affairs and Security Policy as well as the EU Special Representative for Human Rights can also participate in the High-Level Segment and expert meetings of the HRC respectively (Smith 2010).

To ensure and finally benefit from brokerage with institutional and organizational stakeholders, the EU diplomatic network continues to intensively cooperate with the HRC mandate holders of the Special Procedures, notably, via the OHCHR and mandate holders' briefings before the Political and Security Committee on Brussels (Kaddous 2015: 38). The EU Special Representative for Human Rights (EU SR) communicates to non-governmental stakeholders at the HRC side events, delivers speeches at the HRC, addresses the HRC sessions on behalf of the EU's High Representative for Foreign Affairs and Security Policy, cooperates with the HRC special procedures and with the OHCHR, and ensures the implementation of the EU human rights guidelines. The EU network includes the outcomes of the HRC sessions in bilateral human rights policies that further reach civil society of third countries. In Geneva, the EU, together with the other countries, NGOs, representatives of international organizations, delivers demarches and declarations. The Union finally ensures worldwide monitoring through interconnection between the EU Fundamental Rights Agency and the EU Human Rights Focal Points with civil society organizations. The EU also includes human rights as essential elements of agreements, and promotes human rights through the other instruments and bodies, e.g. the Development Cooperation Instrument (Smith 2015).

Conclusions

The network perspective on competition in world politics stresses that scarcity in competition is a dynamic multidimensional phenomenon. In this regard, international organizations ensure communication flow for an increasing complexity of actors and stakeholders in world politics. The formal procedures of international organizations, and particularly, of the UN HRC, ensure sustainable communication within the levels of governance, i.e.

states with states, international institutions with international institutions, NGOs with NGOs, and so on. The formal procedures lead to the emergence of within-level networks. But what about communication flow across levels of governance? The institutional setting of the UN HRC is open for participation of NGOs, but NGOs or institutions do not bear the same capacities in decision-making as states do. Therefore, brokerage in communication across levels of governance becomes a scarce object in network competition at international organizations.

Brokerage in communication flow could be performed not only by 'great powers' but also by complex coalitions of states, NGOs, and international institutions. According to dominant schools of IR theory, competition in world politics is an exclusive prerogative of states, or even of just a few 'great powers'. The network perspective highlights the dynamic character of network competition in international organizations. Competition for brokerage is conditioned on communication flow and not on the formal decision-making of an international organization.

Acting as network power Europe, the EU exerts its economic, social and political influence through complex network relationships at international organizations, and particularly at the UN HRC. The EU exercises this power to compete for the scarce object of brokerage in world politics. There are three main types of brokerage depending on the actors and stakeholders involved: the EU becomes a network broker in intergovernmental affairs, the EU performs brokerage between third state-parties and NGOs, and the EU bridges non-state organizations from the EU and non-EU member states. The competition for brokerage is exercised via complex networks of the EU member states, institutions, institutional bodies, and civil society organizations.

References

Beckfield, Jason (2008): "The Dual World Polity: Fragmentation and Integration in the Network of Intergovernmental Organizations." In: Social Problems 55/3, pp. 419-442.

Biedenkopf, Katja/Petri, Franziska (2019): "EU Delegations in European Union Climate Diplomacy: The Role of Links to Brussels, Individuals and Country Contexts." In: Journal of European Integration 41/1, pp. 47-63.

Blauberger, Michael/van Hüllen, Vera (2020): "Conditionality of EU Funds: An Instrument to Enforce EU Fundamental Values?" In: Journal of European Integration, open access (doi:10.1080/07036337.2019.1708337), pp. 1-16

Borgatti, Stephen/Mehra,Ajay/Brass, Daniel/Labianca, Giuseppe (2009): "Network Analysis in the Social Sciences." In: Science 323/5916, pp. 892-895.

Bousquet, Antoine/Curtis, Simon (2011): "Beyond Models and Metaphors: Complexity Theory, Systems Thinking and International Relations." In: Cambridge Review of International Affairs 24/1, pp. 43–62.

Bovaird, Tony (2008): "Emergent Strategic Management and Planning Mechanisms in Complex Adaptive Systems." In: Public Management Review 10/3, pp. 319-340.

Bradford, Anu (2020): The Brussels Effect: How the European Union Rules the World, New York: Oxford University Press.

Buzan, Barry/Lawson, George (2015): The Global Transformation, Cambridge: Cambridge University Press.

Buzan, Barry/Albert, Mathias (2010): "Differentiation: A Sociological Approach to International Relations Theory." In: European Journal of International Relations 16/3, pp. 315-337.

Castells, Manuel (1999): The Rise of the Network Society, Oxford: Blackwell.

Chané, Anna/Sharma, Arjun (2016): "Universal Human Rights? Exploring Contestation and Consensus in the UN Human Rights Council." In: Human Rights & International Legal Discourse 10/2, pp. 219–247.

Cudworth, Erika/Hobden Stephen (2010): "Anarchy and Anarchism: Towards a Theory of Complex International Systems." In: Millennium 39/2, pp. 399-416.

Damro, Chad (2012): "Market Power Europe." In: Journal of European Public Policy 19/5, pp. 682-699.

Dehousse, Renaud (1997): "Regulation by Networks in the European Community: The Role of European Agencies." In: Journal of European Public Policy 4/2, pp. 246-261.

Delreux, Tom/Keukeleire, Stephan (2017): "Informal Division of Labor in EU Foreign Policy-Making." In: Journal of European Public Policy 24/10, pp. 1471-1490.

European Union (2012): "EU Strategic Framework and Action Plan on Human Rights and Democracy", Council of the European Union Doc. 11855/12, June 25, Luxembourg.

European Union (2015): "Council Conclusions on the Action Plan on Human Rights and Democracy 2015-2019", Council of the EU, Doc. 10897/15, July 20, Brussels.

Freedman, Rosa/Houghton, Ruth (2017): "Two Steps Forward, One Step Back: Politicisation of the Human Rights Council." In: Human Rights Law Review 17/4, pp. 753-769.

Freeman, Linton (2004): The Development of Social Network Analysis: A Study in the Sociology of Science, Vancouver: Empirical Press.

Glaser, Charles (2010): Rational theory of international politics: the logic of competition and cooperation, Princeton: Princeton University Press.

Gloor, Peter (2017): Sociometrics and Human Relationships: Analyzing Social Networks to Manage Brands, Predict Trends, and Improve Organizational Performance, Bingley: Emerald Publishing.

Grieco, Joseph (1988): "Anarchy and the Limits of Cooperation: A Realist Critique of the Newest Liberal Institutionalism." In: International Organization 42/3, pp. 485–507.

Hafner-Burton, Emilie/Kahler, Miles/Montgomery, Alexander (2009): "Network Analysis for International Relations." In: International Organization 63/3, pp. 559-592.

Kaasch, Alexandra/Martens, Kerstin (2015): "Actors and Agency in Global Social Governance". In Kaasch, Alexandra/Martens, Kerstin (eds.), Actors and Agency in Global Social Governance, Oxford: Oxford University Press, pp. 3-17.

Kaddous, Christine (2015): The European Union in International Organizations and Global Governance, Oxford: Hart Publishing.

Kahler, Miles (2009): "Networked Politics: Agency, Power, and Governance." In: Miles Kahler (ed.), Networked Politics, New York: Cornell University Press, pp. 1-20.

Keohane, Robert/Nye, Joseph (1972): Transnational Relations and World Politics, Cambridge: Harvard University Press.

Klein, Robert (1974): Sovereign Equality Among States: The History of an Idea, Toronto: University of Toronto Press.

Koch, Martin (2009): "Autonomization of IGOs." In: International Political Sociology 3/4, pp. 431-448.

Koch, Martin (2015): "World Organizations—(Re-)Conceptualizing International Organizations." In: World Political Science 11/1, pp. 97-131.

Krotz, Ulrich/Maher, Richard (2016): "Europe's Crises and the EU's 'Big Three'." In: West European Politics 39/5, pp. 1053-1072.

Kwon, Seok-Woo/Rondi, Emanuela/Levin, Daniel/de Massis, Alfredo/Brass, Daniel (2020): "Network Brokerage: An Integrative Review and Future Research Agenda." In: Journal of Management 46/6, pp. 1092-1120.

Lock, Karen (2006): "Statement on behalf pf the Group of 77 and China by Ms. Karen Lock", New York, March 9 (https://www.g77.org/Speeches/030906.htm).

Manners, Ian (2002): "Normative Power Europe: A Contradiction in Terms?" In: Journal of Common Market Studies 40/2, pp. 235-258.

Mathieu, Emmanuelle (2016): Regulatory Delegation in the European Union: Networks, Committees and Agencies, London: Palgrave Macmillan.

Maurer, Heidi/Morgenstern-Pomorski, Jost-Henrik (2018): "The Quest for Throughput Legitimacy: The EEAS, EU Delegations and the Contested Structures of European Diplomacy." In: Global Affairs 4/2-3, pp. 305-316.

Mearsheimer, John (1994): "The False Promise of International Institutions." In: International Security 19/3, pp. 5-49.

Okano-Heijmans, Maaike/van der Putten, Frans-Paul/van Schaik, Louise (2019): "Welcoming and Resisting China's Growing Role at the UN", Clingendael Magazine, February 8 (https://www.clingendael.org/publication/welcoming-and-resisting-chinas-growing-role-un).

Orbie, Jan (2008): Europe's Global Role. External Policies of the European Union, Aldershot: Ashgate.

Shaw, Malcolm (2008): International Law. Cambridge: Cambridge University Press, 6th edition.

Smith, Karen (2010): "The European Union at the Human Rights Council: Speaking with One Voice but Having Little Influence." In: Journal of European Public Policy 17/2, pp. 224-241.

Smith, Karen (2015): "The EU as a Diplomatic Actor in the Field of Human Rights." In: Joachim Koops/Gjovalin Macaj (eds.), The European Union as a Diplomatic Actor, London: Palgrave Macmillan, pp. 155-177

Smith, Karen (2017): "Group Politics in the Debates on Gender Equality and Sexual Orientation Discrimination at the United Nations." In: The Hague Journal of Diplomacy 12/2-3, pp. 138-157.

Tallberg, Jonas/Dellmuth, Lisa/Agné, Hans/Duit, Andreas (2018): "NGO Influence in International Organizations: Information, Access and Exchange." In: British Journal of Political Science 48/1, pp. 213-238.

Tallberg, Jonas/Sommerer, Thomas/Squatrito, Theresa/Jönsson, Christer (2013): The Opening up of International Organizations: Transnational Access in Global Governance, Cambridge: Cambridge University Press.

Tawhida, Ahmed/de Jesús Butler, Israel (2006): "The European Union and Human Rights: An International Law Perspective." In: European Journal of International Law 17/4, pp. 771-801.

Weber, Steven (1995): "European Union Conditionality." In: Jürgen von Hagen/Paul Welfens/Barry Eichengreen/Michele Fratianni/Patrick Minford/Jeffry Frieden (eds.), Politics and Institutions in an Integrated Europe, Heidelberg: Springer, pp. 193-220.

Werron, Tobias (2014): "On Public Forms of Competition." In: Cultural Studies—Critical Methodologies 14/1, pp. 62-76.

Werron, Tobias (2015): "Why Do We Believe in Competition? A Historical-Sociological View of Competition as an Institutionalized Modern Imaginary." In: Distinktion: Journal of Social Theory 16/2, pp. 186-210.

Willa, Rafał (2017): "EU–UN Relations. How Much of a Partnership?" In: European Review 25/2, pp. 337-350.

Wouters, Jan/Chané, Anna (2016): "Brussels Meets Westphalia: The European Union and the United Nations." In: Piet Eeckhout/Manuel Lopez-Escudero (eds.), The European Union's External Action in Times of Crisis, Oxford: Hart Publishing, pp. 299-324.

Zacher, Mark (1966): "1966 Prize Award Essay the Secretary–General and the United Nations' Function of Peaceful Settlement." In: International Organization 20/4, pp. 724-749.

Zaru, Davide/Geurts, Charles-Michel (2012): "Legal Framework for EU Participation in Global Human Rights Governance." In: Jan Wouters/Hans Bruyninckx/Sudeshna Basu/Simon Schunz (eds.), The European Union and Multilateral Governance, London: Palgrave Macmillan, pp. 49-65.

Social Mobility in the Global Order
Rising Powers and the Convertibility of Capitals

Katja Freistein & Thomas Müller

World politics—just like world society more broadly—is witness to many forms of competition. Diverse (state) actors strive to increase their shares of socially valued goods, ranging from status over wealth and military capabilities to political authority. Many of these goods are sought after because they constitute what Pierre Bourdieu (1984) called "capitals": sources of power that enable actors to shape their environment in ways favorable to their aspirations. This can refer to material forms of capital such as economic wealth, but also to non-material forms such as the reputation for being effective in fighting a pandemic disease. In this chapter, we explore the politics of capital conversion in world politics, which we conceptualize as the translation of capitals accumulated in one field of competition into another field of competition as well as the struggles over the rules governing this translation. Our approach is not strictly Bourdieusian, since we acknowledge the difficulties of translating his insights to the realm of world society, alongside their applicability to non-domestic settings. At the same time, we think that Bourdieu's ideas of multiple capitals and capital conversion are compelling enough to further pursue them.

More specifically, we focus on 'rising powers' such as China or India and their capacity to convert their rise into positions and conditions that enable them to more strongly shape global order according to their aspirations. Thinking about global relations in terms of the 'rise' and 'fall' of states has a long tradition. Recent discussions about the potential danger or chances of an empowered China (Edelstein 2018) or a confrontation between China and the US (Mearsheimer 2010; Allison 2017) are but the latest episode in this tradition. The literature on emerging powers mostly concentrates on the political implications and dynamics created by the rise of non-Western states, notably the pressure to adapt and reform the institutional arrangements of global order to the changed stratification of world politics.[1] While the literature highlights the status conflicts that arise in such situations, it usually takes the existence of the patterns of stratification as a given and has paid little attention to how these patterns are produced and reproduced in the first place. By focusing on status conflicts, it moreover tends to overemphasize one dimension of the patterns of stratification—namely status hierarchies—and to bracket their multidimensional nature.

We offer two arguments. First, in order to understand the link between rising powers and the evolution of global orders, it is important to account for the possibilities and limits of capital conversion which shape how social mobility—that is, the rise (or fall) of individual states—translates into changes in the institutions, cleavages and policies that together constitute the global order. The politics of capital conversion actualize and alter the prevalent conceptions of stratification, including the criteria for ranking states in status hierarchies, and are thus integral to the reproduction of the patterns of stratification. Second, the institutional dimension of global order is key to the politics of capital conversion. Contrary to recent claims (Nexon/Neumann 2018), we argue that a hegemon—that is, the most powerful state—does not act as the symbolic hegemon setting the rules and rates of conversion. World politics is today much more institutionalized and polycentric than it was in previous phases of world history. Institutionalized settings have thus become important battle grounds for the production of equality and inequality (Fehl/Freistein 2020a, b; Müller 2019)—and hence also for the politics of capital conversion. Rising states strive to convert the capital they accumulated into more advantageous institutional positions while the established (Western) powers, who experience the relative gain in status of others as their own downward social mobility, seek to use the institutional settings to establish and uphold conditions for how capital conversion can take place that preserve their advantageous positions. Conversely, powers that experience relative decline are likely to seek to preserve institutional arrangements with fit to their capitals and strategies of capital conversion. They may however also—as the UK did with Brexit—re-evaluate their membership in certain institutions when they perceive these institutions to hamper rather than foster their chances for future capital accumulation and conversion.

In the following, we first elaborate on our notions of stratification and social mobility (section 2). We then discuss the processes and politics of cap-

---

1   For good discussions of this literature, see Ward (2017) and Zarakol (2019).

ital conversion that are at play in world politics (section 3). Subsequently, we highlight three (non-exhaustive) changes in the institutional settings that drive and shape the current politics of capital conversion. First, several non-Western states have pursued a strategy of capital pooling by forming a club of their own—the BRICS[2]—in parallel to the existing Western club of the G7. Second, the established Western powers have tried to retain control over the conversion rates by themselves opening a new club, the G20, that brings together the established with some of the rising states; thus initiating the formation of a new 'upper class' of states. Third, the biggest of the rising powers—China—has attempted to subvert (or at least challenge) the rules of conversion set by the established powers by creating institutional infrastructures of its own preferences for conversion rates. Taken together, the three dimensions underscore the importance of institutions as both sites and means in the political struggles over the adaptation of global order to social mobility.

Social Stratification and Mobility

Stratification denotes the ordering of actors into superior and inferior social positions based on their relative shares of socially valued goods (Grusky 2001). Stratification is a key concept in sociology, where it is often used synonymously with 'inequality'. While some authors in the field of international relations (IR) similarly employ the concept (Keene 2013a, b; 2014; Fehl/Freistein 2020a, b; Müller 2019), most talk of asymmetries (Philips 2017) or social hierarchies (Lake 2009) rather than social stratification, while avoiding the term inequalities. The concept of stratification we refer to here mostly corresponds to what Bially Mattern and Zarakol (2016: 629) call the "broad conception" of hierarchies in which hierarchies are understood as "(intersubjectively) organized inequality".

Stratification researchers define *social mobility* as the presence of opportunities for the improvement of life situations during and across lifespans (Grusky 2001: 12). Adapted to world politics, social mobility can be understood as changes in the chances of states to realize their aims that arise out of increases or decreases in their shares of various forms of capital. These chances depend on the criteria for social mobility that underpin the social

---

2   The BRICS group comprises Brazil, Russia, India, China, and South-Africa.

order. Social mobility can in this sense be analyzed in two ways: as the im-provement of the relative position of individual states (e.g. 'China is rising') and, in aggregate, as the overall level of changes in the relative positions of states within international society (e.g. 'there is not much social mobility in international society'). This conceptualization differs from that underpinning social identity theories in the status literature in IR. In social identity theo-ries, social mobility refers to the emulation of "the values and practices of the higher-status group with the goal of gaining admission into elite clubs" (Lar-son/Shevchenko 2010: 67). This literature assumes that all states share similar status aspirations. Following stratification researchers, we argue that emu-lation is but one possibility of how actors seek to convert increases in their shares of capital into more advantageous social positions. Social mobility is in this perspective, first, about the potential for changes in the patterns of stratification and, second, about the effects of the changes on the ability of states to shape their own fates.

Sociological approaches to stratification stress its multidimensional na-ture. We draw especially on Pierre Bourdieu's conceptualization of stratifica-tion as a *multidimensional distribution of various forms of capital* that actors accu-mulate and use (Bourdieu 1985). The notion of capitals refers to resources over which actors compete and which allow actors to control the relative shares of socially valued goods. Bourdieu identified four types of capital: economic, social, cultural, and symbolic. As Bourdieu developed this set of capitals for the analysis of the social mobility of individuals in mostly national societies, it has to be modified for the analysis of social mobility among states. States are, notably, corporate actors and the forms of capitals that matter in national so-cieties are not necessarily the same capitals that matter in world politics. We therefore assume that capital can take a variety of forms in world politics, in-cluding economic wealth, military capabilities, crucial governance positions and privileges, status, reputation and so on. The form and salience of capitals are field-specific and, like fields themselves, subject to change (Bigo 2011: 245). Moreover, their distribution varies both across social fields—that is, arenas in which actors compete over capitals (Go 2008)—and over time.

States seem to strive to accrue various forms of capitals. Even states with enormous economic or military capital seek for other forms of capital to en-hance the legitimacy of their social positions and demands, particularly be-cause international relations have become more legalized and institutional-ized (Hurd 2017). The position of an actor in a social system such as world pol-itics accordingly depends on the "overall volume of the capital they possess" relative to other actors across all fields as well as the "composition of their capital", that is, the "relative weight of the different kinds of assets within their total assets" (Bourdieu 1985: 724). If actors increase their relative shares, they move 'upwards'. If, on the contrary, their relative shares decrease, they move 'downwards'.

The patterns of stratification are socially organized in a twofold sense. First, social systems consist of multiple, overlapping *social fields* in which actors *compete over socially valued forms of capital*. These fields are defined by an interplay of material and social factors. Julian Go, for instance, identifies two key dimensions of "global fields": the objective configuration of actor-positions and the subjective meanings guiding actors in the struggle (Go 2008: 207). Fields are constituted and structured by what field theories call 'rules of the games'—understandings, norms and principles that assign value to particular forms of capitals and that specify the appropriate forms and dynamics of the competition over these capitals. These rules are not uncontested. In fact, their definition and interpretation are often part of the very struggle that shapes the various fields.

Second, actors perform various *symbolic practices* through which they seek to *impart meaning into the distribution of capitals* in selecting fields as well as across fields. In world politics, for instance, a prominent representation of the distribution of capitals is the classification of states in terms of classes of 'powers' or into 'developed' and 'developing' countries. To produce such representations of the distribution of capitals, actors employ practices of categorization and classification. If the categorization and classification practices of different actors clash, they engage in what Bourdieu calls "symbolic struggles". What "is at stake" in these symbolic struggles "is the very representation" of "the hierarchy within each of the fields and among the different fields" (Bourdieu 1985: 723). In a Bourdieusian perspective, hierarchies therefore arise and are maintained through symbolic practices that order and structure the distribution of capitals by dividing states into groups with different privileges (or duties). The power of classification is not a simple politics of language. It has manifest consequences for the way different forms of capital are distributed among those who have been classified.

Representations can also be dynamic and describe processes of social mobility. The "rise and fall" of powerful states is a prominent narrative in IR and International History (see pars pro toto Kennedy 1989). The 'rising powers' debate is the latest iteration of this narrative. The debate often associates the shift in the patterns of stratification with the rise of the BRICS. This label, originally developed by a Goldman Sachs analyst, gained prominence in world politics when the five states appropriated it as name for their newly created political group in 2009 (Zarakol 2019: 216). The social mobility described by the 'rising powers' debate predominantly relates to two forms of capital: a growing economic output and an increasing political influence in world politics. What the 'rising powers' narrative masks however, especially in its BRICS version, are the vast differences in capitals among the rising powers. To name but two: China's economic output dwarfs that of the other four BRICS members. Two of the five—China and Russia—are already permanent members of the UN Security Council whereas the others—Brazil, South Africa and India—strive to become permanent members of this coveted governance club (Dijkhuizen/Oderco 2019), similar to supposedly 'established' economic powers, as do Germany and Japan. Moreover, the five states differ in their trajectories of social mobility. Most notably, Russia is in some respects a declining rather than a 'rising' power, especially compared to its Cold War status as a superpower, whereas China is widely regarded to be on its way to becoming a superpower alongside the USA and above all other states. Given this heterogeneity of the group, the validity of the BRICS category has been repeatedly challenged, with scholars also pointing to the lack of concerted influence (e.g. Pant 2013; Hurrell 2018).

However, since we are interested in the rules and categorizations that shape social mobility in world politics, we will not evaluate the actual current status of the group itself. What makes the common categorization of these five states so interesting is that they are widely categorized as 'non-Western', giving rise to a social mobility narrative emphasizing the fall of Western powers and the rise of non-Western powers. It is in other words a striking example of how observers mobilize symbolic capital to frame the same instance of social mobility in different ways: as problem for the West (the Western perspective) or as distributional conflict between the developed and developing parts of the world in which the BRICS side with the developing countries (the BRICS perspective).

Rules of Capital Conversion

The multidimensional nature of stratification means that distributional conflicts are likewise multidimensional. They play out at two levels. The first is the competition over capital in distinct social fields, which most likely differs between domestic settings and world society. The second relates to the inter-play between diverse social fields, and especially the possibilities and limits of converting capital gains in some fields into capital gains in other fields.[3] In the present section, we discuss this second level in more detail. We conceptu-alize conversion rates as part of socially negotiated rules of the game, argue that these rules are not set by a single symbolic hegemon but rather negoti-ated in institutional settings, and discuss the mechanisms through which the institutional settings shape the conversion of capitals.

Conversion Rates as Rules of the Game

Although the very notion of 'capital' might suggest that capital can easily be transferred from one field to another, there are limits to the conversion of capital. Some of these limits stem from the characteristics of the respective forms of capital. Nuclear weapons, for instance, are crucial assets in the mili-tary competition among states, but have little to no value in their competition over international markets.[4] Most of the limits, however, are *socially negotiated rules of what actors can do and cannot do with different forms of capital*. A state could use nuclear weapons to blackmail another state to cede territories or money, which—if successful—would constitute a form of capital conversion. But as there is practically a taboo on using nuclear weapons (Tannenwald 2007), this form of capital conversion is regarded as illegitimate. The rules of the game in this sense set conversion rates for the *legitimate translation* of some forms of capitals into other forms.

The rules of the game change over time, which means that new forms of capital may emerge, or other forms can be de- and revalued. To continue the

---

3   While we focus on capital conversion in the context of social mobility, capital conver-sion does not necessarily involve social mobility. Moreover, the conversion does not always involve the translation of gains accumulated in one field to another field. Only sometimes, as in the case of small states developing a reputation as trustworthy neu-tral intermediaries, the lack of certain forms of capital (economic, military power) can be translated into gains in other forms of capital (political influence).

4   Nuclear weapons may help states to 'win' an economic competition if they force their opponents into nuclear arms races that they, but not their opponents, can sustain with-out depleting their economy. But this strategy is only available among nuclear powers and thus, importantly, not for their economic competition with non-nuclear powers. And among nuclear powers the strategy works only among rivals but not among allies.

example: while military capabilities were used in the past to acquire new territories or to transform political entities into colonies (and were regarded by the European powers, though not the oppressed polities, as legitimate means for doing so), the UN Charter restricts the legitimate use of military force, thus outlawing its use as part of territorial expansionism. To put it differently: military capabilities are no longer as convertible as they used to be. But rules can be broken. Sometimes, states are ready to face the consequences and convert capital in ways deemed illegitimate by the community of states. Russia, for instance, used its military superiority to annex Crimea from Ukraine in 2014, albeit under the pretense of a referendum, which catered to the present rules of the game (Burke-White 2014). That certain modes of capital conversion are delegitimized does therefore not mean that they do no longer happen.

The notion of 'conversion rates' denotes the ease or difficulty with which capitals can be translated from one field to another. In present world politics and world society, the most easily convertible form of capital is economic wealth (both for individuals and for states). Economic wealth enables states to maintain larger diplomatic networks, to build up better military capabilities and to finance the programs of international organizations that they favor. Economic wealth enables actors like Bill Gates and his Gates Foundation to become major players in global health, competing with states to influence policies. The primacy of economic capital reflects the historically contingent, but nonetheless deeply engrained, capitalist nature of modern world politics and world society (Buzan/Lawson 2014).

Most narratives of the rise and fall of states depict the patterns of stratification as a hierarchy of 'powers'. The current rising powers debate is no exception, nor is the current status literature.[5] As the literature on power emphasizes (Baldwin 2016; Guzzini 2009), such a representation folds the multiple dimensions of stratification into a one-dimensional ranking of states according to their 'overall' power. Such narratives thus aggregate—usually based on implicit understandings about conversion rates, including the primacy of certain forms of power (in particular military and economic power)—the diverse distributions of capitals across the fields of competition that form part of world politics. Without implicit or explicit understandings about conversion

---

5   The status literature acknowledges that there are multiple dimensions of status—and hence multiple particular status hierarchies—but nevertheless argues that status usually refers to the relative position in the "general status hierarchy" defined as the "generalized hierarchy of importance in international politics" (Renshon 2017: 41).

rates, it is not possible to speak of 'the' distribution of power in world politics and hence the rise and fall of 'powers' in 'the' stratification of world society.

Institutions, not Hegemons

Within states, governments often act as (legitimate) symbolic hegemons that set conversion rates. Nexon and Neumann (2018) have recently suggested that hegemonic states perform a similar role in world politics. These hegemons are said to possess and use a special form of capital called "meta-capital" to "set the rate of exchange among kinds of capitals—within and across fields—and, more broadly, to structure fields themselves" (Nexon/Neumann 2018: 696). For the same reason that power does not automatically translate into authority (Clark 2011: 23-28), we are skeptical that preponderant political, economic and military capabilities automatically grant a state the symbolic power to define the rules of the game. In line with Pouliot (2016: 81), we contend that there is no symbolic hegemon in world politics and that the rules of the game are negotiated in a more diffuse and complex way, involving struggles among diverse state and non-state actors over the representation of the patterns of stratification as well as the conversion rates for the various forms of capital in world politics.

Over the last one and half centuries, international relations have become both deeply and widely legalized and institutionalized (Alvarez 2006; Gold-stein et al. 2000). While bilateral politics continue to play an important role in world politics, it is often regional and global institutions where decisions about the recognition of states and non-state actors or about military and ju-dicial interventions are made, where financial loans, aid or emission rights are distributed and where international trade rules are negotiated. Therefore, in-ternational institutions are implicated in providing capital and are sites where the conversion of capital from one field to another takes place. They have be-come an important source of legitimizing and delegitimizing certain forms of capital, for instance by codifying that the above-mentioned use of force is only legitimate as self-defense.[6]

International institutions do not end the competition among states but channel it into acceptable forms. International institutions circumscribe and

---

6   This resonates with Max Weber's observation that competition is only "formally peace-ful" (Russ/Stafford, this volume) while simply remaining a latent condition of world politics.

tame some forms of competition (e.g. military competition) while promoting other forms (e.g. economic competition). Moreover, as international institutions mirror or even initiate the functional differentiation of world politics, they contribute to an increase in the variety and forms of capitals for which states (as well as non-state actors) compete. Furthermore, by publishing comparative statistics and rankings on the performance of states, international institutions fuel the competition among states over soft goods such as legitimacy and reputation (Werron 2012).

How Institutions Matter for the Politics of Capital Conversion

Institutions are sites, instruments, and agents in the politics of capital conversion. The power vested in institutions can be understood as "a kind of 'world-making power' in the sense that it involves the ability to construct and impose the 'legitimate vision of the social world of its divisions'" (Eagleton-Pierce 2013: 3). This power is, for instance, exerted through "the role of classifications, the organization of arguments into orthodox and heterodox opinions and the social valuation of particular contexts and speakers" (ibid: 63). There are three main ways in which institutions shape the conversion of capitals:

First, *institutions distribute capitals among their members both via their institutional design and via the policies that they decide upon and implement* (Fehl/Freistein 2020a) The most relevant aspect of institutional design is arguably the allocation of voting rights within and across the institution's decision-making bodies (similarly Peters 2020). Institutions such as the UN grant special privileges—that is, particular forms of political capital—to members that have exceptional shares of capital outside the institution. Institutions thus practice social closure, creating privileged groups monopolizing certain forms of capitals while excluding others. Social closure is usually justified by ascribing different traits to insiders and outsiders or by reference to achievements that deserve merit and reward (Grusky 2001: 6). Institutions can practice social closure by internally differentiating voting rights or—as the G7 and G20 do—by only admitting certain states to the institution and to its deliberations and decision-making. The institutionalized differences in political capital give the privileged states a greater say over the policies that the institutions pursue and consequently also over the distributional effects that these policies have.

Second, *institutions shape the discourse about world politics and consequently also about the value and convertibility of different forms of capitals* (similarly Viola 2020). Institutions perform symbolic practices that legitimize certain distributions of capitals and delegitimize and problematize other distributions of capitals. They are involved in the identification and framing of the problems that world politics is supposed to address and solve. Their 'world-making power' goes beyond simple agenda-setting. It affects the salience that is attributed to different social fields and the capitals that states (and other actors) compete for in these social fields. If key international institutions such the UN, the World Bank or the G20 declare some problems and policy fields to be the most pressing issues the international community has to address, then they also empower the actors working in these fields, and having accumulated capitals relevant to these fields, to play more prominent and more influential roles in world politics.

Third, and consequently, institutions are structures of temporally stabilized visions of world politics and distributions of capital. States that socially move upwards have two principal options: They can seek to *change the distribution of capital in the existing institutions* and to translate their rise into more privileged positions within these institutions. Some distributions of privileges are however hard to reform, as the so far unsuccessful debates on the reform of the UN Security Council or reforming the voting rights in the International Monetary Fund testify to. The alternative option therefore is to *create new institutions with more favorable conversion rules and distributions of capitals* and to seek to make these institutions more relevant in world politics. The struggles over capital conversion in this sense happen both within international institutions and between them.

The Politics of Capital Conversion

In this section, we use the example of current rising powers to highlight some of the strategies and politics through which the rules and rates of capital conversion are renegotiated between established and rising powers in world politics. Challenges to an established stratified global order make stratification, or the rules of the game, more visible and show how state competition over them operates. The first strategy we analyze is capital pooling by forming clubs of rising powers. The BRICS group is a key example of this strategy. The second strategy is the attempt of established powers to retain the control over conversion rates by creating a new governance club that includes the rising powers but whose membership—and thus capital conversion possibilities—are selected by established powers. The G20 is a case in point. The third strategy is the creation of new institutional infrastructures and networks in parallel to the institutions created by the established powers. We illustrate this strategy with the BRICS's New Development Bank and China's Belt and Road Initiative. These are neither the only strategies that established and rising powers pursue nor are the three institutions the sole institutions implicated in the politics of capital conversion. Our aim is not to comprehensively map these politics but to highlight that institutions matter for how the politics of capital conversion are enacted and play out in world politics (similarly Stephen 2012).

Capital Pooling Through Group Formation

In their quest to enhance their political capital in world politics, the BRICS states formed a political group in 2009 and have met for annual summits since then. In important respects, this pooling strategy follows the earlier example of the G7, another club of economically powerful states that sought to pool their economic and political capital in order to steer the economic and financial fields in ways favorable to them. The agenda of the BRICS summits initially centered on the "global economy" and "global development" (see BRICS 2009: 1) but, similar to the evolution of the G7, has expanded over time, both in terms of additional topics addressed at the annual summits and in terms of additional forums and meetings on several of these topics on a ministerial level. The growing scope and level of activities was showcased at the end of the Johannesburg Declaration on the occasion of the 10th BRICS summit in July 2018. A "plan of action" was attached to this declaration, which lists on six pages the various ministerial meetings, senior official and sectoral meetings that the BRICS had held and were still going to be held during South Africa's period as chair of the group (BRICS 2018: 18-23). The list covered a wide range of topics, including meetings dedicated to foreign affairs, trade, industry, agriculture, health, education, environmental affairs, and financial regulation.

In their statements, the BRICS frame their main capital for social mobility in economic terms. They allude to their growing salience in the global economic field that follows from their economic growth. At the margins of the 2019 G20 summit, notably, the BRICS issued a joint statement in which they emphasized that "the BRICS countries have been the main drivers of global growth over the last decade, and currently represent close to a third of the global output". This salience was projected to continue in the future: "(...) the

BRICS will continue to account for more than half of global economic growth through 2030" (BRICS 2019: 1).

The BRICS have however been careful not to frame their demands in exclusive terms as demands of a small group of powers rising into the top class(es) of international society. Rather, they have been seeking to accrue additional political, social, and symbolic capital by framing their demands as demands of a broader segment of international society, namely that of (all) developing countries. The first BRICS statement argued "for a more democratic and just multi-polar world order based on the rule of international law, equality, mutual respect, cooperation, coordinated action and collective decision-making of all states" (BRICS 2009: 2), thus taking up the demands for a more inclusive, equality-based global order voiced by developing countries and the Non-Aligned Movement (see also Cai 2013: 780-783), which resurface today with a reformed agenda. This linkage to the agenda of developing countries has deep historical roots. Two of the BRICS states, Brazil and India, were founding members of the group of developing countries (the G77), a third, South Africa, later became a member and a fourth, China, has for a long time supported the group. The BRICS thus mobilize symbolic frames that restructure the political battles over the distribution of capitals as struggle between West vs. non-West as well as developed vs. developing countries and firmly position themselves on the side of non-Western and developing countries.[7]

Regulating Access to Governance Clubs

As stratification research has shown time and again, moves towards greater equality have often been countered by strategies to safeguard privileges by changing the standards for capital conversion (Fehl/Freistein 2020b; Prys-Hansen 2020). In Bourdieu's writing, the aristocratic elites protected themselves against the *nouveaux riches* through small aesthetic distinctions (i.e. cultural capital), which would recreate the distance that money (i.e. financial capital) had started to close. The founding of the G20 (which did not replace the then G8, of course) can be read as such an example. The founding of the G20 exemplifies how social closure may be strategically decreased without changing the overall rules of the game. Standards for capital conversion have

---

7   The BRICS, though, are not fully representative of the developing countries (Thakur 2014). After all, they are major economies in terms of their absolute economic output, rather than—as many of the developing countries—small economies.

been slightly changed, but—and this is vital—kept entirely within the groups of those already endowed with privilege. As a consequence, social closure may thus actually be reinforced again and the overall chances for social mobility reduced even further.

The G20 first met at the level of heads of government and state in 2008, but its membership structure was already determined a decade earlier when the Western powers created a new G20 finance minister forum in 1999 during the late stages of the Asian financial crisis. In 2008, the established powers elevated the importance of this forum, which also allowed them to downplay questions about the arbitrariness of membership by portraying the G20 as a continuing, rather than a new, format (Cooper/Pouliot 2015: 343-344). The new G20 was designed as an extension of the G8 to a more 'inclusive club' in order to gain more legitimacy for Western-dominated club governance vis-à-vis 'the rest' of the world. As an insider account of the creation of the G20 finance minister forum reveals, the club was designed in a peculiar way, with some select Western politicians mixing several criteria to create its membership list:

> "As crisis followed crisis, Mr. Martin, then Canada's finance minister, became convinced that major developing nations had to be given a voice—not just an ultimatum—when it came to discussing their place in the global economy. [...] Mr. Summers quickly agreed. But that was the simple part. Much thornier was the issue of who would be admitted to the club. With the manila envelope in hand, the two began jotting down countries. China, India, Brazil, Mexico—these were obvious choices. So was South Africa, the biggest economy on its continent. But who else? 'I felt very strongly that it had to be the regional powers,' recalls Mr. Martin. 'Larry felt that, and then he also had geopolitical concerns. I would love to say we sat down and ran the numbers on whose GDP was bigger, but we didn't. We both had a pretty good perspective on where things lay'" (Ibbitson/Perkins 2010).

By delineating the membership of the G20 in this way, the Western leaders determined the new conversion rates for club governance. While GDP was apparently seen as the most obvious measure for determining the economic capital that new members had to have, it was not applied systematically as a criterion. GDP considerations mattered, but the G20 was not designed as the club of the 20 states with the highest GDP. Other criteria—and thus forms of capital—also mattered. Phrases such as "major developing nations", "geopolitical concerns" and "regional powers" suggest that political and social forms

of capital likewise played a role. How the different forms of capital were related to each other, and were weighted relative to each other, remains implicit.
For the Western leaders, though, the conversion rates seem to have nevertheless been clear, as they "had a pretty good perspective on where things lay".

Geopolitical concerns seem to make sense intuitively, since expanding the
group to the G20 was all about opening it up to countries beyond the powers represented in the G8, similar to debates about opening the UN Security
Council up to countries from all world regions. The broad set of capitals is
nonetheless surprising given that the self-proclaimed role of the G20 is to
regulate the global economy: "[R]epresenting more than 80% of the global
GDP, the G20 has made continuous efforts toward achieving robust global
economic growth" (Ministry of Foreign Affairs of Japan 2019). As said above,
GDP was not the decisive selection criterion, although the global field in which
the G20 were to become active was and is the global economy.[8] Having the
best-suited (in terms of functional contributions) new members thus could
have been assumed to depend on their conversion of previously earned economic capital, e.g. their economic growth or GDP.

The making of the membership list, therefore, is a telling example of
how the rules of capital conversion can be rewritten. The membership criteria—meaning the access to the exclusive club G20 and the political capital
that its exclusiveness provides—were not changed to make the club more
inclusive. They were determined rather arbitrarily based on vague assumptions of economic, but relatedly also social and cultural capital, which those
acceding states were assumed to possess—knowing 'where things lay'. The
founding of the G20 therefore resulted in greater global social closure. The
G20 was founded by a one-time invitation, based on opaque criteria and implicit notions of relevant forms of capital that were not being communicated.
Every country that had not been invited, accordingly, can never become a
member, as it was (and remains) unclear what capital it would have to acquire
in order to be considered for membership. The G20 seeks to counter criticism
of this social closure by inviting guest countries to their summits, but the
criteria for the invitations are likewise somehow unclear (see Cooper/Pouliot
2015: 345). As a result, the G20 alleged to be more inclusive than the G8, but
actually cemented a global status order in which status was determined by

---

8   Lora Viola (2020) makes similar arguments regarding the notion of the G20 members
     as systemically significant states.

the global elite (the G8) and underlined by the setting of new criteria for capital conversion, which set a precedent for future political processes.

Creating New Institutional Infrastructures and Networks

With regard to the global institutional architecture—the organizations that structure global governance—Western states thus still dominate (Hurrell/Woods 1999) and are consequently still able to shape the ways in which capital conversion works in the global order (Eagleton-Pierce 2013). As several recent studies have demonstrated (Cooper/Pouliot 2015, Pouliot 2016), the hierarchies within these institutions and those they create or reproduce in their environment are difficult to overcome. One way in which the BRICS side-step the control of the established powers over the means of capital conversion is by creating new, alternative institutional settings of their own design. These institutional settings allow them to translate their capital into formal structures and to create alternative, and additional, opportunities for capital conversion.

The BRICS states do so partly as a group and partly as individual states. The most prominent group project is the establishment of the New Development Bank (NDB) by the five BRICS members in 2014 (Cooper 2017). The NDB serves not only to showcase the group agency of the BRICS despite the differences in their interests and trajectories. It also amounts to an institutional setting that allows the BRICS to create new conditions and opportunities for capital conversion. In contrast to other development banks such as the International Monetary Fund, the NDB is based on a principle of equality, with all five founders contributing the same share to the bank. The bank's goal is to lend at least 50% of its money in local currencies rather than in US dollars, which, if implemented, would challenge the salience of the US dollar and thus economic and financial capital of the US (Financial Times 2019). The bank's focus on investment in green and sustainable infrastructure projects moreover can help the BRICS states to garner cultural and social capital as states that actively contribute to the global climate change agenda (Suchodolski/Demeulemeester 2018: 583-584).

Despite their joint summits and institutions, however, the interests of the BRICS states do not fully overlap and sometimes clash. This is not surprising, given the already mentioned stark differences and their varying shares of capital and trajectories of social mobility. Some BRICS members relatedly complement the pooling strategy with individual projects of institution-building.

The most prominent example is probably the One Belt and One Road Initiative (OBOR), which China has pursued since 2013. Originally designed to promote trade in Asia and with Europe, China has over time expanded OBOR to a global development program that fosters "policy coordination, connectivity of infrastructure, unimpeded trade, financial integration, and closer people-to-people ties" (Office of the Leading Group 2019). The initiative is open to all states and China has already signed cooperation agreements with 136 states and 30 international organizations (Belt and Road Portal 2019). OBOR builds, as did the Western powers with the liberal economic order, a system of "deep interdependence" that enhances the "structural power" of its creator (Lairson 2018). In terms of capital conversion, OBOR thus constitutes an investment of economic capital to create structural relations and conditions which allow China to accrue more economic capital while at the same time also increasing its chances to accumulate other forms of capital. The more states participate in OBOR, the more important the international organizations around which it is built become, such as the Asian Infrastructure Investment Bank that China dominates. This, in turn, enhances China's political capital. Moreover, closer contacts among peoples have the potential to increase China's cultural and social capital and the investment in strategic ports potentially boosts its military capital by giving the Chinese navy access to a global network of ports.

Conclusion

Capital conversion can be understood as a special case of the 'Matthew effect', which is known in the sociological inequality literature as the cumulative advantages of certain groups that produce further advantages for them. Do those that succeed in some fields of competition also succeed in other fields? As we have argued in this chapter, the conversion of capital is heavily shaped by the established rules of the game in world politics and international institutions are key to the making and re-making of these rules. Social mobility—the rise and fall of states—is a test case for how interlinked different fields of competition are and gives insights into how fluid or rigid the conversion rates and the hence the patterns of stratification are.

The answer that our chapter suggests is that social mobility leads to a renegotiation of conversion rates but overall reinforces rather than undermines the stratified nature of world politics. Competition does not happen on a level-playing field, as international institutions only equalize some conditions but not others. They also create new inequalities, notably through social closure. Despite the rhetoric of the BRICS in favor of more equal international relations, their politics of capital conversion are not really aimed at levelling the playing field for all states, but rather only between them and the established powers. Their aim is to cash in on their rise and to accumulate forms of capitals—especially political and symbolic capitals—that allow them to rewrite the conversion rules in ways that befit their ambitions and that enhance their chances to further enhance their share of capitals. The struggles over capital conversion between established and rising powers are consequently about whether the 'losers' should give their shares to the 'winners'. It is about the shape of the distribution of capital, not about the fact that capital is distributed unequally. In their current form, the politics of capital conversion thus perpetuate the stratification of world politics.

References

Allison, Graham (2017): Destined for War: Can America and China Escape Thucydides's Trap?, Boston: Houghton Mifflin Harcourt.

Alvarez, José E. (2006): "International Organizations: Then and Now." In: American Journal of International Law 100/2, pp. 324-437.

Baldwin, David A. (2016): Power and International Relations: A Conceptual Approach, Princeton: Princeton University Press.

Belt and Road Portal (2019): "Six Years of 'Belt and Road'!", October 11, 2019 (https://eng.yidaiyilu.gov.cn/search/newSearch.jsp?q=six+years&t_i d=366&pageSize=15&qIndex=1&siteId=CMSydylyw&qIndex=1&catId=).

Bially Mattern, Janice/Zarakol, Ayşe (2016): "Hierarchies in World Politics." In: International Organization 70/3, pp. 623-654.

Bigo, Didier (2011): "Pierre Bourdieu and International Relations: Power of Practices, Practices of Power." In: International Political Sociology 5/3, pp. 225-258.

Bourdieu, Pierre (1984): Distinction: A Social Critique of the Judgement of Taste, Cambridge, MA: Harvard University Press.

Bourdieu, Pierre (1985): "The Social Space and the Genesis of Groups." In: Theory and Society 14/6, pp. 723-744.

BRICS (2009): "Joint Statement of the BRIC Countries' Leaders. Yekaterinburg, June 16, 2009.", September 5, 2019 (http://www.brics.utoronto.ca/d ocs/090616-leaders.html).

BRICS (2018): "BRICS in Africa: Collaboration for Inclusive Growth and Shared Prosperity in the 4th Industrial Revolution. Johannesburg Declaration, 10th BRICS Summit, July 26, 2018.", September 5, 2019 (http://www.brics.utoronto.ca/docs/180726-johannesburg.html).

BRICS (2019): "Joint Statement on BRICS Leaders' Informal Meeting on the Margins of G20 Summit. Osaka, June 28, 2019", September 5, 2019 (http://www.brics.utoronto.ca/docs/190628-osaka.html).

Burke-White, Willliam W. (2014): "Crimea and the International Legal Order." In: Survival 56/4, pp. 65-80.

Buzan, Barry/Lawson, George (2014): "Capitalism and the Emergent World Order." In: International Affairs 90/1, pp. 71-91.

Cai, Congyan (2013): "New Great Powers and International Law in the 21st Century." In: European Journal of International Law 24/3, pp. 755-795.

Clark, Ian (2011): Hegemony in International Society, Oxford: Oxford University Press.

Cooper, Andrew F./Pouliot, Vincent (2015): "How Much is Global Governance Changing? The G20 as International Practice." In: Cooperation and Conflict 50/3, pp. 334-350.

Cooper, Andrew F. (2017): "The BRICS' New Development Bank: Shifting from Material Leverage to Innovative Capacity." In: Global Policy 8/3, pp. 275-284.

Dijkhuizen, Frederieke/Onderco, Michal (2019): "Sponsorship Behavior of the BRICS in the United Nations General Assembly." In: Third World Quarterly 40/11, pp. 2035-2051.

Eagleton-Pierce, Matthew (2013): Symbolic Power in the World Trade Organization, Oxford: Oxford University Press.

Edelstein, David M. (2018): "Cooperation, Uncertainty, and the Rise of China: It's About 'Time'." In: The Washington Quarterly 41/1, pp. 155-171.

Fehl, Caroline/Freistein, Katja (2020a): "Organising Global Stratification: How International Organizations (Re)produce Inequalities in International Society. Introduction to Special Issue." In: Global Society 34/3, pp. 285-303.

Fehl, Caroline/Freistein, Katja (2020b): "(Un)making Global Inequalities: International Institutions in a Stratified International Society." In: Journal of International Relations and Development Online first, https://doi.org/10.1057/s41268-020-00190-z.

Financial Times (2019): "'BRICS Banks' Seeks Move Away from Dollar Funding", August 6, 2019 (https://www.ft.com/content/76707e22-b433-11e9-8c b2-799a3a8cf37b).

Go, Julian (2008): "Global Fields and Imperial Forms: Field Theory and the British and American Empires." In: Sociological Theory 26/3, pp. 201-229.

Goldstein, Judith/Kahler Miles/Keohane Robert O./Slaughter, Anne-Marie (2000): "Introduction: Legalization and World Politics." In: International Organization 54/3, pp. 385-399.

Grusky, David B. (2001): "The Past, Present, and Future of Social Inequality." In: David B. Grusky (ed.), Social Stratification: Class, Race, and Gender in Sociological Perspective, Boulder: Westview Press, pp. 3-51.

Guzzini, Stefano (2009): On the Measure of Power and the Power of Measure in International Relations, Copenhagen: DIIS Working Paper, 28.

Hurd, Ian (2017 [2011]): International Organizations. Politics, Law, Practice, Cambridge: Cambridge University Press.

Hurrell, Andrew (2018): "Beyond the BRICS: Power, Pluralism, and the Future of Global Order." In: Ethics & International Affairs 32/1, pp. 89-101.

Hurrell, Andrew/Woods, Ngaire (eds.) (1999): Inequality, Globalization, and World Politics, Oxford: Oxford University Press.

Ibbitson, John/Perkins, Tara (2010): "How Canada Made the G20 Happen." In: The Globe and Mail, June 18, 2010 (https://www.theglobeandmail.com/ne ws/world/how-canada-made-the-g20-happen/article4322767/).

Keene, Edward (2013a): "Social Status, Social Closure and the Idea of Europe as a 'Normative Power'." In: European Journal of International Relations 19/4, pp. 939-956.

Keene, Edward (2013b): "International Hierarchy and the Origins of the Modern Practice of Intervention." In: Review of International Studies 39/5, pp. 1077-1090.

Keene, Edward (2014): "The Standard of 'Civilisation', the Expansion Thesis and the 19th-Century International Social Space." In: Millennium—Journal of International Studies 42/3, pp. 651-673.

Kennedy, Paul M. (1989): The Rise and Fall of the Great Powers: Economic Change and Military Conflict from 1500 to 2000, New York: Vintage Books.

Lairson, Thomas D. (2018): "The Global Strategic Environment of the BRI: Deep Interdependence and Structural Power." In Wenxian Zhang/Ilan Alon/Christoph Lattemann (eds.), China's Belt and Road Initiative: Changing the Rules of Globalization, Cham: Palgrave Macmillan, pp. 35-53.

Lake, David A. (2009): Hierarchy in International Relations, Ithaca: Cornell University Press.

Larson, Deborah W./Shevchenko, Alexei (2010): "Status Seekers: Chinese and Russian Responses to U.S. Primacy." In: International Security 34/4, pp. 63-95.

Mearsheimer, John J. (2010): "The Gathering Storm: China's Challenge to US Power in Asia." In: The Chinese Journal of International Politics 3/4, pp. 381-396.

Ministry of Foreign Affairs of Japan (2019): "What is the G20 Summit", June 15, 2020 (https://www.mofa.go.jp/policy/economy/g20_summit/osaka19/en/summit/about/).

Müller, Thomas (2019): "The Variety of Institutionalised Inequalities: Stratificatory Interlinkages in Interwar International Society." In: Review of International Studies 45/4, pp. 669-688.

Nexon, Daniel H./Neumann, Iver B. (2018): "Hegemonic-order Theory: A Field-Theoretic Account." In: European Journal of International Relations 24/3, pp. 662-686.

Office of the Leading Group (2019): "The Belt and Road Initiative Progress, Contributions and Prospects", (https://eng.yidaiyilu.gov.cn/zchj/qwfb/86739.htm).

Pant, Harsh V. (2013): "The BRICS Fallacy." In: The Washington Quarterly 36/3, pp. 91-105.

Peters, Dirk (2020): "Justifying Inequality as Equality: Germany and the Reform of Voting Weights in the Council of the European Union." In: Global Society 34/3, pp. 370-387.

Philips, Nicola (2017): "Power and Inequality in the Global Political Economy." In: International Affairs 93/2, pp. 429-444.

Pouliot, Vincent (2016): International Pecking Orders: The Politics and Practice of Multilateral Diplomacy, Cambridge: Cambridge University Press.

Prys-Hansen, Miriam (2020): "Differentiation as Affirmative Action: Transforming or Reinforcing Structural Inequality at the UNFCCC?" In: Global Society 34/3, pp. 353-369.

Renshon, Jonathan (2017): Fighting for Status: Hierarchy and Conflict in World Politics, Princeton: Princeton University Press.

Stephen, Matthew D. (2012): "Rising Regional Powers and International Institutions: The Foreign Policy Orientations of India, Brazil and South Africa." In: Global Society 26/3, pp. 289-309.

Suchodolski, Sergio G./Demeulemeester, Julien M. (2018): "The BRICS' Coming of Age and the New Development Bank." In: Global Policy 9/4, pp. 578-585.

Tannenwald, Nina (2007): The Nuclear Taboo: The United States and the Non-Use of Nuclear Weapons since 1945, Cambridge: Cambridge University Press.

Thakur, Ramesh (2014): "How Representative are BRICS." In: Third World Quarterly 35/10, pp. 1791-1808.

Viola, Lora A. (2020): "'Systemically Significant States': Tracing the G20's Membership Category as a New Logic of Stratification in the International System." In: Global Society 34/3, pp. 335-352.

Ward, Steven (2017): Status and the Challenge of Rising Powers, Cambridge: Cambridge University Press.

Werron, Tobias (2012): "Worum konkurrieren Nationalstaaten? Zu Begriff und Geschichte der Konkurrenz um 'weiche' globale Güter." In: Zeitschrift für Soziologie 41/5, pp. 338-355.

Zarakol, Ayşe (2019): "'Rise of the Rest': As Hype and Reality." In: International Relations 33/2, pp. 213-228.

Knowledge, Ideology and Competition

The Civilizing Force of National Competition
U.S. Nationalist Reasoning in the Mid-to-Late Nineteenth Century

Johannes Nagel & Tobias Werron

The United States represents a particularly interesting case in the history of nationalism. Perhaps more than others, U.S. nationalism is a case of 'nationalism in the world'—not just a national but a global phenomenon. The nationalist transformation of the U.S. took place in the mid-19th to early 20th century, in an era of European domination shaped by the attempt of the great powers to establish a balance among themselves. This was also the period of a New Imperialism, when the Western powers re-discovered large parts of Asia and Africa as targets of their imperial ambitions, colonial exploitation and civilization mission (see e.g. Ballantyne/Burton 2014).

U.S. nationalism did not fit easily into this world. Although the U.S. was a rising power, it was neither defined by imperialist ambitions nor by anti-imperialist resistance. While the nationalism of European powers was connected to imperialist projects, amounting to what Jürgen Osterhammel (2009: 904) calls "expansionist nationalism", and while Asian and African nationalism was fueled by the mobilizing powers of anti-colonial resistance, or "counter nationalism" (ibid), U.S. nationalists had to find a way of reconciling North America's history of anti-colonial resistance with its own ambition as a rising international power. Thus, U.S. nationalists faced the challenge of combining the founding narrative of the post-colonial nation with the ambitions of a rising power,—to define their nation as one that rejects imperialism while also starting and legitimizing their own brand of imperialism.

The present paper explores in how far U.S. nationalist reasoning in the mid-to-late 19th century can be understood as an answer to this challenge. Against the background described above, it is clear from the outset that studying U.S. nationalist reasoning requires close attention to the nexus between nationalism and the wider world. Only then can we see how global connections shaped this world and how nationalist reasoning tried to make sense of those connections. We will do so by focusing on a type of nationalist reasoning that revolves around ideas of scarcity and competition, on the one hand, and ideas of growth, wealth and progress, on the other. Because notions of scarcity are central to this reasoning, we conceptualize it as a type of 'scarcity nationalism'. This political-economic type of nationalism has been largely neglected in the literature but has played a major role in shaping the U.S. nationalist discourse since the mid-to-late 19th century. We show how contributions to this discourse linked U.S. interests with a vision of a world beneficial to all nations, and thus allowed nationalists to imagine both an increasing competition between nations and a future world beyond competition. By navigating tensions between notions of scarcity and growth, and of national and global development, they were able to define the U.S. as a self-interested competitor in an emerging world of nation-states, while also claiming for the U.S. the role of a standard-bearer of cosmopolitan values and global progress. In a study of the debates about protectionism and navalism we try to demonstrate that studying this type of nationalism is relevant beyond U.S. history for understanding how modern nationalism has established itself as the historical force it is today.

We start by introducing our concept of scarcity nationalism. We argue that scarcity nationalism is a discursive mechanism, which links notions of scarcity to the imagining of competition and which has played an important, though neglected, role in the making of modern nationalism. The second section presents two empirical cases which develop and test this conceptualization by looking at major strands of the U.S. political discourse of the mid-to-late 19th century. We consider first the debate about protectionism, which pitted supporters of 'free trade' against the supporters of a protectionist view who—inspired by the German economist and politician Friedrich List—emphasized the need to develop and protect national industrial capacities. We then consider debate about navalism, where questions of naval armament were discussed as part of a wider struggle over the position and role of the U.S. as an emerging major (military) power. In both cases, we focus on how debates about the pursuit of U.S. American interests made use of notions of scarcity and competition and connected them with conceptions of the world. Both studies call attention to ideas that emphasize *transitional stages of development*. By drawing on such ideas, American nationalists could position the U.S. as an emerging power which, though prioritizing its own interest *in the present*, would contribute to the development of humankind *in the future*. It was this temporalization of human progress, and its embedding in nationalist thinking, which allowed U.S. nationalists to balance anti-imperial, particularly anti-British, sentiments with U.S. expansionist ambitions as a rising power. The paper concludes with some remarks on how this analysis, beyond our two case studies, could inform our understanding of current variants of nationalism.

Constructing Competition from a National Point of View: Conceptual remarks on 'scarcity nationalism'

How does modern nationalism relate to the production and transformation of competition in world politics, and how is this relationship reflected in the U.S. discourse of the mid-to-late 19th century? The present section addresses these questions by providing, firstly, a preliminary understanding of the defining characteristics of modern nationalism. In our view, modern nationalism is a discourse that combines particularistic ideas (the construction of collective identities) with universalistic ones (ideas of world order). Secondly, the questions require an understanding of how nationalism can contribute to the social construction of competition. In this part, we show that and why the introduction of competition into the international system relies on historically changing notions of scarcity. In the 19th century emerged a particular type of nationalism which we call 'scarcity nationalism'.

Modern Nationalism as Global Nationalism: A Working Definition

Building on constructivist contributions to the nationalism literature, particularly Craig Calhoun (1997) and Umut Özkirimli (2017), we suggest an understanding of modern nationalism as a *discourse*. By understanding nationalism as a discourse, we capture both the ideological and institutional dimensions of nationalism. A discourse can be the outcome of aggressive struggles between conflicting ideological positions as well as of routinized ways of writing, speaking and interaction. Both dimensions are relevant for the production and global institutionalization of modern nationalism. We distinguish between a cultural, political and global element in this discourse to draw attention to the historical relationships between them. The construction of collective identities constitutes the cultural element; the legitimization of the political claims of these identities, such as popular sovereignty, the political element; and the idea of a world order divided into nations, or nation-states, the universal or global element.

The relation between the first two has been discussed in the literature on nationalism for quite some time and is famously captured in Ernest Gellner's description of modern nationalism as aiming at a "marriage" between nation and state (Gellner 1983). The third, global element has attracted less attention. However, it explains best why nationalism, irrespective of differences of opinion between 'modernists' and 'anti-modernists' in the nationalism literature (Gorski 2000; Smith 1998), should indeed be considered a modern institution, by calling attention to the historical process in which nationalism has helped transform the early modern state system into a global nation-state system over the last two centuries. By establishing the principle of national legitimacy as a universal model, nationalism has transformed the European 'international society' in two ways: It has helped expand the outer limits of the state-system "to a point where they are coextensive with those of the globe" and it has encouraged the "penetration of central government activity", both internally, by expanding state power and responsibility, and externally, by increasing the range and density of international relations (Mayall 1990: 33-34).

This conceptualization of nationalism emphasizes the modernity of nationalism and of the nation-state system, without denying continuities with the early modern system. Core institutions of the early modern system such as sovereignty, diplomacy or international law are just as characteristic of today's global nation-state system. Yet, it was nationalism which first introduced a source of legitimacy with universal, and thus potentially global, scope. It therefore attracted all kinds of social groups that were looking to legitimize their state-building projects in an increasingly globalized environment—including anti-colonial movements and potential 'great powers' outside of Europe.

Nationalism, Scarcity and Competition: Introducing Scarcity Nationalism

Competition, too, had been an integral part of the European state-system even before the advent of modern nationalism. As Charles Tilly (1975) and others have convincingly argued, military and political competition was largely responsible for the modernization of state structures in the early modern European state system, particularly by creating a constant need for the refinancing of wars and the bureaucratic organization of tax collection. According to this view, 'hard' power competition for territories, as well as cultural and human resources, was as important a trigger of modernization processes as other, more peaceful and 'rational', developments like industrialization, differentiation or the division of labor. These insights are reflected in traditional views of competition in the international system, which imagine the nation-state system as shaped by constant competition for power and prestige.

However, the rise of modern nationalism changed the rules and forms of competition in the international system. In U.S. debates of the mid-to-late 19th century, this was reflected particularly in the tendency of U.S. speakers and writers to combine traditional understandings of power competition with novel ideas of economic and political development. These new ideas linked national prestige with the ability of nations to participate in and contribute to the economic, cultural, and political development of mankind. In so doing, these debates reflected the formation of new forms of competition for 'softer' goods such as attention, legitimacy, or prestige of societal development, whose rise can be traced back to the late 19th century as well (Werron 2015; 2020a). These 'soft' aspects seem particularly significant in the genesis of American nationalism, since the United States participated only peripherally in the dynamics of military-political-fiscal competition in the first place and traditionally avoided any 'entanglement' in the European balance of power. The fact that the United States, despite its regionally distinct development, became a modern nation-state and participant in world politics at the turn of the century raises the question of the influence of the world culture of nationalism.

To make sense of these changes, we understand competition as a social form based on overlapping notions of scarcity. In this view, competition describes the case of (at least) two parties attempting to acquire a good at the expense of the other. This requires shared notions of scarcity and, in many cases, third parties observing and constructing the competition (Simmel 1955; Werron 2014). Often, the connection between competition and notions of scarcity appears too obvious to attract scholarly attention. When two nation-states, under the condition of exclusive ownership of territory, compete for a certain piece of land, it appears self-evident that the land can only be acquired by one of the states at the expense of the other. It is scarce because it exists only once and because all parties involved are aware of that.

In other cases, notions of scarcity are less self-evident to nation-states and are subject to historical change. Indeed, nationalism and state competition are connected through changing notions of scarcity and, by implication, new forms competition. We suggest thinking about such forms of nation-alism in terms of 'scarcity nationalism' (Werron 2020b: 164, 168-173). In the world-view of scarcity nationalism, the world is a place scarce of resources, forcing all nations to fight constantly for their piece of the cake. Scarcity na-tionalism introduces notions of scarcity to specify the goods for which nations and nation-states are supposed to compete, and it imagines nations and na-tion-states as competitors for those scarce goods. There is a long list of goods that can be, and often are, imagined as scarce, ranging from territories, nat-ural and human resources, and selling opportunities on national and global markets to 'soft' goods such as attention, legitimacy, and prestige. Moreover, the relevance of these 'goods' is not stable, and scarcities are discursively re-imagined all the time. This affects if and how state leaders and nationalist movements around the world perceive each other as competitors.

In the mid-to-late 19th century, an increasingly interconnected world urged nationalists worldwide to redefine their own brand of nationalism in a globalized environment. It urged them to think, in particular, about how to define their own national interests while also conceptualizing their nation as part of a larger world shared with other nations. In the case of the United States, two public debates, about protectionist trade policies and about naval armament and strategy, seem to have been particularly influential in (re-)shaping U.S. nationalism. Both were directly concerned with the role of the U.S. as a rising power in the world, and both addressed this role in terms of scarce resources and competition.

'Listian Nationalism' in the U.S.

The mid-to-late 19th century U.S. debate about trade policies pitted support-ers of free trade policies against proponents of protectionist policies, forming two political camps that are still relevant today. The debate did not follow party lines but took place within the new Republican party. Founded in 1854, this went on to dominate U.S. politics on the federal level until the First World War, and has remained a part of the two-party-system ever since. In his sem-inal book about this debate, Marc-William Palen (2016: xvi) argues that eco-nomic historians have long focused on the free trade proponents of the time, even though the protectionists were as active in the debate as the former and arguably more successful in shaping actual politics. Palen calls the protection-ists "Listian nationalists" to emphasize that they were heavily influenced by

the works of the German economist and politician Friedrich List. In this section, we briefly describe the key elements of List's view (including its arrival
in the U.S.) and then show how they were reflected in the U.S. debate of the
mid-to-late 19th century.[1]

Friedrich List's Economic Nationalism: the Core Ideas

Friedrich List's view on political economy developed over the course of two
decades before his major work, *The National System of Political Economy* (Originally *Das nationale System der politischen Ökonomie*) was published in 1841 (List
1922). List agreed with liberal economists that the long-term goal should be
free trade between all nations, but argued that underdeveloped nations should
employ short-term protectionist policies to be able to catch up with the developed nations. Since David Ricardo's work on comparative advantages (1817),
the liberal doctrine assumed that free trade was mutually advantageous under any circumstances. In contrast, List held that selling opportunities on
global markets were scarce and that competition between nations for their
share of these markets was unavoidably fierce. In other words, he saw *scarcities* where the free traders saw nothing but opportunities for common growth
and wealth. Therefore, developing nations should be allowed to help domestic companies to develop their products and production capacities on national
markets before entering global competition. Only after having developed a vi-
able 'people's economy' (*Volkswirtschaft*, in contrast to the 'national economy'
as understood by British economists), would these countries be able to join
the global system of free trade and participate in common growth. On these
grounds, he opposed the theory of free trade as a political ideology used by
Britain to legitimize its own interests and force its superior industry on its
competitors.

It is essential to grasp the *temporal* element of this view: List combined a
short-term emphasis on scarcities and national competition with a long-term
belief in common growth and prosperity. He was able to merge these ideas
by arguing for protectionism *without* buying into the old mercantilist worldview of permanent zero-sum competition and without buying completely into

---

1   The following section is heavily indebted to Palen's (2016) analysis, building on both
     his sources and historical interpretation. It aims, however, to add a sociological inter-
     pretation that draws attention to the role of scarcities, or constructions of scarcity, in
     the debate.

the liberal concept of free competition. Instead, he defined free competition on *global* markets as an ideal that could only be reached by establishing free competition on *national* markets. The combination of these ideas afforded List with the ability to integrate his protectionist nationalism into a cosmopolitan vision: the former to be practiced in the present, the latter to be pursued in the future. In this temporal sense, List took pride in having discovered the 'national principle' as the basis of a functioning *global* economy.

Nationalists around the world quickly recognized that these ideas could be applied to different geographical, political and cultural contexts (e.g. Bayly 2004: 300-302). Before his arguments could influence the U.S. debate, List's thinking was influenced by his own experiences in the U.S. List's influence in the U.S. even preceded the publication of *The National System*. Born in 1789, List worked as a public servant and as a professor of economics in the German state of Württemberg from the late 1810s to the early 1820s. Based on his administrative experiences, he argued for the abolishment of customs within the German states to advance industrialization in Germany. In the realm of foreign trade, the young List by and large was a proponent of free trade, though he was growing sympathetic to protectionist ideas. However, he was also a liberal constitutionalist who pushed aggressively for political reforms. Exiled from Württemberg for his liberal activism, List went to the U.S., where between 1825 and 1832 he worked as a coal and railways entrepreneur as well as a political publicist (he had entered the U.S. on recommendation from Marquis de Lafayette, a prominent figure of both the American and the French revolutions). In his *Outlines of American Political Economy in a Series of Letters*, published in 1827 and addressed to Charles J. Ingersoll, Vice-president of the "Pennsylvania Society for the Promotion of Manufactures and the Mechanic Arts", he gave the first systematic explanation of his protectionist ideas, promoting them as a contribution to the building of an "American System".[2]

It was here that List for the first time developed his theoretical argument that the national element had been neglected in political economy.[3] He pointed out a curious gap in the thinking of the British economists, which he

---

2   The expression "American System" likely alluded to the fact that List's thinking at this stage was influenced by Alexander Hamilton's late 18th century writings.

3   The exact timeline of List's theory development is hard to determine, but it appears that the first mature version was indeed developed, at least published, in the U.S. Later on, in the 1830s, when he was working on *Das nationale System*, List was also influenced by Adolphe Thiers and other French liberal protectionists (cf. Todd 2015: 146-153).

referred to as "Adam Smith and Co." "In consequence of my researches," wrote List, "I found the component parts of political economy to be—1, Individual economy; 2, National economy; 3, Economy of mankind." Of these, however, Smith treated only the first and the last, and did not account for the national element in the global political economy: "he has entirely forgotten what the title of his book, 'Wealth of Nations,' promised to treat." (List 1827: 7)

List went on to explain why accounting for the national element implied criticism of the teachings of free trade. Specifically addressing his U.S. audience, he started his reasoning with a comparison between the United States and the world:

"If the whole globe were united by a union like the 24 States of North America, free trade would indeed be quite as natural and beneficial as it is now in the union. There would be no reason for separating the interest of a certain space of land, and of a certain number of human beings, from the interests of the whole globe and of the whole race. There would be no national interest, no national law contrary to the freedom of the whole race, no restriction, no war." (ibid)

For List, modelling the political organization of the world after the current state of the U.S. described a desirable future, "a postulate of reason, that nations should settle their differences by law as now the United States do among themselves." (ibid). However, he also argued that, *for the time being*, the world was indeed separated by national interests. In such a world, it would be as unwise for the U.S. to embrace the ideology of free trade as it would be for a secretary of war to refuse to arm his soldiers (ibid).

On a more theoretical level, List contrasted these insights with "the Scots theory", which, by ignoring the significance and interests of nations, had in fact ignored the 'political' in political economy by jumping straight to a 'cosmopolitical economy'. As opposed to "individual and cosmopolitical economy", which are only about wealth, "national wealth is increased and secured by national power, as national power is increased and secured by national wealth. Its leading principles are therefore not only economical, but political too." (List 1827: 10)

On this basis, to make his point for protectionism and, again, connect his arguments to the U.S. discussion, List described protectionist policies in the U.S. as a means of preparation for times of war: In times of peace, he argued, "it may be quite indifferent to a Pennsylvanian whether the manufacturer who gives him cloth in exchange for his wheat, lives in Old England or in

New England; but in time of war and of restriction, he can neither send wheat to England nor import cloth from there, whilst the exchange with New England would forever be undisturbed." (ibid). With arguments like these, List managed to draw an immediate connection between economic nationalism and the security interests of the U.S.

British-American Relations and the Repeal of the Corn Laws (1846) as a Catalyst of the Debate

List's ideas gained traction in the U.S. discourse in the 1850s, when they became useful arguments against the increasingly influential proponents of free trade. The latter were called 'Cobdenites' by their critics, referring to the leading British ideologist of free trade, Richard Cobden, who had become (in)famous as the leading figure of several major free trade initiatives, including the Anti-Corn Law League (1838) and the Cobden-Chevalier Treaty (1860).[4]

The conflict between 'Cobdenites' and 'Listian nationalists' shaped the development of 'Listian nationalism' in the second half of the 19th century. The supporters of free trade in the North were closely aligned with the antislavery movement, which in turn was supported by British antislavery activists. Partly for this reason, the lines of the debate neither followed the north-south pattern of the Civil War nor party lines. This would have suggested alliances between the protectionists and the industrial North, on the one hand, and, on the other, between free traders and the agricultural, trade-dependent South. Rather, in the 1830s to 1850s, British abolitionists such as George Thompson went to the U.S. to help link the antislavery cause with the cause of free trade and to join forces with American activists (e.g. Joshua Leavitt, William Cullen Bryant, William Lloyd Garrison, Reverend Henry Ward Beecher, Ralph Waldo Emerson, Charles Sumner)—to the point that leading "Anglo-American Cobdenites [were] a regular *who's who* of radical abolitionists" (Palen 2016: 15).

The rise of Listian nationalism in the newly founded Republican party can be understood as a counterreaction to the influence of these abolitionists-cum-free traders. The opposition was fueled by a general skepticism of British power politics, and sometimes outright Anglophobia, that was rooted in the founding of the United States and was present across political debates

---

4   We should note that the term 'Cobdenite Cosmopolitans' was used by economic nationalists to attack their opponents, whereas 'Listian nationalists' was introduced by Michael Palen after the fact.

in the 19th century (including, most notably, over the Mexican-American War in 1848). Opposition was also sparked by sheer success: from the mid-1840s onwards, the influence of proponents of free trade on politics became noticeable. The first concrete evidence that the 'Cobdenites' were a force to be reckoned with was the repeal of the British Corn Laws in 1846. This had tangible consequences for the North of the United States: it meant that the U.S. lost their backdoor trade route through Canada, which, as a British colony, had been protected by the Corn Laws (implying that the U.S., too, had been indirectly protected by the Corn Laws). The repeal of the Corn Laws, therefore, in the late 1840s led to increasing competition between U.S. and European agricultural exports to the British Empire and to a considerable fall of agricultural prices in Canada and North America (Palen 2016: 27). U.S. farmers and their political representatives could experience the price-drop as a negative consequence of free trade. More generally, they could see it as evidence for the protectionist argument that international trade opportunities were, in fact, a scarce good, and that the advantages of free trade were primarily enjoyed by the British empire—at the expense of producers in North America.

Protecting American Interests While Furthering Human Progress: Fortifying the American System

These experiences help explain why 'Listian nationalists' gained a stronghold within the young Republican party. Since the 1850s, Republican politicians continued List's intellectual work on an 'American system'. Leading figures of the new party like Henry C. Carey, James G. Blaine and William McKinley attacked the cosmopolitan ideology of free trade on all levels of the domestic debate—from systematic book-length studies to the daily infighting in Congress—as a vehicle of British imperial power politics. As an alternative, they made the case for an 'American System' that would effectively protect U.S. interests.

The leading theorist of the American School was Henry C. Carey (1793-1879), a political economist who became chief economic advisor of President Abraham Lincoln (1860-1865). In the 1850s and 1860s, Carey wrote a number of influential books in which he harshly criticized what he called 'the English System' and in which he outlined the characteristics and virtues of 'the American System'. Both his critique of the British economists and his use of the term 'American System' are clearly reminiscent of Friedrich List. In contrast to List, though, he presented himself as an admiring supporter of Adam Smith, focusing his critique on Smith's successors, particularly on David Ricardo and on what he called "the tendency of the Ricardo-Malthusian system to produce intensity of selfishness" (Carey 1851: 64).

Carey developed the notion of the 'American System' into a proper system of thought. He aimed at protecting American interests and claimed for the U.S. the role of a standard-bearer of human progress. In *The Harmony of Interests, Agricultural, Manufacturing and Commercial* (1851), Carey explained what in his view distinguished the American system from the British:

> "[T]wo systems are before the world; the one looks to increasing the proportion of persons and of capital engaged in trade and transportation, and therefore to diminishing the proportion engaged in producing commodities with which to trade, with necessarily diminished return to the labor of all; while the other looks to increasing the proportion engaged in the work of production, and diminishing that engaged in trade and transportation, with increased return to all, giving to the laborer good wages, and to the owner of capital good profits." (Carey 1851: 228; emphasis in the original)

The 'American system' was beneficial to everyone, because it focused on expanding production and on reducing the number of 'unproductive' middle men.

According to Carey, this system was not just a superior guideline for U.S. economic policies, but a model for the world at large. This instilled the U.S. with a mission and responsibility that reached beyond its own interests while, happily, not contradicting them:

> "One looks towards universal war; the other towards universal peace. One is the English system; the other we may be proud to call the American system, for it is the only one ever devised the tendency of which was that of ELEVATING while EQUALIZING the condition of man throughout the world. Such is the true mission of the people of these United States. To them has been granted a privilege never before granted to man, that of the exercise of the right of perfect self-government; but, as rights and duties are inseparable, with the grant of the former came the obligation to perform the latter. Happily their performance is pleasant and profitable, and involves no sacrifice. To raise the value of labor throughout the world, we need only to raise the value of our own." (Carey 1851: 228-29; capitalisation in the original)

By introducing protectionist policies as part of an 'American System', which positions the U.S. both as a rising power in international politics and as a beacon of the progress of human civilization, Carey had devised a powerful ideological weapon: a theory of political economy that managed to reconcile national selfishness with global responsibility. The theory acknowledged the necessity of competition now and aimed at a future with common growth and mutual cooperation—allowing for the pursuit of national interests without bad conscience. This clearly met a demand within the Republican party, where morally conscious movements like abolitionism were hugely influential and where the strong rejection of British imperial power politics was shared by many. It thus comes as no surprise that this line of argument was used extensively within the Republican Party in the decades to come, culminating in the McKinley Tariff of 1890 and the presidency of William McKinley at the conclusion of the century.

Listian Nationalism as a Case of Scarcity Nationalism

Listian economic nationalism in the 19th century U.S. can be seen as a form of scarcity nationalism. In tracing the development of this economic nationalism, we have shown how it introduced the 'the nation' as a central concept of political economy, built on negative experiences with free trade (after the repeal of the Corn Laws in 1846) that reflected a scarcity of trade opportunities, flourished as part of an on-going conflict between proponents of free trade and proponents of protectionist policies, and was integrated into a theoretical model of national economic policies ("American system") which argued that such a national system was necessary not just to protect the short-term interests of the U.S., but in the long run to advance the wealth and progress of humankind. In this worldview, economic nationalism, based on 'realistic' insights into scarcities of trade opportunities, was at the same time a vehicle of an 'idealistic' vision for the world at large that argued for protectionist policies in the present to advance a cosmopolitan world of free trade in the future. In other words, it saw economic nationalism as a necessary stage in the development of humankind.

While this view united all 'Listian nationalists' in their struggle against the 'Cobdenites', they had considerable disagreements about its wider implications. Among the matters of contention was whether the 'American System' could be combined with imperial power politics of the military kind, that is, whether it could be part of an "imperialism of economic nationalism" (Palen 2016: 100). Henry C. Carey, the leading thinker of 'Listian nationalism', clearly opposed any such combination, as he thought that "to improve the political condition of man throughout the world, it is needed that we ourselves should remain at peace, avoid taxation for the maintenance of fleets and armies" (Carey 1851: 229). Other economic nationalists in the Republican Party were much less cautious when it came to the pursuit of power politics—as the case of navalism will illustrate.

The Case of Navalism

The debate over naval reconstruction and strategy is another example that shows how scarcity nationalism played a role in the redefinition of the U.S. in the world at the end of the 19th century. Navalists argued for naval reconstruction and a strategic reorientation of the U.S. navy. In their arguments, they also touched on questions of nationalism, scarcity, imperialism, and American participation in world politics. Previously, the U.S. navy had been seen as a tool of a lesser power primarily concerned with commercial diplomacy. Since the mid-1880s, however, navalists redefined American interests in the world and the navy's role. Like previous naval thinkers, the new navalists believed in universal progress through commercial interdependence and a special role of the U.S. navy in developing global civilization. Unlike their predecessors, however, they perceived world politics as increasingly characterized by scarcity and competition. They called for a new strategic outlook: if the United States wanted to be an agent of civilization in the future, it had to prepare for war in the present.

The Old Navy: Advancing Commerce and Civilization Within the British Imperial System

To understand what was new about the navalists' scarcity nationalism, it might be useful to first consider what preceded it. Before the 1890s, the U.S. was a lesser naval power with political interest confined to its own region, but no aspirations outside the Western hemisphere beyond expanding its trade. U.S. foreign policy traditionally accepted and even embraced a peripheral status in world politics.

This outsider status was a result of both geography and ideology. On the one hand, America enjoyed "free security" after the Civil War, since potential enemies were either too weak or too remote (Woodward 1997: 2). On the other hand, U.S. republican exceptionalism actively rejected the idea of participating in great power struggles. Politicians throughout the 19th century affirmed the guiding motto: "Peace, commerce, and honest friendship with all nations—entangling alliances with none." (Jefferson 1801, cited in Cleveland 1885) This also included a rejection of peacetime military buildup and power competition. One secretary of the navy stated: "It is not now, and it never has been, a part of that [national] policy to maintain a fleet able at any time to cope on equal terms with the foremost European armaments." (Chandler 1883: 8-9) As "a powerful though peaceful nation" (Robeson 1874: 24), the U.S. was also not supposed to participate in any competition over colonies.

Nevertheless, American republicanism had a strong universalist component. On the one hand, the U.S. was supposed to be a model for the world. On the other hand, American elites in the late 19th century believed it to be the vanguard of an "industrial civilization" that would eventually overcome the European-led "militarist civilization" and form a better global civilization (Ninkovich 2009: 316-323). As a result, U.S. foreign and naval policy focused on the promotion of economic interdependence around the world.

The navy served as a tool for this commercialist foreign policy, while also contributing to the construction of a global maritime infrastructure. It was dispersed into regional squadrons across the globe, protecting U.S. citizens abroad, "showing the flag" in foreign ports, and negotiating trade deals. This was a technologically modest "cruising navy," not designed for fighting great wars, but for participating in a global order upheld by the Royal Navy. Especially in East Asia, the U.S. acted as sidekick of British power, based on the assumption of a Euro-American harmony of interests (Burk 2018: 158-159, 203). If the U.S. navy employed force in foreign waters, it used it against 'semi-civilized' powers or groups designated as criminals and pirates, and in cooperation with European navies. The U.S. navy also contributed to exploration, hydrographic mapping, the construction and maintenance of submarine telegraph cables, and other responsibilities of a power contributing to global civilization. There was no security competition between the U.S. and European powers and both wealth and security were perceived as plentiful.

The traditional ideology of the U.S. navy of this time is exemplified by Commodore Robert W. Shufeldt (1850-1934). As a naval officer, commercial agent, and diplomat, Shufeldt sailed to Africa and Asia between 1878 and 1880 and negotiated the 'opening of Korea' in 1882. The purpose of the U.S. navy, according to Shufeldt, was "[...] cruising abroad among the semi-barbarous peoples, because a navy not only protects commerce, it creates it." Gunboat imperialism—the opening of foreign markets with the help of naval power—was "the secret of half the success of the British commerce" which should be emulated (Shufeldt 1884: 21-22). In his quest for access to overseas markets, Shufeldt did not shy away from employing force. Like most naval officers during the 1880s, however, he was opposed to European-style colonialism (Hagan 1973), which was "not employed to 'civilize' orientals—but to subordinate them [...]." U.S. foreign policy, however, "should take higher grounds [...]" (Shufeldt 1880, cited in Drake 1984: 252).

Shufeldt opposed both colonial imperialism and great power competition. In his view, the U.S. should focus on expanding its trade abroad, while cooperating with European powers and avoiding military conflicts. Most naval politicians and officers shared this view before the 1890s, which explains why the U.S. maintained a comparatively weak and outdated fleet. For its strategic purpose of commerce protection and gunboat diplomacy, the old wooden navy was entirely adequate (Buhl 2008). The contribution this small navy was to make to global civilization was not military, but commercial and developmental. Since security was seen as a given and trade as plentiful, there was no need to compete with European navies. Great power prestige was of no concern to most naval decision makers (Hagan 1973: 188).

According to 'old navy' thinking, the navy served the protection and expansion of U.S. commercial interests. This included occasional 'gunboat diplomacy' vis-à-vis underdeveloped parties, but not competition and conflict with other naval powers. Naval politicians and officers did not perceive any threat to U.S. security but enough economic opportunities at the periphery of the Eurocentric world system. The navy shared in the American foreign policy objective to remain outside of the European 'balance of power' and avoid competition.

The New Navalism: Choosing Competition

Traditional ideas about the purpose of the navy were challenged by navalists such as Captain A. T. Mahan (1840-1914) and his mentor Rear Admiral S. B. Luce (1827-1917), who took up many established ideas from professional naval discourse but reinterpreted them based on the assumption of scarcity nationalism. Since the mid-1880s, navalists publicly argued that in an increasingly interdependent world, wealth and security were becoming scarce and the U.S. had to compete with other powers to secure its position in world politics. Subsequently, naval reformers in the legislative and executive branches advocated for the construction of a 'big navy' centered on battleships and a strategic shift towards an offensive defense. In 1890, Mahan published the first volume of "The Influence of Sea Power Upon History", which contributed to popularizing navalism across the U.S. and global public. Mahan's ideas were not entirely original but synthesized years-long professional debates on naval policy. His book and many articles show how the new navalism redefined U.S. nationalism by framing global politics as a zero-sum game and legitimizing the participation of the U.S. in great power competition. This competition, however, would eventually contribute to universal progress. In this, navalists followed established discourses of American exceptionalism and global-developmentalist optimism, but they argued for a temporary necessity of participating in great power naval competition.

Navalists argued for naval buildup on political-economic considerations but introduced a new argument about scarcity. Since political discussions of foreign and naval policy had traditionally focused on commercial interests, navalists expressed their agenda in similar terms. Their view of the global economic system differed from their predecessors', however, in that they perceived economic interdependence as the basis for a zero-sum, not positive-sum commercial politics. According to Mahan, sea power determined the rise and fall of great powers. Sea power was not a purely military concept since it included a power's capacity to participate in and (if necessary) control parts of global maritime trade routes and access to overseas markets. Mahan took a zero-sum view of commerce-as-power: "The history of sea power is largely, though by no means solely, a narrative of contests between nations, of mutual rivalries, of violence frequently culminating in war." At the center of this lay the struggle over the sources of "growth and prosperity" and every nation tried to "secure to one's own people a disproportionate share of such benefits" (Mahan 1890: 1). This understanding of economic and naval power, which he derived from his analysis of the 17th and 18th centuries, Mahan applied to his own time. In the late 19th century, he perceived another cycle of great power competition: "Everywhere nation is arrayed against nation; our own no less than others" (Mahan 1917a: 18). It was not just access to trade routes and markets, however, that Mahan—in opposition to traditional naval commercialism—conceptualized as scarce. The infrastructure of globalization itself made conflict more likely and U.S. isolationism an anachronistic strategy: "[...] Proximity, as has been noted, is a fruitful source of political friction, but proximity is the characteristic of the age. The world has grown smaller. Positions formerly distant have become to us of vital importance from their nearness" (Mahan 1917c: 148).

Similarly, security could no longer be taken for granted. A new wave of imperialist competition increased other powers' interests in the Western hemisphere and the technology-aided shrinking of the world transformed the oceans from strategic barriers into highways. Potential adversaries included not just traditional European powers, but also the rising naval powers Japan and Germany, which became increasingly active in the Atlantic and Pacific (Millett/Maslowski 1994: 317). On the other hand, the conversion of fleets to steam propulsion made all naval powers more dependent on naval bases. Whereas sail ships had been able to operate independently for months, steam navies were reliant on a network of bases (and supply lines) for weekly maintenance and refueling (Hobson 2002: 29). Because "fuel is the life of modern war [...]," wrote Mahan, around logistical questions would "cluster some of the most important considerations of naval strategy. In the Caribbean and the Atlantic we are confronted with many a foreign coal depot [...]" (Mahan 1917a). The U.S., too, needed to establish such bases as long as locations were still available. There was only a limited number of islands in the Pacific and Atlantic where such stations could be established. A race for such islands seemed imminent which increased the danger of European intervention in the Western hemisphere.

Another technological development that seemed to make hemispherical security into a scarce good was the anticipated construction of a Central American canal. Such a canal, navalists reasoned, would increase maritime commerce and create a new source of tension between the naval powers, akin to the Suez Canal completed in 1869. It would be "nothing but a disaster to the United States, in the present state of her military and naval preparation. It is especially dangerous to the Pacific coast" (Mahan 1890), which could be reached more easily by European naval powers once the canal would be completed. (In today's security parlance, the Central American canal is one of multiple "maritime chokepoints", which are today characterized as "increasingly scarce natural resources" (Nincic 2002: 144).) This situation required a new strategy focused on gaining command of the sea and confronting other naval powers with an offensive battleship fleet. The coercive acquisition of coaling stations was seen as a legitimate move in ensuring strategic and operational autonomy for the U.S. navy. Therefore, the increasing scarcity of security necessitated a strategic shift and reconstruction of the navy.

Since interdependence increased scarcity and the potential for conflict, the U.S., according to the navalists, had no choice but to give up its traditional isolation and prepare for war. The main political obstacle to this was the traditional U.S. isolationism and distrust of expensive standing militaries. To overcome this, navalists redefined the role of the U.S. in the world and legitimized great power competition in the context of American ideology. By focusing on the prestige that would come with naval power, navalists tried to reconcile American universalism with a militarist agenda that might otherwise have been perceived as too European. Navalists argued that in order to "take rank" in the world, the U.S. required a European-style battleship navy (Tracy 1889: 3). The navalists' focus on battleship-building (rather than cheaper alternatives such as torpedo-boats) suggests the importance of modernity prestige in naval reconstruction. Mahan tried to overcome the contradiction between traditional and new naval policy by temporalizing both America's earlier "policy of isolation which befitted her infancy", and, to a lesser extent, his own proposed naval strategy (see further below): "[…] whereas once to avoid European entanglement was essential to the development of her individuality, now to take her share of the travail of Europe is but to assume an inevitable task […]" (Mahan 1917b: 122-123). Although there is little to suggest that Mahan closely followed discussions on political economy or was involved with the business world, it is noteworthy that he chose to make a temporally defensive argument similar to Listian protectionist reasoning.

Great Power Competition and America's Contribution to Global Civilization

Despite his embrace of power competition, Mahan also retained the traditional American belief in global progress and America's special role as agent of civilization. Mahan's starting assumption was that great power competition itself was a mechanism to bring about peace and development. Ridiculing the liberal internationalism of the 'Cobdenites' he claimed that "[n]ot in universal harmony, nor in fond dreams of unbroken peace, rest now the best hopes of the world […]." Instead, he identified "the competition of interests[,]" the "reviving sense of nationality" and "the jealous determination of each people to provide first for its own, of which the tide of protection […] is so marked a symptom" as forces which, in the long run, would foster the "common interests of civilization" (Mahan 1917b: 122-123). He suggested at least three specific mechanisms:

First, naval buildup would deter European powers from the Western hemisphere and establish a mutually beneficial regional division of labor, thereby integrating the U.S. into a common global security system with

Europe. Initially, the navalists sought to make the Western hemisphere safe from European intrusion. Their proposed offensive navy was not just designed to counter German and Japanese, but also British naval power. U.S. demands for international recognition of regional autonomy (the Monroe Doctrine) was first and foremost motivated by a desire for security. However, this also made the Americas a zone of influence for the U.S., and the U.S. an "international police force," as President Theodore Roosevelt, himself a navalist, declared in 1903. Mahan's reflections on the future Anglo-American relationship show that the claim to regional autonomy and security enabled to think about Anglo-American cooperation on a global scale (Mahan 1917b). Hemispheric security, therefore, implied integration into a global power system.

Second, competition would force the U.S. to take up its responsibility as participant in the "outward impulse of all the civilized nations of the first order of greatness" (Mahan 1917d: 225). By this Mahan both referred to a great inter-civilizational struggle between "Eastern or Western civilization" as well as global development more generally. After the Spanish-American War in 1898, when the U.S. acquired overseas territories, he increasingly believed such "duties which must be accepted" to include colonial development in Cuba and the Philippines (Mahan 1907: 324-325).

Third, Mahan argued that great power competition between nations would eventually have to give way to a new world order, in which competition might take a new form and even be reduced. Reflecting on the coming 20th century, Mahan speculated that warfare as a means of naval competition between the great powers might become obsolete since no state could command the immensity of future sea power by itself. He, therefore, envisioned a "multinational consortium" (Sumida 2000) of naval powers which would shape the world together: "it is improbable that control ever again will be exercised, as once it was, by a single nation." Competition between nations would lay the groundwork for this by encouraging military preparedness and creating "a common standard of moral and intellectual ideas" (Mahan 1917b: 124–125). National interest would thus make international cooperation necessary and therefore inevitable lead to a transcendence of nationalist competition. In the future, the U.S. might act in accordance with European powers to check the rising power of East Asia, or in an alliance with Britain, Germany and Japan to balance Russia (Mahan 1917d: 256-258; Sumida 2000: 95). Paradoxically, while the naval buildup of the 1890s was directed against the Royal Navy, many navalists were also Anglophiles hoping for Anglo-American naval cooperation in the future. In 1895/1896, such an understanding emerged when Britain recognized U.S. hegemony in the Western hemisphere by accepting the American offer to act as arbitrator in a British-Venezuelan border dispute (Schake 2017: 148). This even gave rise to ideas of supra-national "imperial federation" and "race patriotism" (Mahan 1917d: 225, 243). While Mahan seems to have been unable to conceive a world beyond power competition, he did think nationalist competition might lead to and give way to supra-national cooperation. This did not just serve a global balance of power, but also the protection of maritime commerce, which Mahan saw as the main source of prosperity for all nations.

To conclude, the navalist discourse continued previous naval debates on economic interdependence and the role of the US in fostering global civilization but reframed the problem by conceptualizing both naval security and economic power as scarce. Security depended on the control of limited geographic points, while prosperity depended on the ability to control maritime trade routes and access points to overseas markets. Therefore, the 'shrinking of the world' intensified great power competition. If the U.S. wanted to survive this struggle, it had to compete with European naval powers on their terms. To reconcile this 'realist' thinking with traditional American universalism, Mahan made a temporal argument both regarding traditional isolationism and the newly proposed navalist strategy. While the former was appropriate to an earlier stage in history, the latter was an adequate response to the contemporary strategic situation. Ultimately, however, competition among nation-states would give way to intra-civilizational cooperation. This way, Mahan reconciled the 'idealist' universalism of U.S. ideology with 'realist' thinking about scarcity and competition. By entering into competition with the European powers, U.S. nationalism would eventually contribute to global civilization.

Conclusion

In this chapter we have tried to show how U.S. nationalist outlooks on the world in the mid-to-late 19th century built on notions of scarcity. Our analysis of debates in trade and naval policy shows how notions of scarcity—particularly, regarding trade opportunities and security—were used to define U.S. interests, while also embedding these interests in worldviews that, at least rhetorically, cared for the well-being of humankind as a whole. For American nationalists, conceptualizing national competition as a stage on the road to universal 'civilization' might also have been a way to reconcile the anti-colonial legacy of 1776 with national self-interest and new imperial aspirations.

Based on these historical accounts, there is much to be said for the idea that this tension between 'realist' assumptions of scarcity (and associated ideas of competition) and 'idealist' conceptions of human development and progress characterizes the mainstream of political thought today. At the very least, it is characteristic of nationalist reasoning that is present in current debates about economic nationalism vs. "globalism" around the world, and in the U.S. in particular.

In the field of economic policies, there is even is a figure that could be described as a modern-day Friedrich List: the Korean economist Ha-Joon Chang (2002, 2008), who has been arguing for years that the free trade ideology as represented in the "Washington consensus" and similar global policies is oblivious of the fact that today's rich countries were yesterday's 'developing' countries, dependent on the very protectionist policies they now declare as incompatible with enlightened economic thought. By insisting on free trade policies, according to Chang, developed countries are "kicking away the ladder" (2002) they once used themselves. With this thinking, Chang would certainly have found friends and admirers among Listian nationalists of the 19th century.

In the realm of power and military politics, too, variants of nationalism can be observed that resemble developments of the late 19th century. China and the U.S. are now engaged in a competition not unlike that of the great naval powers around 1900, centered around maritime trade routes and scarce strategic points. At the same time, both compete over prestige and influence in the world, with China increasingly presenting itself as another provider of 'global public goods' and its rise to power as beneficial to the world. In the current constellation, then, it seems that it is China which has adopted the kind of nationalist reasoning described here, where national power politics based on notions of scarcity meet cosmopolitan leadership on behalf of human civilization.

As these examples indicate, nationalist reasoning that connects ideas about scarcity, competition, globalization and utopias of human civilization is as prevalent today as it was in the mid-to-late 19th century. In other words, the blueprints of scarcity nationalism as invented in the 19th century are still in use today. Studying them, therefore, is important not just to the history of nationalism, but also its current state.

References

Ballantyne, T./Burton, A. M. (2014): Empires and the Reach of the Global, 1870-1945, Cambridge, MA: Belknap.

Bayly, Christopher A. (2004): The Birth of the Modern World 1780-1914, Oxford: Blackwell.

Buhl, Lance C. (2008): "Maintaining an American Navy, 1865–1889." In: K. J. Hagan/M. T. McMaster (eds.), In Peace and War: Interpretations of American Naval History, Westport: Praeger Security International, pp. 112–133.

Burk, Kathleen (2018): The Lion and the Eagle. The Interaction of the British and American Empires 1783-1972, London: Bloomsbury.

Calhoun, Craig (1997): Nationalism, Minneapolis: University of Minnesota.

Carey, Henry C. (1851): The Harmony of Interests. Agricultural, Manufacturing & Commercial, New York: Myron Finch.

Chandler, William E. (1883): Annual Report of the Secretary of the Navy, Washington, D.C.: Government Printing Office.

Chang, Ha-Joon (2002): Kicking Away the Ladder. Development Strategy in Historical Perspective, London: Anthem Press.

Chang, Ha-Joon (2008): Bad Samaritans. The Myth of Free Trade and the Secret History of Capitalism, New York: Bloomsbury.

Cleveland, Grover (1885): "First Inaugural Address, 4 March 1885." Miller Center: Presidential Speech Archive. Available at: https://millercenter.org/the-presidency/presidential-speeches/march-4-1885-first-inaugural-address (last access: 01.02.2020)

Drake, Frederick C. (1984): The Empire of the Seas. A Biography of Robert Wilson Shufeldt, USN, Honolulu: University of Hawaii Press.

Gellner, Ernest (1983): Nations and Nationalism, Oxford: Basil Blackwell.

Gorski, Philip S. (2000): "The Mosaic Moment—An Early Modernist Critique of Modernist Theories of Nationalism." In: American Journal of Sociology 105: 1428-1468.

Hagan, K. J. (1973): American Gunboat Diplomacy and the Old Navy, 1877–1889, Westport: Greenwood Press.

Hobson, Rolf (2002): Imperialism at Sea. Naval Strategic thought, the Ideology of Sea Power and the Tirpitz Plan 1875–1914, Boston: Brill.

List, Friedrich (1827): Outlines of American Political Economy in a Series of Letters, Philadelphia: Samuel Parker.

List, Friedrich (1922 [1841]): Das nationale System der politischen Oekonomie, Erster Band. Der internationale Handel, die Handelspolitik und der deutsche Zollverein, Jena: Gustav Fischer.

Mahan, Alfred T. (1890): The Influence of Sea Power Upon History, 1660–1783, Boston: Little.

Mahan, Alfred T. (1917a [1890]). "The United States Looking Outward." In: A. T. Mahan (ed.), The Interest of America in Sea Power, Boston: Little, pp. 3–30.

Mahan, Alfred T. (1917b [1894]). "Possibilities of an Anglo-American Reunion." In: A. T. Mahan (ed.), The Interest of America in Sea Power, Boston: Little, pp. 107–134.

Mahan, Alfred T. (1917c [1895]): "The Future in Relation to American Naval Power." In: A. T. Mahan (ed.), The Interest of America in Sea Power, Boston: Little, pp. 137–172.

Mahan, Alfred T. (1917d [1897]). "A Twentieth-Century Outlook." In: A. T. Mahan (ed.), The Interest of America in Sea Power, Boston: Little, pp. 217–268.

Mahan, Alfred T. (1907): From Sail to Steam: Recollections of a Naval Life, New York, London: Harper & Brothers.

Mayall, James (1990): Nationalism and International Society, Cambridge: Cambridge University Press.

Millett, A. R./Maslowski, P. (1994): For the Common Defense: A Military History of the United States of America, New York: Free Press.

Nincic, Donna J. (2002): "Sea Lane Security and Maritime Trade: Chokepoints as Scarce Resources." In: S. J. Tangredi (ed.), Globalization and Maritime Power, Washington D.C.: National Defense University Press, pp. 143–169.

Ninkovich, Frank A. (2009): Global Dawn: The Cultural Foundation of American internationalism 1865–1890, Cambridge, MA: Harvard University Press.

Osterhammel, Jürgen (2009): Die Verwandlung der Welt. Eine Geschichte des 19. Jahrhunderts, München: C. H. Beck.

Özkirimli, Umut (2017): Theories of Nationalism. A Critical Introduction, New York: Palgrave.

Palen, Marc-William (2016): The 'Conspiracy' of Free Trade. The Anglo-American Struggle Over Empire and Economic Globalisation, 1846–1896, Cambridge: Cambridge University Press.

Robeson, George M. (1874): Annual Report of the Secretary of the Navy, Washington, D.C.: Government Printing Office.

Schake, Kori. N. (2017): Safe Passage: The Transition from British to American Hegemony, Cambridge, MA: Harvard University Press.

Shufeldt, Robert. W. (1884): "Views of Rear-Admiral Shufeldt, 17.01.1884." In: 48th Congress, 1st Session, Senate Report 161, appendix 7, Views submitted to the Committee on Naval Affairs, Washington, D.C.: Government Printing Office, pp. 12–22.

Simmel, Georg (1955): Conflict and the web of group-affiliation, New York: The Free Press.

Smith, Anthony D. (1998): Nationalism and Modernism. A Critical Survey of Recent Theories of Nations and Nationalism, London: Routledge.

Sumida, Jon T. (2000): Inventing Grand Strategy and Teaching Command: The Classic Works of Alfred Thayer Mahan, Baltimore: Johns Hopkins University Press.

Tilly, Charles (ed.) (1975): The Formation of National States in Western Europa, Princeton: Princeton University Press.

Todd, David (2015): Free Trade and Its Enemies in France, 1814–1851, Cambridge: Cambridge University Press.

Tracy, Benjamin F. (1889): Annual Report of the Secretary of the Navy: Part I. Washington, D.C.: Government Printing Office.

Werron, Tobias (2014): On Public Forms of Competition. Cultural Studies <> Critical Methodologies 14/1, pp. 62-76

Werron, Tobias (2015): "What Do Nation-State Compete For? A World-Societal Perspective on Competition for "Soft" Global Goods." In: B. Holzer/F. Kastner/T. Werron (eds.), From Globalization to World Society. Neo-Institutional and Systems-Theoretical Perspectives, London: Routledge, pp. 85-106.

Werron, Tobias (2020a): "Global Publics as Catalysts of Global Competition: A Sociological View." In: V. Huber/J. Osterhammel (eds.), Global Publics. Their Power and Their Limits, 1870-1990, Oxford: Oxford University Press, pp. 343-366.

Werron, Tobias (2020b): "Nationalism as a Global Institution." In: M. Albert/T. Werron (eds.), What in the World? Understanding Global Social Change, Bristol: Bristol University Press, pp 157-176.

Woodward, Comer V. (ed.) (1997): The Comparative Approach to American History, Oxford: Oxford University Press.

'Free Trade' and the Varieties
of Eighteenth-Century State Competition

James Stafford

The ideology of free trade is commonly associated with an idea of the peaceful interdependence of states and peoples. Eighteenth-century philosophers such as Montesquieu and Immanuel Kant believed that growing commerce between European states could (at the least) set limits to the duration and intensity of modern wars (Hirschman 2013). In the nineteenth century, free trade was associated with a normatively charged, civilizational rhetoric of human progress—one that provided a justification for the violent opening of China and Japan to British, American and French goods and merchants (Todd 2008). Liberal and neoliberal narratives of the twentieth century collapse of this European civilization, meanwhile, attribute significant blame to the failure to rebuild an open and coherent trading system in the aftermath of the First World War (Link 2018).

This understanding of the history of free trade emphasizes the distinction it draws between price competition within global markets for goods and services—involving firms, workers and consumers—and the political rivalries of trading states (Neff 1990). The maintenance of this distinction between state and market competition lies at the heart of modern organs of liberal economic governance, such as the European Union (Patel and Schweitzer 2013) and the World Trade Organization (Howse 2016). As a reading of the political character and historical origins of a policy of 'free trade', however, is at best partial. By drawing a line from the French *doux commerce* thesis of the eighteenth century through the *pax Britannica* of the nineteenth and the 'rules-based order' of the post-war period, it misses out a crucial chapter in the origin story of 'free trade'. This is the distinct case made by a range of British intellectuals and merchants for a transformation of the imperial "fiscal-military state" (Brewer 1989) during its late eighteenth-century apotheosis.

During this period, the case for 'free trade' in Britain was not articulated as a "vision of global order" (Howe 2007). It was not yet linked to either the bleak verities of Evangelical Christianity (Hilton 1988), nor the expansive cosmopolitanism of the Manchester manufacturer Richard Cobden and the Anti-Corn Law League of the 1840s (Howe 1998). Instead, free trade was discussed as a strategy for imperial fiscal reform, aimed at securing Britain's prosperity and security against its main imperial rival: Bourbon France. Far from seeking to insulate market competition from state competition—still less, as Cobden and his allies would later demand, to effectively replace the latter with the former—eighteenth-century British advocates for 'free trade' claimed that opening and integrating the markets of the British Empire could enable it to more durably sustain the costs of its security and expansion.

A policy of free trade would lower the cost of food and raw materials, maximize tax revenue and increase export competitiveness, improving productivity and driving the efficient allocation of scarce capital. It would remove the inefficiencies and distortions created by what the famous eighteenth-century advocate for 'free trade', the Scottish jurist and moral philosopher Adam Smith, called Britain's "mercantile system" (Smith 1976a: IV.I.1). Most of all, it would limit the growing danger of imperial and military and over-reach, generated by the pathological insistence of powerful mercantile lobbies on the necessity for wars of colonial conquest. Unlike their nineteenth-century successors, eighteenth-century British free traders argued against these wars on grounds of prudence, not morality. "Going to war for the sake of trade" (Tucker 1776: 59) ultimately served only to increase the profits of merchants and war contractors, and forced successive British government to expand the national debt to a degree that would fatally undermine the commercial prosperity of the empire. Yet the threat of France remained real, and war was always to be expected. 'Free Trade' was allied to a policy of strategic restraint and even neutrality, rather than a cosmopolitan vision of the British empire as an indispensable agent of peace and human progress.

The idea that the "cosmopolitical economics" of free trade were ultimately self-serving was most famously articulated by the German economist Friedrich List and his US-American followers in the nineteenth century (Palen 2016; see also Nagel/Werron in this volume). Britain, these charged, had only adopted a policy of free trade once its dominance of global markets had been assured through unrestrained naval warfare, protectionism, and colonial exploitation; all of which enabled Britain to build up overwhelming manufacturing and shipping capacity that no other power could match.

List's argument remains a topic of lively debate among historians of Britain's 'Industrial Revolution' (Ashworth 2017; Mokyr 2009). Yet it serves further to highlight the under-rated distinctiveness of the case made for free trade *before* victory in the Napoleonic wars secured the British Empire's nineteenth-century political-economic hegemony. Before it was the hypocritical doctrine of a global empire built through protection, slavery and military conquest, 'free trade' was understood as an alternative path to power, as well as a means of slowing (if not eliminating) the very cycle of global colonial and commercial rivalry that would ultimately deliver Britain to its commanding position in nineteenth-century world politics.

The present contribution seeks to reconstruct this distinctive perspective on the logics of political and commercial competition in the eighteenth-century European world in the decades before the French Revolution. Alongside Smith, it focuses on a lesser-known economic thinker, the Anglo-Dutch merchant and financier Matthew Decker. Both Smith and Decker made distinct arguments for free trade as the solution to the political and commercial challenges facing the British empire in the era of the War of the Austrian Succession (1740-48), the Seven Years' War (1756-63) and the War of American Independence (1776-1783). Smith is more usually credited as the intellectual progenitor of Britain's nineteenth-century turn to free trade. Yet, as the following will show, it was Decker's expansive vision of Britain as a giant 'Free Port' that most clearly anticipated the fiscal and naval politics of the nineteenth-century empire.

The next section outlines the global political and economic context for the Franco-British confrontation of the eighteenth century, and the nature of contemporary British ambitions for an 'empire of the seas' that could check French ambition on land. Inter-imperial rivalry was reflected by a conscious process of emulation in the design of policies and institutions, with the emergent 'science' of commerce at its center (Adelman 2015; Reinert 2011). In this context, it was unthinkable to pursue 'free trade' as a strategy of cosmopolitan benevolence. The case for a radical reform of the British imperial system necessarily rested on the argument that free trade would ultimately enable the empire to better secure its competitive position in relation to its French rival.

The subsequent two sections deal with two contrasting variants of free trade strategy in eighteenth-century Britain. Matthew Decker advanced a case for free trade that rested on Britain's unique ability to dominate European and colonial shipping networks through the abolition of the seventeenth-century

'Navigation Acts' that restricted access to British and imperial ports to ships carrying the flag of Great Britain. Adam Smith, by contrast, argued for the preservation of the Acts as a vital bulwark of imperial security. Behind the wooden walls of a British navy sustained by a national shipping monopoly, the gradual removal of duties and prohibitions and the integration of the imperial fiscal state would enable an explosion of manufacturing productivity and export competitiveness. The resultant tax revenues would save the empire from its nemesis: the public debt that had built up over decades of unnecessary wars of colonial aggression.

The fourth and final section considers what this historical reconstruction of what we might think of as a 'realist'—even nationalist—variant of free trade has to tell us about the relationship between state and market competition in a multipolar global political economy. Contemporary observers present at the inception of economic liberalism in eighteenth-century Britain well understood that 'free trade', while opening the possibility to positive-sum exchanges among market actors residing in different polities, meant a reconfiguration, not an abandonment, of pre-existing patterns of political competition between the European powers. While this involved a retreat from direct military conflict, it also intensified the pressure of economic competition, rendering productivity and social discipline under open market conditions the indispensable condition of national security.

The Competitive Conjuncture of the Eighteenth Century

Political and economic relations in eighteenth-century Europe was defined by the coexistence of significant commercial expansion with an escalating cycle of global military conflict. These two circumstances were connected at a fundamental level by the challenges of financing expanding and modernized armed forces, which were in turn required to defend the sources of revenue that guaranteed rival powers' ability to triumph in future wars. From the Nine Years' War of 1689-97 to the French Revolutionary and Napoleonic Wars of 1789-1815, the 'long eighteenth century' witnessed recurrent warfare that spread, through the expansion of European colonial and naval power, to South Asia, the Americas and the Caribbean (Baugh 2011). While less catastrophic in their regional effects than the seventeenth century's wars of religion, the eighteenth century's conflicts over the European 'balance of power' were more far-reaching in their consequences for a global conjuncture defined by the consolidation of wealth and military force in Western Europe.

The entanglement of European power-politics with colonial expansion was driven by the circumstances of what the historian Christopher Bayly has termed "archaic globalization" (Bayly 2004: 52). As recovery from the seventeenth century's "general crisis" (Parker 2017) gathered pace, European elites engaged in the consumption of new commodities acquired through slavery, settler colonialism, and new economic institutions, such as the Dutch and British East India Companies. South American coffee and cocoa, Chinese teas, Caribbean sugar and Indian calicoes became central parts of European material culture. In combination with more locally-routed developments—the expansion of working time (the so-called "industrious revolution" (De Vries 1994)), the rise of scientific, 'improving' agriculture (Jones 2016), and a demographic recovery following the wars and epidemics of the seventeenth century (Alter/Clark 2010: 52-53)—the expansion of long-distance trade in mass 'luxury' goods created a new and more widely diffused sense of prosperity among an emergent bourgeoisie: especially, though not exclusively, in England, France and the Dutch Republic.

It also, however, placed control of colonial trade routes and trading posts at the center of European geopolitical competition. The first major inter-state wars explicitly justified as being in the defense of trading interests—over and above those of confessional or dynastic alignment— were between England and the Dutch Republic in the 1660s (Pincus 1996). By the War of the Spanish Succession (1702-14), English and Dutch opponents of the French King Louis XIV's bid to install his grandson as King of Spain were united in their terror of a 'universal monarchy' (Pincus 1995) that would combine France's landed military might with Spain's control of the slave and bullion trade to South America. "Trade", observed the widely-travelled Scottish mercenary, parliamentarian and pamphleteer Andrew Fletcher in the early years of that conflagration, "is now become the golden ball, for which all nations of the world are contending" (Fletcher 1997: 193).

Why was political control over growing markets in goods and slaves valued so highly in eighteenth-century Europe? Status and prestige were, in the first instance, a crucial factor: a succession of different powers learned to 'emulate' one another's attempts to secure wealth, security and renown through trade and colonization (Adelman 2015). The rise of the Iberian empires in the Americas in the sixteenth century had inspired the first English reflections on the prospects for a limitless "empire of the seas'" (Armitage 2000: 100-124), while the rapid rise of the Dutch Republic following its successful revolt against Spain's global mercantile empire inspired emulation of its commercial and financial policies in both France (Isenmann 2017) and England (Jardine 2009).

The value of trade in European politics, however, was far from purely symbolic. It was linked, through the nexus of the gold and silver coinage, to the seventeenth-century "military revolution" (Rogers 2018). New and expensive developments in technologies for shipbuilding, fortification, small arms and artillery demanded that the emergent 'fiscal states' of early modern Europe discover new sources of revenue. These necessarily took the form of gold and silver money acquired through trade on international markets. This was indispensable because it offered a uniquely fungible means of paying troops and sailors in whatever jurisdiction they happened to be serving (Ashworth 2003: 29; Mann 2012: 52–58). Gold and silver were similarly indispensable as an "anchor" for the inter-personal systems of informal credit that underpinned everyday life throughout much of early modern Europe (Muldrew 2001: 84); it was with good reason, therefore, that an influential body of seventeenth-century English economic thinkers believed metal coinage to be the "blood" of the body politic (Wennerlind 2013). It was in England, too, that a specie-backed system of state debt and paper currency became indispensable to the financing of military conflict, releasing precious gold and silver for use abroad (Dickson 1967).

The centrality of specie currency to war finance and domestic economic growth created a perverse set of incentives for participants in eighteenth-century European power competition: one that was the object of a growing volume of criticism from philosophers and reformers from the second quarter of the eighteenth century. The security interests and domestic stability of European polities seemed increasingly to depend on their ability to command reliable access to a portion of the global supply of gold and silver. The military conquest and domination of colonies, shipping lanes and trading posts, combined with the pursuit of monopoly control over a limited number of exported goods, was indispensable to securing that access. Yet efforts to maintain and expand that control themselves generated fresh pressures to go in search of new markets, new colonies and new revenues; or at least to prevent rivals from doing the same. The nexus of war finance and foreign trade seemed thus to presage an inescapable, escalating cycle of conflict, in which each war laid the foundations for the next. As the philosopher David Hume complained in 1742, it produced an ambient condition of "jealousy of trade", in which every state pursued a "malignant policy" that sought to undermine the prosperity of its neighbors (Hume 1985).

"Jealousy of trade" magnified and altered pre-existing religious, dynastic and national animosities; interdependence, proximity and relative cultural homogeneity expanded, rather than diminishing, the scope for military conflict. "The historic union of the nations of Europe has entangled their rights and interests in a thousand complications," observed the Genevan philosopher Jean-Jacques Rousseau in a despairing commentary on the prospects for peace in Europe, composed at the height of the Seven Years War. "They touch each other at so many points that no one of them can move without giving a jar to all the rest; their variances are all the more deadly, as their ties are more closely woven." (Rousseau 1991: 91).

Given this bleak prospect, thinkers and politicians in eighteenth-century Europe sought, with increasing urgency, to reconceptualize the relationship between commerce and politics: both to help their own polities better understand their true interests, and to think (like Rousseau) at a more systemic level, asking how "jealousy of trade" might be tamed or transcended. These efforts were informed by, and continuous with, a flourishing political-economic literature in every European language, with a lively culture of translation promoting the circulation of key manuals of policy among a growing body of experts in the 'science of commerce' (Reinert 2011).

Without too much oversimplification, we can arrange eighteenth-century projects for the reform of European political economy into two main categories. The first sought to sever permanently the pathological relationship between cash, commerce and war. Advocates of 'perpetual peace'—including the Quaker merchant and North American colonist William Penn, the Saxon philosopher Gottfried Wilhelm Leibniz, the French diplomat the Abbé Saint-Pierre and (most famously) the Prussian philosopher Immanuel Kant—advocated a transformation of the rules of international conduct, encouraging Europe's states (often, though not always, through a degree of compulsion by a hegemonic power, commonly France) to agree to new systems of international arbitration capable of supplanting military conflict (Stafford 2021). Monetary reformers, such as the Scottish gambler and erstwhile French finance minister John Law (Shovlin 2016), the Irish philosopher George Berkeley (Kelly 1985) and his later eighteenth-century Prussian counterpart Johann Gottlieb Fichte (Nakhimovsky 2011), meanwhile demanded the establishment of national fiat currencies (backed by land, labor, patriotic contributions of plate and jewellery, stocks in trading companies, or a combination of all four) that would enable the relative or absolute separation of their respective polities from the vicissitudes of globally circulating metal currencies.

Neither Matthew Decker nor Adam Smith engaged in this kind of utopian speculation. They formed part of a broader mainstream of European thinking on the relationships between war trade: one that sought not to escape the underlying drivers of inter-state competition, but to limit the continued escalation of "jealousy of trade" while continuing to advance the power interests of their own polities. The 'Gournay circle', eighteenth-century French followers of Louis XIV's finance minister Colbert, can be placed in this category (Charles et al. 2011); as can the most influential international jurist of the period, the Neuchâtel diplomat Emmerich de Vattel (Nakhimovsky 2007).

The lesson these thinkers took from the ultimate failure of Louis XIV's efforts to create a 'universal monarchy' in Europe and the Atlantic was that the rise of commerce had rendered wars of conquest too costly to sustain. While war and conquest would not be eliminated through the interdependence created by commerce, their attraction would certainly, over time, be reduced. "Jealousy of trade" might be replaced by a new kind of statecraft fitted to new times: one that sought to preserve a European balance of power through the peaceful expansion of domestic economic capacities, but which did not seek to commit the wealth and armed forces thereby developed to war at the slightest provocation. It is in this light that we should view the interventions made by Decker and Smith in the landscape of British political-economic debate in the third quarter of the eighteenth century, to which we will now turn.

Britain as a 'Free Port': Matthew Decker's *Essay on the Causes of the Decline of Foreign Trade* (1744)

Sir Matthew Decker was born to an Amsterdam merchant family in 1679. His fortunes in business and politics followed those of the Dutch Republic: as it gradually ceded commercial and financial pre-eminence to England in the early decades of the eighteenth century, Decker settled in the City of London and was naturalized as an English subject in 1704. During the War of the Spanish Succession, he built up a commanding fortune based on Anglo-Dutch trade while exploiting his political connections to acquire lucrative directorships at the East India and South Sea Companies, alongside (for a time) a seat in Parliament (Gauci 2016). His major intervention in British political-economic debate, *An essay on the causes of the decline of the Foreign Trade, and con-*

sequently the value of the lands of Britain (1744; 2nd edn. 1750), occupied a minor but distinguished position in subsequent canons of British free trade: one that justifies its selection as a case-study here. 'There are few if any of the older works on commerce,' wrote the Scottish Ricardian economist James Ramsay McCulloch in 1845, 'that have so many well-founded claims to attention, or that embody so many enlightened, ingenious and original views' (McCulloch 1845: 46).

The reason for McCulloch's retrospective praise is obvious. Decker's *Essay* advocated the same, or similar, reforms to those demanded by Victorian economic liberals: the abolition of customs duties and the recentering of the tax base on domestic consumption, the opening of British and colonial ports to vessels under any flag, and the abolition of the very monopoly trading companies on whose boards Decker had served. Yet if its prescriptions seemed—with the benefit of McCulloch's supremely confident hindsight—to anticipate the free trade politics of the Victorian era, its context and motivations could not have been more different. Decker's *Essay* was not concerned, like McCulloch and his contemporaries, with the working-out of incipient class antagonisms within a rapidly industrializing and urbanizing society that faced no serious geopolitical rivals. It offered instead a stark warning about the risks posed to British security by France's successful "cultivation of the arts of peace", and an urgent call to radically reform the British tax system as a means of preserving—and expanding—British naval power (Decker 1750: 156).

The immediate context for Decker's work was the renewal, after a generation of peace, of an intense rivalry between Britain and France. The nature of this rivalry had shifted in emphasis since the seventeenth-century wars waged by Britain and the Dutch republic against Louis XIV's threatened 'universal monarchy'. Whereas in the previous century, England's trading and colonial wealth had been a means of funding a land war against France in the Holy Roman Empire and the Low Countries, confrontation now centered on the high seas: control of lucrative transatlantic trades in sugar and slaves, as well as in contraband with Spain's declining South American empire (Wilson 1988: 77f). The continental 'balance of power' still mattered, but the question of whether to divert scarce resources to the land warfare or to sea defense was increasingly contested in British politics. Foreign and commercial policy was coming under the influence of an emergent 'patriot' faction, hostile to the continental commitment of ministries aligned with the Kingdom's Hanoverian ruling dynasty, but determined to uphold Britain's trading supremacy through an aggressive posture in seaborne warfare and colonial conquest (Harris 2002: 115-120).

The naval and mercantile politics of oppositional English 'patriotism' found an echo in Decker's *Essay*, which closed with a fantasia of British naval dominance that placed 'free trade' at the heart of a revised strategy for containing French power. This provided an apt summary of the British mode of war against a range of European opponents over the subsequent two centuries:

> If *France* can give Laws by Land, *Britain* can do it by Sea; and in a little time the Sea will command the Land, for our Men of War can destroy their Ships, ravage their Coasts, batter down their Forts, and burn their Sea-Port Towns: this must ruin their Trade, as Trade goes so must their Money, and when the Money is gone the Armies cannot be supported, they must be drawn from the Countries they invade, or they will desert rather than perish with Hunger for want of Pay (Decker 1750: 152-153).

Decker's ambitions for British sea power were commonplace in metropolitan political debate at mid-century. What was an unusual about the *Essay* was the means proposed to ensure that Britannia did indeed 'rule the waves'. Decker argued that a radical liberalization of British trade would rebound to the benefit of the commercial and naval supremacy his patriotic contemporaries so valued. Britain, he declared, was possessed of "natural advantages" that neither France nor the Dutch republic, "our great Rivals in Trade", could boast. Its island situation and temperate climate, its "mild" form of constitutional monarchy, a "plenty of provisions" that enabled workers to be cheaply fed and ships provisioned, and an abundance of natural resources, alongside a workforce that was naturally "brave, laborious and strong" all but guaranteed the Kingdom's European pre-eminence (Decker 1750: 75-76).

Why, then, as Decker and so many of his contemporaries complained, was British trade "in decline" (Harris 2002: 240-243)? The answer could be found in the heavy taxation and monopolistic policies pursued by successive English and British governments over the past century. Britain's high taxes had acted to raise the prices of the provisions its workers and sailors lived upon (Decker 1750: 10). The consequences were far-reaching, affecting the production, export and re-export of British and colonial goods at every stage (Decker 1750: 18). Monopoly trading companies meanwhile diverted trade from provincial ports to London, adding land transport costs to those required by import and export by sea, and reduced demand for ships and sailors to ply the long routes to India, the Ottoman Empire and the South Pacific (Decker 1750: 44). The Navigation Acts—seventeenth-century legislation permitting only British flagged vessels to bring goods to and from British ports—contributed to the high price of provisions and manufactured by limiting the supply of ships serving the country (Decker 1750: 41-42). The restrictions imposed on Irish and colonial exports and shipping left these imperial possessions under-taxed yet impoverished, increasing the burden on British taxpayers: under present policy, Decker lamented, "we drive one part of our People out of Trade by Monopolies, and the other by Taxes" (Decker 1750: 40-41).

The antidote to the British Empire's tottering edifice of taxation and monopoly, Decker urged, was to turn Britain into a "Free Port". What Decker proposed, however, was on a much grander scale than this name suggests, encompassing not just a single city but the entire island of Britain. This was to become a "universal Storehouse", capable of assuming a dominant position in world trade by becoming Europe's most attractive location for merchant capital and the re-export of imported colonial goods. The revenue lost from customs duties would be recouped, Decker argued, through a tax on "luxuries"—coaches, silver plate, jewelry, coffee, wine and chocolate—products which, for Decker, constituted the "bane of Virtue and Industry" (Decker 1750: 17).

In combination, Decker claimed, the abolition of monopolies and customs duties and the introduction of a luxury tax would produce a revolution in British trade. The driver of this transformation would be an expansion of price competition throughout the British economy, enabling the cheapest possible production of goods and the disciplining of excesses of 'luxury' consumption among the mercantile class. Opening British ports and shipping to the cheapest provisions from around the world would mean that "our Labor would be so cheap, that we could send all our Goods to foreign Markets cheaper than any People, by reason of our superior Natural Advantages" (Decker 1750: 105). Imposing a tax on luxuries would remove the burden of customs duties and thereby enable a proliferation of new merchant houses capable of subsisting on lower starting capitals, and who were thus "less liable [...] to combine together to impose on the People extravagant Prices of their Goods" (Decker 1750: 102). It would have the additional effect, moreover, of pushing imported luxury goods back out into the re-export market for other nations to consume, rather than trapping them (and their baneful social effects) within Britain behind walls of customs duties. It was luxury consumption, not luxury trade, that was for Decker the most legitimate object of state taxation (Decker 1750: 22-23).

The goal of Decker's proposed suite of radical fiscal reforms was to bring what he termed the "natural advantages" of Britain—its landscape, institutions and laboring people—to the fore, clearing away the artificial distortions of complex taxation and monopoly policies that did nothing but undermine the ultimate goals of British power and security. Decker urged Parliament, instead of legislating explicitly to exclude France from access to British ports and product markets, to construct a fiscal regime capable of maximally extending Britain's ability to build up a commanding merchant marine and a dominant position in export and re-export markets for colonial commodities and domestic manufactures alike. "The certain way to be secure", Decker claimed, "is to be more powerful, that is, to extend our Trade as far as it is capable of; and as Restraints have proved its Ruin, to reject them, and depend on Freedom for Security" (Decker 1750: 151-52).

The Nationalism of Adam Smith's *Wealth of Nations* (1776)

Placing Adam Smith's *Wealth of Nations* (Smith 1976a) a canonical work of political and economic theory, alongside a polemical *pièce d'occasion* like Decker's *Essay* may seem like a lopsided comparison. Commonly styled as the 'inventor of modern economics', Smith is associated above all with an ambition to create abstract models of perfectly functioning markets, and with a doctrinal commitment to cosmopolitan 'free trade' as the logical extension of a coldly utilitarian conception of 'economic man'. As generations of scholarship on Smith have now shown, however, Smith's political economy was but a small part of a much larger intellectual project, centered on the moral philosophy of his *Theory of Moral Sentiments* (Smith 1976b), and above all the legal theory he taught as Professor of Jurisprudence at Glasgow University (Phillipson 2010). The *Wealth of Nations* was also a profoundly *political* work, designed at least in part as an intervention in the controversies of its own time, and with a stark message about the kind of polity that was likely to succeed in the highly competitive political and economic juncture of the later eighteenth century (Hont 2005: 1-128).

Over the three decades that separated Smith's *Wealth of Nations* from Decker's *Essay*, Britain had triumphed over France in both the War of the Austrian Succession and the Seven Years' War. The latter conflict, however, had left the empire perilously overstretched, confronted with the challenges of ruling vast new territories in Canada and India, and panicked by the specter of ever-inflating debts (Elliott 2006: 294-307). The result was a frantic search for new revenues, particularly from the increasingly wealthy North American colonies. The details of the famous dispute over the Westminster Parliament's right to levy taxes on British subjects in North America, which led ultimately to the foundation of the modern United States, lie beyond the scope of this chapter. Instead, we will consider how the central messages of the *Wealth of Nations* related to the fiscal and imperial predicament of Britain in the 1760s (when the work was already in preparation) and 1770s, when colonial rebellion and European isolation threatened to end the empire's all-too rapid rise to global pre-eminence.

The principles of commercial policy outlined in Smith's work can be simply and briefly summarized. There could be no more efficient means of guaranteeing the ability of the nation to defend itself than through the expansion of the productive capacities that would guarantee ready access to the gold, silver and public credit necessary for war fighting when required (Smith 1976b: V.iii.5-8). These, in turn, could only be maximized by extending—as far as was commensurate with political prudence—a "perfect liberty" of domestic and foreign trade, one that would allow the local knowledge and intersubjective social discipline of the autonomous moral agents who made up "commercial society" to direct both labor and "stock" to those places where they would be most profitably employed (Smith 1976b: II.v). Attempts to render the British empire a closed system, obsessed with securing positive balances in gold and silver currency, were hugely damaging to the productive capacity that could alone guarantee both wealth and security. They raised the prices of food and other inputs needed for British manufactures, limited the opportunities for export, and caused the misallocation of capital to long-distance trade and commercial shipping. Worst of all, the military defense of colonial possessions forced the diversion of productive capital into unsustainable war debts (Smith 1976b: V.iii.52-56). If colonies were to be retained, then they needed to accept a simplified and uniform system of taxation, rather than the maze of different prohibitions, subsidies and customs duties that constituted what he termed the "mercantile system" (Smith 1976b: V.iii.69-74). Absent this, it would be better to let them go, and to consider them as colonies on what Smith took to be the 'Greek' model: distinct polities, which could expect little more than an amicable trading relationship with the mother-country (Smith 1976b: IV.vii.a.2).

Smith's political economy, it should already be apparent, had a distinctly national and European orientation. Where Decker deemed of universal naval domination on the basis of Britain become the "universal storehouse of the world", Smith counselled his readers to focus on domestic and regional trade, and to abandon imperial pretensions. Indeed, he constructed his entire account of European history, contained in the third book of the *Wealth of Nations*, around a sustained criticism of the eighteenth-century European turn to colonization and long-distance trade. This, Smith argued, was the product of an "unnatural and retrograde order" of economic growth (Smith 1976b: III.i.9), one that had long favored the interests of merchants over those of the general population, and those of aristocratic luxury over the parsimony and "prudence" required for productive investment (Smith 1976b: II.iii.19).

Correcting this distortion—a legacy of the fall of Rome and the chaos of the Middle Ages—would be the work of many ages, but it was imperative that Britain stop encouraging it by chasing dreams of global mercantile empire. Britain did not need colonies to supply it with commodities or to sustain its status relative to European rivals—it needed productive, tax-paying artisans and small capitalists, capable of driving the accumulation of wealth on which the state could draw in situations of war and emergency. It should come as little surprise, then, that Smith regarded the ultimate loss of the American colonies with an equanimity that was unusual among his devastated contemporaries. In a 1783 letter to the British minister William Eden, written following the concession of American independence and the conclusion of a humiliating peace treaty with France, Smith speculated that Britain might now be able to "open a commerce with the neighbouring nations of Europe, infinitely more advantageous than that of so distant a country as America" (Smith 1977: 271).

Smith's political judgement on Britain's post-war situation was deeply rooted in the account of the relationship between domestic and foreign trade he had laid out in *The Wealth of Nations*. Far from envisaging free trade as a global order upheld by Britain, Smith fancied that the abandonment of colonial monopolies and protective tariffs would promote a reorientation of British trade towards the domestic and European markets. Absent the distorting effects of Britain's "mercantile system", Smith reasoned, the owners of capital would be far more inclined to invest it in productive domestic activity than in lengthy and tenuous dealings across the oceans. They could better trust their own countrymen to honour engagements, and better monitor the condition of their goods and money when these were employed closer to home. "Every individual endeavours to employ his capital as near home as he can," claimed Smith, "and consequently as much as he can in the support of domestick industry" (Smith 1976a: IV.ii.5-6).

The national bias of capitalists had an important political consequence for Smith—one that drove much of his criticism of a British commercial policy that neglected domestic and European trade for the glittering attractions of Asia and the Americas. Goods bought and sold within the country, Smith reasoned, were capable of supporting twice as much domestic "productive labor" as those involving import and export, where some of the labor supported would be foreign. They would also encourage a far more rapid accumulation of wealth. The greater the distance involved in exchange, Smith argued, the less rapidly the capital of the country, and the fund of productive labor that it could support, would be augmented. Trade between England and Scotland might be twelve times faster than trade between England and Portugal.

Slowest and most "uncertain" of all, however, was the "circuitous" or "carrying trade": the exchange of colonial goods for European, constructed on the principles of the "mercantile system". Seeking to purchase European goods with those imported from the colonies, thereby seeking to protect a fictive 'balance of trade' in gold and silver, was the least efficient means of encouraging the expansion of the country's real productive capacities:

> The riches, and so far as power depends upon riches, the power of every country, must always be in proportion to the value of its annual produce, the fund from which all taxes must ultimately be paid. But the great object of the political economy of every country, is to increase the riches and power of that country. It ought, therefore, to give no preference nor superior encouragement to the foreign trade of consumption above the home-trade, nor to the carrying trade above either the other two. It ought neither to force nor to allure into either of those two channels, a greater share of the capital of the country than what would naturally flow into them of its own accord (Smith 1976a: II.v.31)

Allowing the free play of competition to determine the allocation of British mercantile capital would thereby have the happy effects of reorienting it *away* from long-distance trade to the Americas and Asia, and towards a more intensive cultivation of domestic agriculture and manufactures. This shift would not be the product of any protective tariff; although Smith, unlike Decker, was prepared to make an exception from the doctrine of "perfect liberty" in the case of the Navigation Acts. These were deleterious to foreign trade, but indispensable to the maintenance of a merchant marine capable of being turned to the purposes of naval warfare. Since they guaranteed the security of an island nation, the Acts of Navigation were "perhaps the wisest of all the commercial regulations of England" (Smith 1976a: IV.ii.28-30).

Far from being an early exponent Britain's nineteenth-century 'empire of free trade', therefore, Smith prescribed a kind of defensive realism for an over-stretched imperial power. *The Wealth of Nations* offered an argument for a Europeanized Britain, indifferent (though not actively hostile) to colonial adventures, and relentlessly focused on the expansion of productivity in domestic manufactures and agriculture as the key to its wealth and security. Smith urged his compatriots to abandon their addiction to costly global warfare, in pursuit of far-flung possessions of little or no economic utility. Patient, parsimonious, and cautious in its dealings, the free-trade nation of Smith's imagination would forsake the empire of the seas, and "accommodate her future views and designs to the real mediocrity of her circumstances" (Smith 1976a: V.iii.92).

From 'Jealousy of Trade' to International Competition

This chapter has sought to disrupt some commonly received notions about the origins of liberal political economy in eighteenth-century Britain. Against a dominant narrative emphasizing the pacific, cosmopolitan and hypocritical character of British arguments for free trade, it has used the examples of Matthew Decker and Adam Smith to suggest that free trade was initially conceptualized as an alternative strategy for British national power and security in the course of its long rivalry with Bourbon France. It has further sought to demonstrate that arguments against what Smith termed "the mercantile system" could have multiple and conflicting political valences. Decker's demands extended to the abolition of Britain's Navigation Acts and aimed at securing dominance of the global carrying trade by transforming the country into a free port. Smith, by contrast, was actively hostile to grand projects of long-distance trade, and the colonial wars that accompanied them. His vision of a Britain governed by the principles of "natural liberty" centered on the abandonment of imperial pretensions, and the intensive cultivation of the domestic agriculture and manufactures that could alone fund national defense for the long term.

Neither Decker or Smith were able to fully describe or anticipate the interlocking dynamics of military force, capital accumulation and political decision that ultimately rendered Britain the hegemonic power of the nineteenth century. The interest of these texts, however, does not lie in their capacity for prophecy: still less in the success with which they articulate the 'correct' doctrines of latter-day liberal theories of free trade. What is most significant about Decker's *Essay* and Smith's *Wealth of Nations* is what connects them: a new conception of the interlocking relationship between economic and political competition, which emerged in the course of the eighteenth-century debate over "jealousy of trade" and remains relevant even under the radically different circumstances of twenty-first century global political economy.

The explicit purpose of Decker and Smith's reconceptualization of Britain's commercial and political interests was to bring about a pause, or reversal, in an unsustainable cycle of military conflict with France. Attempting to 'force' trade into convenient channels through warfare or legislation was a self-defeating strategy that risked ruining the empire. Allowing market competition to reshape the country's trading relationships, by contrast, could unlock new and more durable sources of revenue that would allow Britain to prevail against, or even dominate, its rivals, without having to resort to continuous warfare of the kind that defined the central decades of the eighteenth century. For both Smith and Decker, however, the struggle of arms would ultimately be replaced by the struggle for productivity and social discipline. Maintaining Britain's relative position in the European scale of wealth and power required constant vigilance and adjustment on the part of both capital and labor: it was for this reason that both Decker and Smith were so preoccupied with the destructive influence of luxury consumption on the national character. The abandonment of aggressive naval warfare enabled a dramatic expansion of the reach of a hybrid form of competition, at once political and economic, that involved the entire population in the collective fate of the economic nation. It is this conceptual shift, rather than their contribution to any canon of liberal economic doctrine, that should inspire continued interest in these historic authors.

References

Adelman, Jeremy (2015): "Mimesis and Rivalry: European Empires and Global Regimes." In: Journal of Global History 10/1, pp. 77-98.

Alter, George/Clark, Gregory (2010): "The Demographic Transition and Human Capital." In: Kevin H. O'Rourke/Stephen Broadberry (eds.), The Cambridge Economic History of Modern Europe, Volume 1: 1700–1870, Cambridge: Cambridge University Press, pp. 43-69.

Armitage, David (2000): The Ideological Origins of the British Empire, Cambridge: Cambridge University Press.

Ashworth, William J. (2003): Customs and Excise: Trade, Production, and Consumption in England, 1640-1845, Oxford: Oxford University Press.

Ashworth, William J. (2017): The Industrial Revolution: The State, Knowledge and Global Trade, London: Bloomsbury.

Baugh, Daniel A. (2011): The Global Seven Years' War, 1754-1763: Britain and France in a Great Power Contest, Harlow: Longman.

Bayly, Christopher (2004): The Birth of the Modern World, 1780-1914: Global Connections and Comparisons, Oxford: Blackwell.

Brewer, John (1989): The Sinews of Power: War, Money and the English State, 1688-1783, London: Routledge.

Charles, Loïc/Lefebvre, Frédéric/Théré, Christine (eds.) (2011): Le cercle de Vincent de Gournay: savoirs économiques et pratiques administratives en France au milieu du XVIIIe siècle, Paris: Institut national d'études démographiques.

De Vries, Jan (1994): "The Industrial Revolution and the Industrious Revolution." In: The Journal of Economic History 54/2, pp. 249-270.

Decker, Matthew (1750): An Essay on the Causes of the Decline of the Foreign Trade: Consequently of the Value of the Lands of Britain, and on the Means to Restore Both, London: Printed for J. Brotherton.

Dickson, P. G. M. (1967): The Financial Revolution in England: A Study in the Development of Public Credit, 1688-1756, London: Macmillan.

Elliott, J. H. (2006): Empires of the Atlantic World: Britain and Spain in America, 1492-1830, New Haven: Yale University Press.

Fletcher, Andrew (1997): "An Account of a Conversation." In: John Robertson (ed.), Andrew Fletcher: Political Works, Cambridge: Cambridge University Press, pp. 129-215.

Gauci, Perry (2016): "Decker, Sir Matthew, First Baronet (1679–1749), Political Economist and Merchant." In: Oxford Dictionary of National Biography. Retrieved 1 Feb. 2021, from https://www.oxforddnb.com/view/10.1093/ref:odnb/9780198614128.001.0001/odnb-9780198614128-e-7408.

Harris, Robert (2002): Politics and the Nation: Britain in the Mid-Eighteenth Century, Oxford: Oxford University Press.

Hilton, Boyd (1988): The Age of Atonement: The Influence of Evangelicalism on Social and Economic Thought, 1795-1865, Oxford: Clarendon Press.

Hirschman, Albert Otto (2013): The Passions and the Interests: Political Arguments for Capitalism before Its Triumph, Princeton: Princeton University Press.

Hont, Istvan (2005): Jealousy of Trade: International Competition and the Nation-State in Historical Perspective, Cambridge, MA: Harvard University Press.

Howe, Anthony (1998): Free Trade and Liberal England 1846–1946, Oxford: Oxford University Press.

Howe, Anthony (2007): "Free Trade and Global Order: The Rise and Fall of a Victorian Vision." In: Duncan Bell (ed.), Victorian Visions of Global Order, Cambridge: Cambridge University Press, 26-46.

Howse, Robert (2016): "The World Trade Organization 20 Years On: Global Governance by Judiciary." In: European Journal of International Law 27/1, pp. 9-77.

Hume, David (1985): "Of the Jealousy of Trade." In: Eugene F. Miller (ed.), Essays Moral Political and Literary, Indianapolis: Liberty Fund, pp. 327-332.

Isenmann, Moritz (2017): "Égalité, Réciprocité, Souveraineté: The Role of Commercial Treaties in Colbert's Economic Policy." In: Antonella Alimento/Koen Stapelbroek (eds.), The Politics of Commercial Treaties in the Eighteenth Century: Balance of Power, Balance of Trade, Basingstoke: Palgrave MacMillan, pp. 77-103.

Jardine, Lisa (2009): Going Dutch: How England Plundered Holland's Glory, London: Harper Perennial.

Jones, Peter (2016): Agricultural Enlightenment: Knowledge, Technology and Nature, 1750-1840, Oxford: Oxford University Press.

Kelly, Patrick (1985): "Ireland and the Critique of Merchantilism in Berkeley's 'Querist'." In: Hermathena 139, pp. 101-117.

Link, Stefan (2018): "How Might 21st-Century De-Globalization Unfold? Some Historical Reflections." In: New Global Studies 12/3, pp. 343-365.

Mann, Michael (2012): The Sources of Social Power, Volume I: A History of Power from the Beginning to A.D. 1760, Cambridge: Cambridge University Press.

McCulloch, John Ramsay (1845): The Literature of Political Economy: A Classified Catalogue of Select Publications in the Different Departments of That Science, with Historical, Critical and Biographical Notices, London: Longman, Brown, Green & Longmans.

Mokyr, Joel (2009): The Enlightened Economy: An Economic History of Britain, 1700-1850, New Haven: Yale University Press.

Muldrew, Craig (2001): "'Hard Food for Midas': Cash and Its Social Value in Early Modern England." In: Past & Present 170, pp. 78-120.

Nakhimovsky, Isaac (2007): "Vattel's Theory of the International Order: Commerce and the Balance of Power in the Law of Nations." In: History of European Ideas 33/2, pp. 157-173.

Nakhimovsky, Isaac (2011): The Closed Commercial State: Perpetual Peace and Commercial Society from Rousseau to Fichte, Princeton: Princeton University Press.

Neff, Stephen C. (1990): Friends but No Allies: Economic Liberalism and the Law of Nations, New York: Columbia University Press.

Palen, Marc-William (2016): The 'Conspiracy' of Free Trade: The Anglo-American Struggle over Empire and Economic Globalization, 1846-1896, Cambridge: Cambridge University Press.

Parker, Geoffrey (2017): Global Crisis: War, Climate Change and Catastrophe in the Seventeenth Century, New Haven: Yale University Press.

Patel, Kiran Klaus/Schweitzer, Heike (2013): "Introduction." In: Kiran Klaus Patel/Heike Schweitzer (eds.), The Historical Foundations of EU Competition Law, Oxford: Oxford University Press, pp. 1-18.

Phillipson, Nicholas T. (2010): Adam Smith: An Enlightened Life, New Haven: Yale University Press.

Pincus, Steven (1995): "The English Debate over Universal Monarchy." In: A Union for Empire: Political Thought and the Union of 1707, Cambridge: Cambridge University Press, pp. 37-62.

Pincus, Steven (1996): Protestantism and Patriotism: Ideologies and the Making of English Foreign Policy, 1650-1668, Cambridge: Cambridge University Press.

Reinert, Sophus (2011): Translating Empire: Emulation and the Origins of Political Economy, Cambridge, MA: Harvard University Press.

Rogers, Clifford J. (ed.) (2018): The Military Revolution Debate: Readings On The Military Transformation Of Early Modern Europe, London: Routledge.

Rousseau, Jean-J. (1991 [1756]) "Abstract and Judgement of Saint-Pierre's Project for Perpetual Peace." In: Rousseau on International Relations, Oxford: Clarendon Press, pp. 53-101.

Shovlin, John (2016): "Jealousy of Credit: John Law's "System" and the Geopolitics of Financial Revolution:" In: The Journal of Modern History 88/2, pp. 275-305.

Smith, Adam (1976a [1776]): An Inquiry into the Nature and Causes of the Wealth of Nations, Oxford: Clarendon Press.

Smith, Adam (1976b [1791]): The Theory of Moral Sentiments, Indianapolis: Liberty Fund.

Smith, Adam (1977): The Correspondence of Adam Smith. Oxford: Oxford University Press.

Todd, David (2008): "John Bowring and the Global Dissemination of Free Trade." In: The Historical Journal 51/2, pp. 373-97.

Tucker, Josiah (1776): Four Tracts on Political and Commercial Subjects, Gloucester: R. Raikes.

Wennerlind, Carl (2013): "Money: Hartlibian Political Economy and the New Culture of Credit." In: Mercantilism Reimagined: Political Economy in Early Modern Britain and Its Empire, Oxford: Oxford University Press.

Wilson, Kathleen (1988): "Empire, Trade and Popular Politics in Mid-Hanoverian Britain: The Case of Admiral Vernon." In: Past & Present 121, pp. 74-109.

The Development of Neoliberal Measures of Competitiveness

Dieter Plehwe

Throughout the last few decades, international rankings and ratings have occupied an important place in the context of international politics. Tools of quantification such as benchmarks, indices, ratings and rankings, measuring countries' democratic systems, levels of transparency and corruption, the quality of health services, creditworthiness and so on, have become abundant and are frequently heeded by actors in international politics (Cooley/Snyder 2015: 2; Krever 2013: 135). Although the quantification of governance as a phenomenon has existed since the late 19th century (Power 1997: 17), its proliferation in the form of global performance indicators (GPIs) aligns with processes of quantification originating in the years following the Second World War.

After 1945, data was collected to establish systematic observation of an ever-increasing number of functional areas relevant to governance. The transformation of information into numerical data facilitated the comparison of a wide range of social systems by way of simplification. Such comparison also established notions of sameness and comparability, driving and driven by the process of intensified globalization (Heintz 201: 169; Wahlberg/Rose 2015). Although a few indices were developed before 1990—notably GDP or the Freedom House Index of Political Freedom—most indicators have been set up afterwards and over 90 per cent after the year 2000 (Cooley/Snyder 2015: 10).[1] Inadvertently, the anarchic system of competing states has been turned into a global system of (e)valuation and competition (Lamont 2012) with considerable influence on the policies of individual states. Furthermore, if competition during the Cold War era was all about system competition pitching the socialist world against capitalism, it has more recently been turned into a

---

1   Bandura (2008) counted 178 quantitative composite indices, 15 of which existed before the year 2000.

global system of competing competitions, depending on rival norms emanating from a greater variety of sources, and the objectives of a diverse set of players.

As a result of these transformations, at least two distinct notions of competition and competitive states need to be acknowledged. A traditional notion of competition is rooted in the (neo-)realist theory of international relations, which sees the international state system as an anarchy in which competing states are vying for power. According to this theory, the order resulting from the competition of states is ultimately decided by state power relations (Waltz 1979). Secondly, another theory of competitive states holds that 'competition states' have advanced to the status of a normative ideal. In this understanding, the question is how to improve the position of the state in a constant process of capitalist locational competition. The local perspective is here determined both by local (immobile) and global (mobile) factors of production (Cerny 2007). Unlike neorealist IR and its notion of competing states in an anarchic world system, this notion of competition understands states as part of a global order of "cosmopolitan capitalism", which subordinates the local political and social system to the prerogatives of an economic system conceived as an inevitably global system (Plehwe/Slobodian 2017). While competition plays an important role in each of the two perspectives, the relevant properties and criteria relevant for states to prevail or succeed are quite different.

Scholars have hitherto explained the rise of global performance indicators (GPI)[2] and the rating and ranking organizations behind them in general with a confluence of three developments: the turn to neoliberalism, specifically the interest in establishing performance metrics; the rise of transnational governance networks; and the evolution of information technology and open data sources (Cooley/Snyder 2015: 10). These approaches, however, understate the importance of new data sources created for the specific purpose of index construction, as I will show below. The concurrent rise of neoliberalism and comparative performance indicators similarly does not address the

---

2   Kelley and Simmons (2019: 492) define GPIs as "a named collection of rank-ordered data that purports to represent the past or projected performance of different units", frequently states or regions, but also organizations. Apart from basic indicators like GDP much use has been made of what the authors call "overtly strategic state rating and ranking systems that package and deploy information intentionally for policy advocacy and implementation." (Kelley/Simmons 2019: 493). The economic freedom indices discussed in this chapter belong to the latter category.

deliberate development of specific GPIs for the purpose of directing neoliberal transformation processes and the rise of the normative ideal of 'competition statehood' in the economic sense.

In order to substantiate this criticism, I will tackle the history and development of the economic freedom indexes of the Canadian Fraser Institute and the Heritage Foundation in Washington, DC. Looking closer at the origins of these "devices" (Bloch/Mitterle 2017: 933), which constitute technologies of knowledge creation, means of communication and, ultimately, "technologies of persuasion" (Porter 1995), allows the substantiation of claims regarding the coincidence of the rise of GPIs and neoliberalism; though we need to think of neoliberal world politics more as a highly contested arena.

Arguments pertaining to the neoliberal character of GPIs conflate neoliberalism and Western traditions of rationality and power. Indicators' power in influencing nation-states or organizations' dynamics of decision-making has stirred up contentious debates in academia and international politics on the issue of global governance. These debates focused on whether indicators were imbued with Western notions of rationality and achievement due to their origins in the Western world, (Cooley/Snyder 2015: 8; Diaz-Bone/Didier 2016; Uribe 2015). In this vein, poststructuralist scholarship in international political economy began to question the claim to neutrality of indicators and other tools of quantification. The research thereby aimed at re-politicizing these tools of global governance and at deconstructing the underlying neoliberal logics (Krever 2013). By seeing all indicators as Western efforts at economic domination, however, this scholarship misses the explicitly strategic nature of neoliberal efforts to counter GPIs of different orientations. Why should neoliberal scholars and activists bother developing specific indexes if the general development works in their favor? If supporters of neoliberalism rightly worry about indexes and rankings that seek to promote social development, social equality, ecological sustainability, or economic democracy, for example, the link between quantification and neoliberalism needs to be understood as tenuous.

While there has been considerable attention to the links between neoliberalism, the transformation of governance and quantification in general, there has been a lack of attention to the substantive influence of neoliberal ideas. Some approaches to the measuring of the world are useful with regard to the theorization needed to guide comparisons (Strang/Meyer 1993) and to secure commensuration, i.e. "the transformation of qualities into quantities that share a metric." (Espeland/Sauder 2007: 16). The example of the economic freedom indexes developed by neoliberal intellectuals and think tanks of and around the Mont Pèlerin Society (Walpen 2004; Plickert 2008, Burgin 2012) in the course of the 1980s provides a powerful example of such theorizing, and a daring commensuration effort seeking to establish a social technology and policy instrument to support neoliberal reform efforts.

The first section provides an account of the intellectual background and the social origins of economic freedom indexes in the 1970s and 1980s. Economic freedom indexes relied on the theoretical work of a group of neoliberals organized in the realm of the Mont Pèlerin Society on the topic of entrepreneurship and competitiveness of the 1970s, and on the legal and institutional turn among public choice theorists. Apart from the key actors situated in academia and civil society, this section explains the dual meaning of competition of states (and regions) and of competition statehood in the global capitalist economic system, which endeavours to enable locations in the competition for local (immobile) and global (mobile) factors of production.

The second section describes how economic freedom indexes were made, focusing on the collection of data, its manipulation, and the distribution of the results to governments and publics worldwide, using the example of the Economic Freedom Index produced by two leading neoliberal think-tanks, the Fraser Institute and the Heritage Foundation in conjunction with partner think tanks and the Wall Street Journal, respectively. The production of Economic Freedom indexes thus is a case of how private think tanks (backed by corporate money) have acted to set the terms of inter-state competition in the economic field. Local conditions are judged according to how well-suited they are for improving conditions for local capital, and attracting and maintaining mobile capital.

The third section then pivots to critically assess the impact of the indexes, according to claims made by the officials and contributors of the ranking and rating organizations, as well as both friendly observers and critics. This section examines the linkages between neoliberal devices such as the Economic Freedom Indexes and the transformation of global and national institutions, which we can altogether describe *grosso modo* as the neoliberal transformation of statehood and governance. To substantiate this claim we will go beyond the discussion of the immediate impact of the economic freedom indexes by way of taking a closer look at subsequent indexes developed to address issues of economic governance. The original efforts of organized neoliberals pale in comparison to the role the World Bank's "Ease of Doing Business Index". At the level of global institutions, a new set of actors come into play, namely state and regional actors who are critical in the social co-production of the public devices that seek to enable and support institutional transformations at regional, national and international levels. The original, civil society-based economic freedom GPIs, nevertheless continue to play a dual role in guiding neoliberal reforms and gauging the state of neoliberal transformation. They thereby inadvertently attest to the conflicted and contested character of the contemporary great neoliberal transformation process at large.

The Economic Freedom Movement and Supply Side Economics

"In the most recent edition of the University of Pennsylvania's Global Go To Think Tanks Report, Economic Freedom of the World was ranked as the fifth most influential report published by the world's 6,618 think tanks. Nobel Laureate Douglass North has called it the 'best available ... description of efficient markets.'" (Fraser Institute, 2020).

The self-described 'economic freedom movement' responsible for the economic freedom indices emerged in the 1970s under the ambit of the Mont Pèlerin Society. It is based in sprawling networks of neoliberal think tanks like the Atlas Economic Research Foundation network linked to the Mont Pèlerin Society (Djelic/Mousavi 2020). Its roots go back to critical assessments of traditional economic indicators, which measured GDP and economic growth (Schmelzer 2016). It aimed at complementing the Freedom House Democracy index, which has measured civil and political rights across the world since 1972. The neoconservative bias of Freedom House (Giannone 2010) notwithstanding, members of the Mont Pèlerin Society were ambivalent concerning the usefulness of an index focused on democratic institutions, doubting whether these could be relied upon to serve their conception of economic freedom. They were also hesitant about the social indicators movement (Andrews 1989), which attempted to measure the wellbeing of citizens and communities in conjunction with public policies designed to improve welfare. As such, social indicator measures also challenged the input focus of traditional economic indicators. The members of the Mont Pélerin Society opposed the discourse leading up to the Global Development Index of the United Nations. Examining the welfare of populations living in different countries and economic systems moved a number of socialist countries in the developing world ahead of their capitalist competitors due to their performance in areas like economic growth or public health—much to the dismay of neoliberals like Peter Bauer who placed a premium value on the economic freedom of capitalists (Plehwe 2009).

In order to understand the history of the economic freedom indexes it is necessary first to examine conceptual developments in economic theories of entrepreneurship, innovation and competitiveness that can be summarily labelled as supply-side economics (Feldstein 1986). These efforts date back to the 1960s and developed rapidly in response to the stagflation crisis of the 1970s, which seemed to neoliberals to prove the failure of Keynesian demand management. A wide range of neoliberal scholars, influenced by Austrian economics in general and Ludwig von Mises in particular, including Herbert Giersch in Germany and Israel Kirzner in the United States, helped to shift the focus of economic reasoning to supply-side conditions. These scholars and many others under the ambit of the Mont Pèlerin society emphasized the importance of entrepreneurship, competitiveness, innovation and economic opportunity (Plehwe 2020).

During the 1980s, the activities of this cohort of supply-side, neoliberal economists provide a clear illustration of the importance of theorizing, and of theoretical simplification, for the development of systems of comparison and quantification (Heintz 2010: 169). Opposed to the ways in which quantification was used to measure economic growth across economic systems, the economic freedom movement was not afraid to construct direct comparisons between conditions of economic freedom, regardless of whether the state in question was one of the richest or poorest in the world. On the basis of a common notion of national competitiveness and the comparison of regulatory and other conditions of private economic activity it became possible to organize the process leading up to the construction of economic freedom indices that thrive on "numerical difference" (Heintz 2010).

The Anglo-Hungarian development economist Peter Bauer's critique of statistical measures of GDP and growth is the best place to retrace the steps from neoliberal criticism of indices and rankings to the construction of these new neoliberal quantification projects. Crucially, these began with a rejection of existing methods of quantification centered on GDP. Bauer's field studies in Africa and the Far East led him to challenge standard statistical efforts, because the collection of data on agricultural work missed the trading activities of peasants, and because subsistence activities escaped measurement altogether (Bauer 1948, 1954). Such concerns with blind spots of mainstream econometrics and GDP measures preceded the broader attack on quantitative GDP measures from a qualitative perspective (Meadows et al. 1972; cf. Schmelzer 2016: 245f.).

After the second world war, neoliberals strongly opposed important features of mainstream neoclassical economics, Keynesian econometrics and modernization theory. Far from being champions of a unitary Eurocentric tradition of quantification, the heirs of Austrian economics in particular attacked prevailing positivist approaches to economics and the use of standardized quantitative data, on the basis of qualitative considerations. Against mainstream recognition of the economic success of the macro-planning efforts of socialist economics, neoliberals raised fundamental objections to the calculation and to a certain extent the planning macro-economic development. Peter Bauer and many other neoliberals emphasized choice and freedom of choice, holding these to be more relevant than wealth. It was only later that neoliberals made the additional claim of a positive correlation of freedom and growth and wealth. This moment coincided with the neoliberal turn towards techniques that claimed to quantify qualitative data (Schmelzer 2016: 288f.).

The rejection of quantification and positivism after the second world war was complemented by another, more important shift of emphasis in neoliberal economics. From the late 1960s, neoliberals orchestrated a revival in concepts and understandings of 'entrepreneurship', based on the original work of Ludwig von Mises. Against the neoclassical emphasis on equilibrium—an ideal of marginal production without profit and loss—von Mises had defended the priority of profit as a critical element of the price mechanism; one that was neglected in mainstream neoclassical economics alongside the key role of the entrepreneur. According to von Mises, every entrepreneur, no matter the size of a company, was a critical person in the relation of demand to supply, which he held to be impossible without profit (Mises 1998 [1949]: 255)

Based on the principled emphasis on entrepreneurship and profit a number of neoliberals worked hard to oppose prevailing notions of the limits and problems of entrepreneurship. Mises' student Isaac Kirzner (1971) attacked Joseph Schumpeter's famous characterisation of entrepreneurship as disruptive, for example, and emphasized the role of entrepreneurs with regard to achieving equilibrium. Germany's early behavioral economist Günther Schmölders, president of the MPS from 1970 to 1972, organized the Society's general conference on the issue of entrepreneurship in Munich in 1970 (Schmölders 1971). Schmölders and colleagues in other countries launched surveys on the image of the entrepreneur in Germany and France, for example. Arguably even more important than Kirzner or Schmölders, however, was Herbert Giersch, the long-time president of the Kiel Institute for the World Economy and president of the MPS from 1984 to 1986.

Giersch published his seminal work on the role of entrepreneurship, "The Role of Entrepreneurs in the 1980s", in 1982, and announced a new age of Schumpeter in 1984 (Giersch 1982, 1984). Contrary to Kirzner's effort to displace Schumpeter, Giersch now claimed to rely on him, albeit selectively. Neoliberals like Giersch proudly professed a new confidence in greatly expanded notions of entrepreneurship, which went far beyond Schumpeter's elitist understanding of successful family business founders who made a difference for macro-economic development. Despite his references to Schumpeter, however, Giersch's theory effectively re-labelled the Mises entrepreneur as the Schumpeter entrepreneur. Unlike Schumpeter's rare species of innovative and successful entrepreneurs, Giersch and Mises saw no limits for entrepreneurs as long as they behaved in an entrepreneurial way. Schumpeter was nevertheless a more attractive name for two reasons. Firstly, Schumpeter was much more widely recognized and respected as a leading economist. Secondly, Schumpeter had an elaborated theory of product and process innovation, which went beyond micro-economic opportunity and which Giersch was ready to combine with the German tradition of location theory. At the center of Giersch's theory of innovation, growth and economic geography was what he called the 'Schumpeter volcano', a center of innovation in a specific location, which would provide the innovating entrepreneur with a temporary monopoly. Once the innovation lava flowed downward and cooled, competitive advantage was lost. The volcano thus must continue producing new innovations (new technologies) or move to the margins in the process of locational competition. In reaction to the slow growth patterns of the late 1970s and early 1980s, Giersch directly opposed Keynesian economics in his nine-point program based on his Schumpeter hybrid. His third point said:

> "What matters most in present circumstances are the driving forces of economic development. Emphasis, therefore, is on the growth and dissemination of knowledge, on path breaking entrepreneurs and eager imitators, on credit creation for the supply of venture capital, and on Schumpeterian competition (i.e. on innovative monopolistic competition rather than sterile perfect competition, on oligopolistic rivalry rather than collusive equilibria and on aggressive trading rather than arbitrage transactions). In the interna-

tional economy, which Schumpeter mostly neglected, emphasis is on free trade rather than fair trade (trade minus competition) and on export orientation rather than import substitution." (Giersch 1984)

Giersch's ninth and last point reads: "Entrepreneurial talent is in almost unlimited supply, but it often finds productive outlets only abroad, or less productive and even counterproductive use in politics and government, public and private bureaucracy or the military" (Giersch 1984).

Against Kirzner, Giersch also chose to reinstate Schumpeter's ideas of innovator-entrepreneurship in his writing. No longer was the concern to make entrepreneurship compatible with neoclassical theories of equilibrium. The new emphasis was on disruption and innovation, which were now considered positive rather than disturbing. The important link between Schumpeter, Schmölders and Giersch was the emphasis on dynamism and change, which required entrepreneurs to manoeuvre. According to Giersch, even the underemployed and unemployed could be turned into self-employed entrepreneurs, provided that political institutions were adequately reformed and the correct incentives put in place. In order to realize this potential, Giersch argued, it was necessary to encourage a society's demand for entrepreneurship: "the demand permitted, induced or actively provoked by the socio-economic structure and the political and cultural environment" (Giersch 1982: 15).

The demand for entrepreneurship, in other words, depended on the social arrangements in support of economic freedom. This was an understanding that Giersch and Kirzner shared. "The central question," Kirzner had written in 1980s, was

> "what *institutional frameworks* are best-suited to tap the reservoir of entrepreneurial alertness which is certainly present among the members of society? ...Entrepreneurial talent is 'switched on' by the prospect of 'pure gain'—broadly defined to include fame, prestige, even the opportunity to serve a cause or to help others." (Kirzner 1980, emphasis added)

Progress in favor of entrepreneurship thus can be measured by reforms dedicated to enable the prospect of pure gain, to advance economic freedom broadly conceived, reaching far into the non-profit sector to advance social entrepreneurship and civic engagement. Progress in favor of entrepreneurship, in this logic, requires the wholesale removal of restrictions on economic freedom including much of the welfare state and the full range of legal regulatory measures that compromise price signals.

Thus, it was possibly most important in the course of the evolution of the economic freedom movement that Giersch, Kirzner and a wide range of other neoliberal economists re-focused economics on the role of political and other institutions conducive to entrepreneurship, articulating a relentless critique of what they held to be the sclerotic developments of the modern welfare state. In 1985, Giersch coined the term "Eurosclerosis" in a paper arguing for comprehensive European deregulation and cross-border liberalisation: the programme to complete the single European market by 1992 (Giersch 1985).

The counter-narrative to state-led development can therefore be considered as a kind of template economy: an ideal-type that serves as a benchmark the distance to which can be judged in the world of individual countries, rich and poor. Economic freedom indexes measure the deviation of the real model of economic governance of a country with reference to what, according to the normative perspective of the neoliberal economic freedom movement, constitutes the universal model of optimal economic governance. Such a conception allows countries to compete with one another in the extent to which they conform to this ideal-type. The closer a country manages to approximate the ideal type of governance tailored to economic freedom, the better it does in the never-ending competition for optimal location according to neoliberal reasoning. This was the backdrop of the initiative taken by the Fraser Institute in Canada, which led the effort to turn verbal assessments and comparative judgements into numerical difference: the social technology of economic freedom indexing and ranking developed into the Economic Freedom Index.

Developing indices: Ideas, Money and Networks

It is illuminating to look at the timeline of global indicator projects related to issues of political, social and economic governance. While we can observe early efforts to promote sustainable and human development, the Index of Sustainable Economic Welfare (later Genuine Progress Indicator) still covers a small range of countries only and has not been fully completed. As will be discussed below, the Human Development Indicator under the auspices of the United National Development Program (UNDP) in 1990 had been one of the reasons for neoliberal circles around the Fraser Institute and the Heritage Foundation to establish the Economic Freedom Indicators. In the meantime, the Fraser Institute in 2018 has added the Human Freedom index (HFI) to the Economic Freedom Index. Adding personal and civil freedom indicators to the staple of economic freedom indicators, HFI was an effort to shield economic freedom from democratic concerns (Slobodian 2019). A decade after the first economic freedom reports were published, the World Economic Forum and the World Bank created indices (Fougner 2008) that build on the ideas put forth by the self-declared "economic freedom movement".

Table one: Economic and political governance indexes, timeline

Year	Index	Organization
1972	Freedom in the World	Freedom House
1980	Freedom of the Press	Freedom House
1989	Index of Sustainable Economic Welfare	Hernan Daly, John B. Cobb (U.S.), Preceeds GPI
1990	Human Development	UNDP
1995	**Economic Freedom**	**Heritage Foundation**
1995	Corruption perception index	Transparency International
1996	**Economic Freedom of the World**	**Fraser Institute**
1996	World Wide Governance	Brookings & World Bank
2003	**Ease of doing business**	**World Bank**
2004	**Global Competitiveness Index**	**World Economic Forum**
2006	Tax Misery and Reform	Forbes
2012	International Property Rights	Americans For Tax Reform
2018	Index of Economic Democracy	New Economic Thinking
???	Genuine Process Indicator (beyond GDP)	Different, EU, changing, still subject to change

Source: Cooley and Snyder 2015, Annex one, author's selection from a total of 95 indexes listed. Indexes in Bold highlighted are subject to closer analysis in this chapter

In the course of the 1980s, Mont Pèlerin Society circles engaged in a multi-pronged effort to develop new ways of advancing policies based on their theories concerning the relationship between entrepreneurship and economic freedom. At the second conference dedicated to developing an economic freedom index organized by the Fraser Institute in Vancouver in 1988, which resulted in a volume titled *Economic Freedom: Toward a Theory of Measurement* (Block 1988), William Hammett of the Manhattan Institute in New York suggested that "people think that entrepreneurship is bad and we are suffering from an overdose of it in this country" (Hammett 1988: 127). Unlike support for political freedom, which is supported as an end in itself, Hammett claimed, economic freedom is considered as a means to the end of wealth, which is frequently hard to sell. Hammett used the difficulties the then-real estate developer Donald Trump faced when he wanted to evict a few rent controlled tenants to illustrate his concern. He went on to report on his limited success in strengthening the link between entrepreneurship and economic freedom on previous occasions:

> "I organized two conferences overseas in the last two years on the topic of growth...In both cases we were trying to energize the debate on lowering taxes and encouraging growth and entrepreneurship...the whole George Gilder scenario, supply-side thing. At neither one of those conferences did the topic of economic liberties ever come up. It was treated strictly as a pragmatic thing. Will this produce more growth and more wealth or will it not? ...We all believe in economic freedoms here, we know what it leads to. But it is almost an impossible chore to try to translate this to the general public who relate much more to the concept of growth, wealth, things like that, which is the end result of economic freedom." (Block 1988: 127).

Sustained efforts to clarify the link between economic freedom and entrepreneurship aimed at defining and determining measurable conditions of economic freedom. The earliest index proposed to measure economic freedom came from Freedom House in the early 1980s. Freedom House emphasized a link between democracy and economic freedom. Subsequent measuring and indexing efforts organized by the Fraser Institute in Canada and funded by the Liberty Fund (Indianapolis) began to de-emphasize democracy and eventually led to the construction of the Economic Freedom of the World Index (Gwartney et al. 1996) and to the Heritage Foundation's Indices of Economic Freedom (published in conjunction with the Wall Street Journal).

Much of the groundwork for these efforts to define and measure economic freedom was carried out by the MPS members Alvin Rabushka (Stanford) and Gerald William Scully (University of Texas), often in close interaction with MPS members from Europe. The 1988 conference proceedings (Block 1988) list (among others) the German libertarian science philosopher Gerard Rad-nitzky; Antonio Martino, a founding member of Forza Italia and later Italian minister of foreign affairs and defense; and the French libertarian essayist Henri LePage. All were members of the Mont Pèlerin Society.

In lieu of an accepted definition of economic freedom, Alvin Rabushka's combination of four central elements of economic liberty were considered by neoliberals to constitute the gold standard:

a) secure property rights;
b) voluntary exchange of individuals within and across borders;
c) absence of governmental control of the terms of transactions of individuals;
d) freedom from governmental expropriation of property (e.g., by confiscatory taxation or unanticipated inflation) (Hanke/Walters 1992, 120-121).

All but the first element (secure right to property) emphasizes the absence of restrictions by governments, not positive rights like a minimum social condition or a clean environment, or the freedom of association. Quite to the contrary: legal rights to form trade unions and mandated minimum wages, for example, are considered restrictions of economic freedom because they impede the price mechanism entrepreneurs depend on to fulfil their function in the economic system, according to the basic understanding laid out by Ludwig von Mises. The terms of transactions of individuals are subject to undesired external influence if trade unions determine the price of labor, rather than shifting conditions of supply and demand.

The data that is collected and prepared for the use in the economic freedom indices is not readily available. Think tanks in the different countries are charged with collecting and interpreting the data in the case of the Fraser Institute effort, for example. Qualitative data (like changes in the tax code etc.) are transformed into numerical data in order to offer an air of quantitative 'exact' assessment. No external and recognized academic council is involved in checking the data or the interpretation for accuracy and reliability. But the large number of countries and the long time period covered in the meantime offers a data source that is now readily available for use by think tank pundits and in universities and academic research institutes. Beyond academic research, the data is widely cited in media outlets and has been used in economic governance reforms at various times in a number of countries, notably in Central and Eastern Europe (Gwartney/Lawson 2003). Heritage indices and rankings are relied upon to allocate US foreign aid through the Millennium Challenge Corporation, for example.[3]

To improve the academic utility of the index, data has also been added for the period before the two economic freedom indexes were started. The extension draws on data sources from OECD countries and goes back to 1850 (Prados de la Escosura 2016). Regardless of the increasing efforts by the producers of the Economic Freedom Index to obtain academic standing, it is essential to take a closer look into the ways in which such ready for use data have been produced. Anybody who relies on the Economic Freedom Index data without subjecting the figures to critical investigation by way of looking into the sources and the ways in which the information has been transformed into quantitative indicators buys into the economic freedom ideology of the producers of the index, which at the same time leads to surprisingly different results in the position of countries like Russia or the Netherlands in the two rankings (Ram 2014).

More important than specific measures and valuations, of course, has been the overall message: economic liberalization will be economically beneficial, supporting entrepreneurship and growth. Regardless of significant qualifications, academic studies that employ the apparently more widely used Fraser Index are held to confirm this expectation (Haan/Sturm 2000). Jeffrey Sachs (2005) disputes such claims, however, and Ram (2014) demonstrates the fundamental flaws of the datasets, which undermines the very possibility of drawing such conclusions. It is in any case fascinating to observe how early neoliberal critiques of indices such as GDP and positivist accounts of economic growth have given way to generate instruments claiming the value of (pseudo-positivist, to be sure) instruments to improve growth. Ironically, the economic freedom movement appears to be complicit in the old bandwagon game: if you cannot beat them, join them. But the shift of attention to institutional conditions of economic activities must still be considered creative, helping to pave the way for the wider concerns of James Buchanan's public choice and Douglass North's new economic institutionalism.

---

3   See www.mcc.gov/who-we-fund/indicators (last access December 18, 2020)

Creating the Data You Need: Using the Index and its Data Sources

MPS members themselves took stock of the impact of the index at the Chattanooga regional meeting in 2003. Among the highlights reported were increasing media coverage of the Economic Freedom Index by quality journals like the *Economist*, the increasing reliance of professional economists on the index data in academic journals, new software projects to make easier use of the data, regional spin off projects in China and North America, a better understanding of the link between institutional environment and investment, and, last not least, a number of individual country examples of policy impact (Gwartney/Lawson 2003). The project has since expanded to cover more developing regions like the Maghreb World.

The history of this collective effort in the social construction of a neoliberal understanding of economic freedom as a precondition for entrepreneurship, and the important differences to the parallel development of national competitiveness indexes (on the International Institute of Management and the World Economic Forum, cf. Davies 2014) have been discussed by MPS member Steve Hanke and his co-author Stephen Walters in the *Cato Journal* (Hanke/Walters 1996). The Global Competitiveness Indicator of the World Economic Forum draws on a wide and diverse set of data including infrastructure, health, education, product and labor market efficiency, state of technological development, and so on. The index relies on both public data sources and perceptions of business leaders. It thus has little in common with GPIs like the economic freedom indices that are designed to address the regulatory framework of private economic activities that are subject to political change. Unlike managerial indices and ratings, the economic freedom indices do not aim at appraising endowments and infrastructures relevant for planning and forecasting. All measures are about institutions that can be changed by political means.

The economic freedom index endeavour has thus been conceived and strategically developed as a comprehensive and universal neoliberal policy tool, directed to remove restrictions on private sector economic activities needed to strengthen—in Giersch's terms—the demand side for entrepreneurship. But this purpose need not to be the only function of the index. Inadvertently and at the same time the yearly results can also be read as a measure of the state of neoliberal transformation. Attacks on neoliberal reforms, like the nationalization of erstwhile privatized companies or significant re-regulation, led to setbacks and roll back of neoliberal reforms in quite a few countries. In particular in times of economic crisis, voters and politicians frequently show a taste for policy preferences that lead to lower values in the economic freedom ranking. The numerical representation allows neoliberal reform forces to point to such decline to voice concern with regard to the conditions of economic freedom in a country, without discussing the details of individual measures. For those who oppose neoliberalism, index data similarly offers opportunities to identify countries in which the opposition to neoliberal reforms has made gains.

A great example of neoliberal data use of the neoliberal production of index data is Johan Norberg's (2001) "In defense of global capitalism", a popular booklet written to provide a counter narrative to the alter-globalisation movement of the late 1990s. Much of the statistical material used to support the claim that free market capitalism is good for development, the environment and gender relations comes from the data sources created by the Fraser Institute and its allies of the Economic Freedom project.

In her work on quantification as a means of communication, Bettina Heintz (2010) de-emphasizes the relevance of social networks in terms of their relevance for globalization processes. She argues that means and modes of communication are more relevant than the social relationships across borders. The social construction and the use and communication of economic freedom data and rankings suggest that we may need to rethink her argument that relies on functional differentiation. In the case of the neoliberal networks in charge of economic freedom indices, production and communication are closely intertwined and embedded in transnational think tank networks.

Arguably even more relevant than the influence exerted by think tank networks and organized neoliberal intellectuals of the economic freedom movement has been the influence of the ideas promoted by these forces on global governance elites in more powerful institutions like the World Bank. While the Economic Freedom Indexes have received a fair amount of criticism from progressive forces, the contested character of neoliberal transformation processes and the pertinent use of indexes and ranking instruments can be clarified best by way of examining the younger but bigger brother of the economic freedom indexes, the World Bank's Ease to do Business Index.

Intermediate Influence: Normalizing and Generalizing
Neoliberal Ways of Thinking

The World Bank's Ease of doing Business Index (EODB) shares with the Economic Freedom Indexes the idea of measuring the quality of the legal institutional environment of private sector economic activity across the different countries. A stylized medium sized company has been imagined for which the conditions are established in the different countries around the globe. The EODB-Index goes deeper into the micro-economic dimension of business activity than do the Economic Freedom Indexes. They add the regulatory dimension of starting a business, of credit facilitation, and employing or firing workers, for example. In principle, however, the World Bank's index follows a supply side economic logic very similar to the economic freedom indexes. How did the index come about?

The key person behind the index is Bulgaria's most illustrious economist, finance minister and World Bank director, Simeon Djankov. As co-founder of the index Djankov worked at the World Bank and was a non-resident senior fellow of the economic think-tank the Peterson Institute before he became deputy prime minister and finance minister of Bulgaria. Apart from his affiliation with high end economic research institutes, Djankov also took part in activities of the Atlas Economic research foundation network of think tanks linked to the Mont Pèlerin Society and the Economic Freedom Movement at large.[4] Djankov can be considered a—if not the—key global intellectual behind the drive toward market oriented institutional reforms. He easily operated in and between academia, think tanks, national government and global institutions illustrating both the interaction and the coalescence of different sources of (epistemic and political, national and international) authority (cf. Zürn 2017 on such "liquid" authority).

Djankov was asked to participate in writing the World Development Report of 2002 titled "Building Institutions for Markets". Djankov turned to Andrei Shleifer, an American economist at Harvard, who had worked on institutions and varieties of capitalism. Schleifer was willing to collaborate on the report if the project involved committing to gathering cross-country datasets

4   See for Djankov's biographical background www.doingbusiness.org/en/about-us/fou nders and https://www.atlasnetwork.org/about/people/simeon-djankov (last accessed 04.01.2021).

on institutions (Djankov 2016: 247). Together with Djankov and a range of colleagues a number of background papers were produced, which relied heavily
on rational choice institutionalism developed by Douglas North and public
choice literature, among other sources. Overlaps with the neoliberal sources
of the economic freedom movement and the producers of the Economic Freedom Indexes are abundant. The first publication on the regulation of market
entry (Djankov et al. 2002) draws on public choice inspired bureaucracy and
corruption theory to develop the comparative framework and criteria for the
index. The other papers backing the index development are written very much
in the same public choice spirit.[5] Unsurprisingly, the EODB-Index has run
into heavy criticism. Arguably because of its success detailed in review papers, which single out the number of academic articles using the data (more
than 1.000 in 2013) and the number of political reforms inspired by the index,
the methodology of the index has been attacked from many sides (compare
"A Review of doing Business" Acemoglu et al. 2013).[6] The strongest defense
of the report by the review committee points to the Scandinavian countries,
which do quite well in the World Bank's index. Accusations of neoliberal deception are unfounded according to the authors, because the index deals only
with about 100 of more than 14.000 regulations of the European Union, for
example (Acemoglu et al. 2013: 6).

This response clearly misses the point. If a set of just one hundred regulations is singled out to compare countries in de-contextualized ways, the
result is quite likely to be skewed. If, for example, regulations to start and run
businesses and to hire and fire workers are quite positive in Scandinavia from
a neoliberal perspective, the ways in which an expanded welfare state and a
high unionization rate mitigate the impact of business flexibility on labor is
obviously not addressed. Such selective representation of facts about a country uses Scandinavia to promote business models that are not very much like
the Scandinavian models taken as a whole.

In some ways the Economic Freedom Indexes are franker and less diplomatic than the EODB-Index because they don't make a secret of their dislike
of labor market deregulation, for example. The reason for diplomacy at the
World Bank is obvious on the other hand. The index ran into serious criticism

5   Compare the compilation of papers at https://www.doingbusiness.org/en/methodolog
     y (last accessed 07.09.2020).
6   350 by 2013 claims the Review paper from 2013, and almost 2000 claims Steve Hanke
     of the Cato Institute (2013).

with regard to the labor market measurements on the one hand, and with regard to the disclosure of income of politicians on the other hand (Djankov 2016: 248). The first measure was dropped from the ranking and the second was not taken up by the World Bank. Even the World Bank project cannot escape contestation and needs to invest heavily in corrections and legitimization efforts, as demonstrated by frequent changes to the methodology between 2005-2017. It appears as if the perceived power of the World Bank's index generates the contestation (Kelley/Simmons 2019; Doshi et. al 2019). Strong criticism of the World Bank's index from China in turn sparked a defensive response from members of the Economic Freedom movement (Hanke 2013).

Apart from the general closeness of the Economic Freedom Index and the EODB-Index, which both are designed to reproduce neoliberal ideas of law in the service of private business activities and entrepreneurship, the two devices both seem to revive ordoliberal ideas of an institutional framework for a market economy as pure as possible. Unlike the Economic Freedom Indexes, the neoliberal assessment of legal institutions gains weight at the World Bank because the index data accrue meaning of standards and instruments of conditionality (Krever 2013).

The neoliberal intellectual efforts behind the economic freedom indices—particularly their shared focus on supply-side reforms, entrepreneurship and public choice-type institutional analysis—conjunction with the personal experience of the decline and eventual collapse of socialist economies have clearly shaped Djankov's economic understanding. The World Bank's index co-developed by Djankov in turn informed the Atlas Foundation's economic freedom campaigns in various countries, notably India. India has been a prominent user of the EODB-Index to guide domestic reforms under Prime Minister Narendra Modi. On top of using the device to promote neoliberal reforms at the national level, his right-wing government replicated the index at the domestic level to push the different provinces in the direction of deregulation (Doshi et al. 2019: 633f.). The creation of the EODB-Index at the World Bank was arguably a significant upgrade for the Fraser and Heritage led efforts. Due to the weight of the World Bank for the international investment and policy-making community, governments are considerably more under pressure from a World Bank rating than from rankings established by civil society-based think tank networks. Unsurprisingly, the "market share" of the EODB-Index among the "cognate economic indicators" (including the two economic freedom indexes studied here) is calculated at 65.26 per cent, compared to 16.46 per cent for the global competitiveness index of World

Economic Forum (WEF); 8.07 per cent for the Heritage Foundation's Index of Economic Freedom, and 2.8 per cent for the Fraser Institute's Economic Freedom Index (Doshi et al. 2019: 618).

The relevance of the Fraser and Heritage efforts can thus be seen less in the institutional weight of the economic freedom indexes as such. They have become stepping stones in the process of redirecting more relevant private (World Economic Forum) and public (World Bank) institutions that provide much more weight and authority to the cause of economic freedom. In addition to the numerical difference of the indicators and rankings we need to consider the institutional difference. Neoliberal ideas become quite a bit more powerful once they enter the realm of the powerful global financial institutions at the core of contemporary global governance and neoliberal transformation processes. In the process of two decades, national and regional competitiveness norms and concerns advanced from the status of pro-business ideology nurtured by neoliberal intellectuals and think tanks to thoroughly institutionalized norms within the hierarchy of intertwined global and domestic institutions—a powerful example of the agenda-setting capacity of neoliberal think tanks.

Conclusion

The impact of the economic freedom indices developed by neoliberal think tanks around the Fraser Institute and by Heritage Foundation and the Wall Street Journal in the 1990s has been underestimated rather than overestimated, even if the indexes remain subject to severe criticism and academic use of the data seems unimpressive. Examining the genesis of neoliberal economic freedom indexes enables us to better comprehend the ability of neoliberal intellectuals to develop new concepts labelled 'supply-side economics', which are based on neoliberal norms and principled beliefs that were subsequently used as critical tools in a wide range of media and policy circles to change perceptions of the world.

The indices provided a policy instrument and knowledge reservoir for a broad range of social actors frequently based in think tanks linked to the Atlas network. The self-declared economic freedom movement behind the push for economic freedom indices focused attention on legal and other regulatory institutions subject to political change. The economic freedom indices were designed as tools of neoliberal policy reforms, guiding the larger process of neoliberal transformation. The development and articulation of a new understanding of entrepreneurship and the institutional requirements for innovation and economic development enabled the economic freedom movement to develop indices and to stage-manage the numerical depiction of alleged economic freedoms. The building of the collective transnational indicators project could draw on neoliberal civil society networks and served to expand and stabilize the work of this group of non-state actors. It attests to the capacity of neoliberal networks of intellectuals and think tanks to institutionalize new expertise and thus to advance an effort to change the global knowledge power structure (Strange 1988) by way of introducing new data sources, institutions, social technologies and communication circuits. Neoliberal networks did not just draw on a wider range of open data resources but displayed a critical ability to generate their own databases tailored to the needs of the economic freedom arguments. Born in critical distance to indices focused on macro-economic growth like GDP measures, economic freedom indices have lately been used to legitimate free market reforms based on claims of a close correlation of economic freedom and growth.

From a historical perspective, such arguments made in favor of economic freedom indices avoid the fundamental question: why have growth rates been higher across the OECD world and the Global South during the time of welfare state expansion and planning compared to the recent era of welfare state retrenchment? The indices are also silent on the crucial issue of asymmetries and uneven distribution. The design of the economic freedom indices suggests a causal relationship between economic freedom and economic benefits for the whole of society, although welfare state regimes and rules benefitting the working class and the poor are cast in a negative light. The evident attempt to support economic freedom for the rich in turn implies the question: what about economic freedom for the rest of us (Stanford 1999)? Indices and ratings are social constructions for discursive and political purposes. The critical use of indices needs to address the purposes for which they have been crafted.

Beyond the results achieved by the own civil society-based effort of the economic freedom movement it is important to discuss the wider influence of neoliberal economic 'freedom' reasoning in other indexes and rankings, which are arguably more influential in the assessment and transformation of economic governance than the Economic Freedom Indices themselves. As one scholar looking at the two most important legal indicator projects, the Ease of Doing Business Index and the Worldwide Governance Indicators argues: "these reproduce a narrow neoliberal conception of law as a platform for private business and entrepreneurial activity, and institutional support for a system of laissez faire markets" (Krever 2013: 131) In addition to the numerical difference Bettina Heintz has explained we need to recognize the institutional difference. It matters which private or public institution generates data and turns it into standards and conditions of the interaction between the public and the private sphere. Contrary to Heintz's particular emphasis on communication, it is necessary to insist on the relevance of social networks and their relevance at the interface of generation and communication of data. The links between the economic freedom movement and the World Bank effort also suggests to keep an eye on the institutional conditions of successful communication.

In addition to the necessary emphasis on "institutional difference" when it comes to global performance indicators, this chapter has demonstrated the ways in which the original neoliberal conceptions of economic freedom and market institutions have been created and strategically advanced. It thereby uncovers a hitherto missing link between the rise of neoliberalism and the rise of global performance indicators. It sheds light on the ongoing competition between different sets of performance indicators, and the ongoing competition of states *through* different sets of indicators in this age of neoliberal transformation.

More research is needed to assess the competition between progressive and neoliberal indicator systems. Even if it is more right than wrong to speak of a neoliberal era, the ideas, concepts and normative leanings of neoliberal agents and agencies are not universally accepted and subject to criticism of countervailing forces, as evidenced by rival indices produced by the Human Development Project or the Real Progress Indicator Project. Yet in spite of such competition, so far, a comprehensive attack on narrow neoliberal economic governance projects and their indicators is largely absent.

References

Acemoglu, Daron/Collier, Pau/Johnson, Simon/Klein, Michael/Wheeler, Graeme (2013): "A Review of Doing Business", May 12 (https://www.doing business.org/content/dam/doingBusiness/media/Methodology/Open-Le tter-Review-of-the-Arguments-on-DB.pdf).

Andrews, Frank M. (1989): "The Evolution of a Movement." In: Journal of Public Policy 9/4, pp. 401-405.

Bandura, Romina (2008): A survey of composite indices measuring country performance: 2008 update, New York: United Nations Development Programme.

Bauer, Peter (1948): Report on a Visit to the Rubber-Growing Smallholdings of Malaya, London: H.M.S.O.

Bauer, Peter (1954): West African Trade, Cambridge: Cambridge University Press.

Bloch, Roland/Mitterle, Alexander (2017): "On Stratification in Changing Higher Education: the 'Analysis of Status' Revisited." In: Higher Education 73, pp. 929-946.

Block, Walter E. (ed.) (1988): Economic Freedom: Toward a Theory of Measurement. Proceedings of an International Symposium, Vancouver: Fraser Institute.

Burgin, Angus (2012): The Great Persuasion, Cambridge, MA: Harvard University Press.

Cerny, Philip G. (2007): "Paradoxes of the Competition State: The Dynamics of Political Globalization." In: Government and Opposition 32/2, pp. 251-274.

Cooley, A./Snyder, J. L. (eds.) (2015): Ranking the World: Grading States as a Tool of Global Governance, Cambridge: Cambridge University Press.

Davies, William (2014): The Limits of Neoliberalism: Authority, Sovereignty and the Logic of Competition, Thousand Oaks: SAGE Publications.

Diaz-Bone, Rainer/Didier, Emmanuel (2016): "Introduction: The Sociology of Quantification—Perspectives on an Emerging Field in the Social Sciences. Historical Social Research." In: Historische Sozialforschung 41/2, pp. 7-26.

Djankov, Simeon (2016): "Correspondence." In: Journal of Economic Perspectives 30/1, pp. 247-248.

Djankov, Simeon/La Porta, Rafael/Lopez-de-Silanes, Florencio/Shleifer, Andrei (2002): "The Regulation of Entry." In: The Quarterly Journal of Economics CXVII/1, pp. 1-37.

Djelic, Marie Laure/Mousavi, Reza (2020): "How the Neoliberal Think Tank Went Global: The Atlas Network, 1981 to the Present." In: Dieter Plehwe/Quinn Slobodian/Philip Mirowski (eds.), Nine Lives of Neoliberalism, London: Verso, pp. 257-282.

Doshi, Rush/Kelley, Judith G./Simmons, Beth A. (2019): "The Power of Ranking: the Ease of Doing Business Indicator and Global Regulatory Behavior." In: International Organization 73/3, pp. 611-643.

Espeland, Wendy Nelson/Michael Sauder (2007): "The Reactivity of Rankings: How Public Measures Recreate Social Worlds." In: American Journal of Sociology 113, pp. 1-40.

Feldstein, Martin (1986): "Supply Side Economics: Old Truths and New Claims." In: American Economic Review 76/2, pp. 26-30.

Fougner, T. (2008): "Neoliberal Governance of States: The Role of Competitiveness Indexing and Country Benchmarking." In: Millennium 37/2, pp. 303-326.

Fraser Institute (2020) "Economic Freedom: History of Free the World", Fraser Institute Website (https://www.fraserinstitute.org/economic-freedom/history-of-free-the-world).

Giannone, Diego (2010): "Political and Ideological Aspects in the Measurement of Democracy: The Freedom House Case." In: Democratization 17/1, pp. 68-97.

Giersch, Herbert (1982): "The Role of Entrepreneurship in the 1980s." In: Kiel Discussion Papers, August 1982.

Giersch, Herbert (1984): "The Age of Schumpeter." In: The American Economic Review 74/2, pp. 103-109.

Giersch, Herbert (1985): "Eurosclerosis—the malaise that threatens prosperity." In: Financial Times, January 2, 1985, p. 9.

Gwartney, James D./Lawson, Robert A. (2003): "The Impact of the Economic Freedom of the World Index." In: Regional Meeting of the Mont Pelerin Society Chattanooga, Tennessee, USA, September 18-21, 2003, Stanford: Hoover Institution, Mont Pelerin Files.

Gwartney, James/Lawson, Robert A./Block, Walter (eds.) (1996): Economic Freedom of the World, 1975-1995, Vancouver: Fraser Institute.

Haan, J. de/Sturm, J.-E. (2000): "On the Relationship between Economic Freedom and Economic Growth." In: European Journal of Political Economy 16/2, pp. 215-241.

Hammett, William (1988): "Discussion of Chapter 4, 'Preliminary Definition of Economic Freedom' by Alvin Rabushka." In: Walter E. Block (ed.), Economic Freedom: Toward a Theory of Measurement. Proceedings of an International Symposium, Vancouver: Fraser Insitute, pp. 127.

Hanke, Steve H. (2013): "Doing Business Singapore Style", Cato Institute, August 20 (www.cato.org/publications/commentary/doing-business-singapore-style).

Hanke, Steve H./Walters, Stephen J. K. (1997): "Economic Freedom, Prosperity, and Equality: A Survey." In: Cato Journal 17/2, pp. 117-146.

Heintz, Bettina (2010): „Numerische Differenz. Überlegungen zu einer Soziologie des (quantitativen) Vergleichs." In: Zeitschrift für Soziologie 39/3, pp.
162–181.

Kelley, Judith G./Simmons, Beth A. (2019): "Introduction: The Power of Global
Performance Indicators." In: International Organization 73/3, pp. 491-510.

Kirzner, Israel (1967): "Entrepreneurship and the Market Approach to Development." In: Floyd A. Harper/Henry Hazlitt/Leonard Read/Gustavo R. Ve-
lasco/Friedrich August von Hayek (eds.), Toward Liberty: Essays in Honor
of Ludwig von Mises, Menlo Park: Institute for Humane Studies, pp. 194-
208.

Kirzner, Israel (1980): "The Primacy of Entrepreneurial Discovery." In: Arthur
Seldon (ed.), Prime Mover of Progress, London: Institute of Economic Affairs, pp. 1-2.

Krever, T. (2013): "Quantifying Law: Legal Indicator Projects and the Reproduction of Neoliberal Common Sense." In: Third World Quarterly 34/1, pp.
131-150.

Lamont, Michèle (2012): "Toward a Comparative Sociology of Valuation and
Evaluation." In: Annual Review Sociology 38, pp. 201-221.

Meadows, Donella H./Meadows, Dennis L./Randers, Jorgen/Behrens, William
W. (1972): The Limits to Growth. A Report for The Club of Rome's Project
on the Predicament of Mankind, New York: Universe Books.

Mises, Ludwig von (1998 [1949]): Human Action: A Treatise on Economics,
Auburn: Ludwig von Mises Institute.

Norberg, Johan (2001): In Defense of Global Capitalism, Stockholm: Timbro.

Plehwe, Dieter (2009): "The Origins of the Neoliberal Economic Development
Discourse." In: Philip Mirowski/Dieter Plehwe (eds.), The Road from Mont
Pelerin. The Making of the Neoliberal Thought Collective, Cambridge, MA:
Harvard University Press, pp. 238-279.

Plehwe, Dieter (2020): "Schumpeter Revival? How Neoliberals Revised the
Image of the Entrepreneur." In: Dieter Plehwe/Quinn Slobodian/Philip
Mirowski (eds.), Nine Lives of Neoliberalism, London: Verso, pp. 120-142.

Plehwe, Dieter, Slobodian, Quinn (2017): "Landscapes of Unrest. Herbert Giersch and the Origins of Neoliberal Economic Geography." In: Modern Intellectual History 16/1, pp. 1-31.

Plickert, Philip (2008): Wandlungen Des Neoliberalismus. Eine Studie zu Entwicklung und Ausstrahlung der 'Mont Pelerin Society', Stuttgart: Lucius
& Lucius.

Porter, T.W. (1995): Trust in Numbers. The Pursuit of Objectivity in Science and Public Life, Princeton: Princeton University Press.

Power, M. (1997): The Audit Society: Rituals of Verification, Oxford: Oxford University Press.

Prados de la Escosura, L. (2016): "Economic Freedom in the Long Run: Evidence from OECD Countries (1850-2007)." In: Economic History Review 69/2, pp. 435-468.

Ram, Rati (2014): "Measuring Economic Freedom: A Comparison of Two Major Sources." In: Applied Economics Letters 21/12, pp. 852-856.

Sachs, Jeffrey (2005): The End of Poverty: Economic Possibilities for our Time, London: Penguin Books.

Schmelzer, Matthias (2016): The Hegemony of Growth, Cambridge: Cambridge University Press.

Schmölders, Günter (ed.) (1971): Der Unternehmer im Ansehen der Welt, Bergisch Gladbach: Lübbe.

Slobodian, Quinn (2019): "Democracy doesn't matter to the defenders of 'economic freedom'", In: The Guardian, November 11 (www.theguardian.com/commentisfree/2019/nov/11/democracy-defenders-economic-freedom-neoliberalism).

Stanford, Jim (1999): "Economic Freedom for the Rest of us", Canadian Economics Association Meeting, Toronto, May 27-30 (www.csls.ca/events/cea1999/stanf.pdf).

Strang, David/Meyer, John W. (1993): "Institutional Conditions for Diffusion." In: Theory and Society 22/4, pp. 487-511

Strange, Susan (1988): States and Markets—An Introduction to International Political Economy, London: Pinter.

Uribe, M. A. P. (2015): "The Quest for Measuring Development: The Role of the Indicator bank." In: S. E. Merry/K. E. Davis/B. Kingsbury (eds.), Cambridge Studies in Law and Society. The Quiet Power of Indicators: Measuring Governance, Corruption and Rule of Law, Cambridge: Cambridge University Press, pp. 133-155.

Wahlberg, A./Rose, N. (2015): "The Governmentalization of Living: Calculating Global Health." In: Economy and Society 44/1, pp. 60-90.

Walpen, Bernhard (2004): Die offenen Feinde und ihre Gesellschaft. Eine hegemonietheoretische Studie zur Mont Pèlerin Society, Hamburg: VSA-Verlag.

Waltz, Kenneth (1979): Theory of International Politics, Boston: McGraw-Hill.

Zürn, Michael (2017): "From Constitutional Rule to Loosely Coupled Spheres of Liquid Authority. A Reflexive Approach." In: International Theory 9/2, pp. 261-285.

Competing Powers
Engineers, Energetic Productivism, and the End of Empires

Daniela Russ & Thomas Turnbull

"Tons of data go with Wilson party," read the *New York Times* of December 4th, 1918. The newspaper article described how three truckloads of geographical and economic records had accompanied President Woodrow Wilson as he had left for the Paris Peace Conference (Smith 2003: 488). The US not only brought money, weapons and soldiers to Europe, but geographic expertise. In September 1917, Wilson had decided to gather a group of experts to quietly prepare the US's position in the post-war scramble for territories among rival and allied powers. Known as 'The Inquiry', the organization was akin to a foreign policy think tank, insofar as it brought together geographers, historians, and economists in the production of an impressive amount of data and reports surveying the post conflict landscape in a purportedly scientific manner (ibid: 119). World War I had swept away empires, and the maintenance of peace was believed to depend on the redrafting of territory on the basis of self-determined nation-states; in effect, the Inquiry's challenge was to assign every European coal mine and river valley to what was deemed its rightful place (ibid: 149).

The geopolitical worldview the US brought to the conference table emphasized a model of economic development freed from the need for territorial expansion. This North American principle had developed since the closing of the frontier and the inter-imperial wars of the late 19th century (see Nagel/Werron this volume). Territorial questions were still at the center of the peace talks, but, according to the Americans, they were the vehicle to achieve that peace, not its purpose. With the territorially defined nation-state came the idea of a world economy in which territorial size no longer determined economic significance (Smith 2003: 141-2). However, territorial *quality* still mattered: questions of resource supply, transport routes, and access to the sea were seen as crucial to the economic survival of nation states. In line with its earlier Open Doors Policy, with regard to trade with China, the US sought a post-war world with free, supposedly non-discriminatory access to goods and capital: a world in which, with America at the helm, territorial conflict would give way to 'peaceful' economic competition (Tooze 2015: 15-16).

In a time of rapid technological change, the economic diagnosis that lay behind the US position was shared by a wider cast of historical actors. Engineers and natural scientists who had risen to managerial or public positions began to articulate a new view of economic progress based on the efficiency of resource use rather than the assumption that monetary economy was alone sufficient to guarantee economic development (Hays 1999; Tyrell 2015). The pursuit of resource efficiency implied a materialist, if relativistic, view of the economy: in contrast to neoclassical economists, these critics defended the idea that wealth must be measured in material terms and pointed out the arbitrariness of the allocation of price by markets alone and the inefficiencies of price-governed forms of economic policy. Moreover, against the scarcity-mongering of some earlier classical economists, they emphasized the emancipatory role of technological progress. The fact that more was increasingly being produced with less introduced a certain relativity to the determination of absolute material limits (Turnbull 2020), while new means of production, particularly those powered by electricity, added plausibility to this new efficiency-centered materialist economics.

Referring to a series of scientific and social initiatives in the 19th century, historian Anson Rabinbach has used the term 'productivism' to describe the widely held belief that 'energy' was the ultimate source of all productive power, human, animal, or mechanical (Rabinbach 1990: 61; Underwood 1995). Drawing on thermodynamics, a vision of an economy governed by contrasting principles of work and waste had been a widely shared belief amongst physicists, engineers, physiologists, and political economists in the mid-19th century (cf. Wise and Smith 1989a; 1989b; 1990). The rise of price-based, neoclassical economics at the end of the 19th century superseded these views, concealing almost all traces of natural-economic thinking in mainstream economics (Mirowski 1989; Schabas 2005). A later productivism, as espoused by German national socialists and Italian fascists, no longer reflected a natural philosophical idea of nature and society united in production, so much as a technocratic idea of total societal management (Maier 1988: 77; Rabinbach 2018). By the 1950s, both forms of productivism were increasingly subsumed under the global rivalry between the capitalist principles of efficient resource allocation and the socialist principle of material balancing (Arvay 1994; Mirowski 2002).

We term this short-lived interest in an energy-based form of materialist economics during the interwar period as 'energetic productivism.' Rather than the gradual decline of materialist economics, we propose to think of energetic productivism as a brief period of enthusiasm for a distinct form of materialist economics. It was not materialism in retreat, but a reformulated reiteration of materialist thinking: a response to the changing technological, economic, and political conditions of the period. Energetic productivism was based on the idea that the amount of energy a state could harness and control was a central indicator of its economic and political power. Energy was understood as a resource but one that was relative to the efficiency of a state's working population, its productive technologies, and the efficacy with which the state was able to configure these productive capacities. Energy availability, in effect, was a function of a state's ability to make advantageous use of material resources. This body of ideas recognized that it was longer a state's absolute amount of territory, its population, or resources that determined its power, so much as the energy that could be productively harnessed from these potentialities.

Energetic productivism, we further argue, implied a form of *indirect competition for a reliable, broad, and efficient use of energy*. While this form of competition clearly did not rule out national conflicts over resources and territories, it created a new medium via which supremacy could be asserted: How long would a country's coal resources last? How much waterpower could be harnessed? How many homes and industries could be electrified? How much mechanical power could an average worker exert? Countries observed each other closely through official statistics, meticulously comparing one another's' energetic capacities, and striving for the recognition of comparative advantages from an increasingly international public sphere. While preferable to direct conflict, we argue that this form of competition was only 'formally peaceful'. As Max Weber stated "only complete political confusion and naive optimism" could mistake pre-war expansion of imperial trade for peaceful economic competition (Weber 1894, quoted in Mommsen 1990: 77). Such a view also applied to competition over energetic productivity in the interwar years.

Energetic productivism changed the terms of geopolitical competition and the nature of imperialism. In the following two parts, we first outline the roots of energetic productivism in the 19th century and show how it related to imperial competition around the turn of the century. We then turn to two forms of energetic productivism that emerged out of two distinct nation states, Great Britain and the Soviet Union. On the basis of these examples, we argue 'power competition' was wedded to two wider political conflicts. The first was between Great Britain and 'rising' rival powers whose ascendence was beginning to end its industrial and political hegemony. The second power competition occurred between the Soviet Union and the capitalist countries whom this experimental new polity sought to supersede. The chapter concludes by contrasting these two iterations of energetic productivism with a more well-known formulation of energetic statehood proposed in the US in the 1930s.

Energetic Productivism

In the interwar years, energetic productivism drew its persuasive power from economic uncertainties, technological change, and visionary plans for the future. Its roots, however, lay in the age of the steam engine and the science of thermodynamics. Rabinbach has traced the metaphorical idea of humans as motors and the idea that society should be governed according to thermodynamic imperatives back to the early 19th century, while others have associated such a view with advances in engineering, political economy and natural philosophy (Rabinbach 1992; Breger 1982). In this 19th century iteration, productivists espoused the idea that humans, animals and nature shared an ability to do work. Productivism linked human life processes to those of other species and to natural processes, such as photosynthesis and the combustion and the generation of heat. Because this productivism rested upon physical principles, its advocates believed it articulated universal principles for the improvement of human existence.

This physicalism was particularly apparent among those who became known as energeticists, a loose group of natural scientists who on the basis of the seemingly universal applicability of the laws of energy ventured into the social sciences at the end of the 19th century. For mathematician Georg Helm, and chemists Ernest Solvay and Wilhelm Ostwald, energy could no longer be solely a matter for engineers and natural philosophers but the basis of a program of societal reform (Müller 2020: 37). Solvay and Ostwald drew a strong moral lesson, an 'energetic imperative' which saw civilizational advancement as something dependent on more efficient use of available energy resources. As Solvay pointed out, this obligation was grounded in human physiology: "The productivist movement has its source in social energetics; it expresses itself physiologically and socially in the law of struggle for the best existence which, itself, is only an expression of the superior physico-chemical law of maximum work" (Solvay 1900: 150, our translation). Under this law, colonial expansion was also cast as an energo-moralistic obligation. The productivist law that "generates the well-being of humanity and will consequently constitute the universal law [...]. It [...] legitimizes from a humanitarian point of view the forced imposition of the system of full productivism or the forced political or territorial occupation of the least developed countries by the most advanced productivist countries." (Solvay 1900: 73, our translation; cf. Ostwald 1912; Rabinbach 2018). For Ostwald's fellow energeticist and Leipzig university colleague, the geographer Friedrich Ratzel, by contrast, colonial expansion was a means for the maximization of resources which fecund but supposedly lesser nations were unable to exploit to their fullest potential. This was a rationale underlying his infamous concept of *Lebensraum*: the idea that state seizure of territory was defensible as a requirement of societal evolution (Livingstone 2008).

Proponents of energetic productivism articulated a belief that mastery over the physics of energy conversion determined economic productivity and the creation of value. But as economies had become more dependent on technology, this energo-physicalism could no longer be quantified solely in terms of population, acres of land or resources. It had become instead a function of the effective use of technology, labor, and nature: in sum, the determinants of a nation's capacity to productively expend available energy. Rabinbach termed such productivism "transcendental materialism" (1993: 4) to characterize how the mobilization of matter via energy transcended and extended conventional materialist economics: as alongside a focus on matter and bodies it stressed that energy offered a unified form of explanation. Manifest in acts of measurement that attested to the efficiency of industrial processes, such potentialities were seen as the energo-material basis of economic life and pitted against economic theories that focused on immaterial and subjective determinations of value (cf. neoclassical orthodoxy). In the productivist view, the financial economy could obscure the true determinant of economic growth and detract attention from the pursuit of technological efficiency. For example, in US institutional economist Thorstein Veblen's radical polemics, the most productive economy would be that which freed itself from the restriction to pursue profit above all else (Veblen 1975).

Like no other technology, electrification exemplified the changes afoot in the pursuit of economic progress. Commercial electricity had begun as a means of lighting and a communication technology. By World War I, it had become the connective tissue of the machine industry that supplied electric power and machinery for all kinds of purposes, spawning new industries such as electrochemistry (Hughes 1993: 285-323, Friedrich/James 2017). By conveying electricity generated by a smaller number of large power plants of greater efficiency than discrete steam engines, and dispersing this across an interconnected grid, significant efficiencies were achieved, and dramatic claims were made about electricity's coal saving capacities (Zimmermann 1933: 569). Moreover, for countries with limited access to coal, or those looking to supplement its power, mechanized industries and infrastructures could be driven by electricity derived from falling water. Electric power could also be used more efficiently than steam in productive processes, it could be split and employed where needed and could replace or amplify human labor. Electrification came to be understood as a lever which, properly employed, could augment economic productivity (Hausman et al. 2008, 27).

Against the backdrop of a confusing and unexplained economic depression, marked by falling prices and competing views regarding business cycle amplitudes, energetic productivism offered a theory of economic development which could draw on the authority of the natural sciences and engineering. This authority was greater than ever after World War I: a conflict that had been fought to a large extent with cutting-edge scientific advancements, which had brought more scientists and engineers into public office, and in which engineering principles had begun to be applied to economic planning (Thomas 2015: 13-21; Meer 2012). Energetic productivist thinking was seemingly most common in the fields of economic geography, industrial chemistry, and electrical engineering, areas in which the efficiency gains and spatial and economic changes heralded by new energy technologies were readily apparent.

Crucial to this world view was a distinct theory of progress, in which civilizational advancement was primarily determined by the predominant source of energy that was used. The rise of electricity coincided with a number of theories of 'energy development', the idea that society progressed through increases in the quantity and quality of energy that was available for use. These theories had found an early expression in the sociology of Herbert Spencer, and subsequent organistic theories of state, which posited that society was an aggregate of evolving energy-dependent organisms (McKinnon 2010). Theories of energy-based societal development found full expression in the work of North American historian-philosopher Lewis Mumford, who saw electricity as an energy form that would allow society to shift from a "paleotechnic" coal-based existence toward a cleaner and more prosperous "neotechnic age" (Mumford 1934). It is perhaps unsurprising that the first reinterpretation of the industrial revolution as a coal-driven historical event emerged around this time (Nef 1932). But however diverse the intellectual threads of energy productivism, they were united by a shared understanding of history as something driven by techno-economic rationales. In attempting to outdo each other in terms of energetic capacity, countries competed via a new form of developmental supremacy.

Energetic Imperialism

The last quarter of the 19th century marked the beginning of a period of intensified rivalry between the great powers. Imperial Germany and the US were rapidly industrializing, and their industrial products had begun to compete with those of Britain (Friedberg 1988: 35). Former outliers such as Tsarist Russia and the Ottoman Empire had built railroads, welcomed some foreign investment, and slowly begun to modernize their economies. When the great powers sought to resolve their territorial rivalries by dividing the African continent among themselves at the 1884-5 Berlin conference, the last 'frontier' of land available to Imperial states was reached. The globe's North and South poles would soon be reached, and just one seventh of the Earth would remain unmapped (Smith 2003: 11). Given evidence of territorial limits to growth, the scramble for the last 'unclaimed' territories had also been fuelled by fears prompted by falling prices and investments, dynamics later classified as perhaps the first 'Great Depression', lasting between 1873 and 1896 (Saul 1985; Hobsbawm 1989). This insecurity raised doubts about the economic advantages of free trade and imperialism and encouraged new forms of economic organization. Many countries introduced tariffs to protect their domestic and colonial industrial interests from international economic competition (Hobsbawm 1989: 39-42).

What made this 'depression' so hard to grasp is that while prices and investment fell, wages and production increased, and profits soared. This discrepancy sparked discussions over the contested relation between productivity and profitability within businesses but also in regard to the wider logics of imperial economies. Businesses responded by attempting to avoid increased competition via cooperation, vertical integration, and scientific management (Chandler 2002). The large shareholder corporation with its meticulous accounting system reached maturity in the late 19th century, soon followed by Taylorist principles of scientific management in the early twentieth century, which espoused the idea that laborers could be disciplined to make more efficient use of time and motion in productive processes (Maier 1970). A tendency toward the formation of monopolies or monopolistic forms of cooperation was particularly great in both new and old networked and energy industries, such as coal, railroads, oil and electric power (Hobsbawm 1989: 44). The large trusts and monopolies of the rising industrial powers—Germany'scoal syndicates and the oil and power companies of the US—exemplified this tendency. By the outbreak of World War I, German and American electric power companies dominated electric development world-wide (Hausman et al. 2008: 75-105).

To some, such end of the century imperial competitiveness and skirmishes over productivity seemed directed more toward the attainment of private profits than national advancement. In *Imperialism: A Study* (1902) British economist John Atkinson Hobson proposed a relationship between domestic underconsumption, foreign investment, and imperial expansion. In his view, there were powerful domestic interests benefitting from imperialism: namely manufacturers and, particularly, investors (Cain 2002: 103-114). In a peculiarly energetic metaphor, Hobson noted that "finance is rather the governor of the imperial engine, directing the energy and determining its work; it does not constitute the fuel of the engine, nor does it directly generate the power." (Hobson 1902: 59) In an expression reminiscent of the later technocratic criticism of "financial managers" (Veblen 1921: 29), Hobson suggested finance was important only in so far as it governed the rate at which energy entered the economy.

The World War made both the dependency on financial markets plainly visible and sparked a hope among some that a new, energo-materially oriented reorganization of economic life might be achieved. The allies had borrowed heavily from Wall Street, creating a strong link between entrenched financial interests and the European conflict. While this was not the trigger for the US joining the war, it established a dependency that could not be neglected: not least because, during the war, the US turned from the world's largest debtor to the largest creditor nation (Wilkins 2009; Tooze 2015). It replaced an international financial system based on the gold standard and centered around London with a new system that gravitated towards Wall Street. However, domestic war economies, particularly the German War Resource Department, were able to prove that another relation between the state and capital was possible: the centralized administration of production, allocation, and consumption that was based not on world market prices but on the material prosperity of the 'nation' or 'community' (Maier 1970; Hardach 1981: 58-62; Michalka 1997).

Colonialism was officially outlawed after World War I but continued under the mandate system of the League of Nations. In fact, the modern oligopolistic oil industry, in which a handful of multinational corporations divided up global oil resources, emerged at that time. The mandate system prohibited annexation but allowed states to administer territories to "promote the wellbeing and development of [its] people" (Snow 1919: 68). Under this system, France and Great Britain split the former Ottoman territories in the Middle East and began to develop oil industries and pipelines in their mandate territories (Sampson 1975; Garavini 2019: 11-52). At the same time, the US oil companies founded the Arabian-American Oil Company (Aramco) outside of the mandate system, but under equally favorable business conditions. These 'post-imperial' undertakings, in which territory was not seized, but access to resources was secured through long-term treaties within mandates or with formally independent states, were often more profitable than direct imperialism (Strachey 1959: 179). This modified colonialism, in which resource access trumped the burdens of territorial ownership, was referred to by Isiah Bowman, geographer advisor to President Franklin Roosevelt, and leading Inquiry member, as 'American Lebensraum', a term not solely applicable to the US but which acknowledged its oversight of this system of access-led resource appropriation (Smith 2003: 27-28).

The new order proved precarious. The national borders carved out at the Paris Peace Conference remained contested and global economic shock waves continued to hit even well-organized *Volkswirtschaften* (national economies). In fact, the suspicion that something was wrong with the international economic order became only stronger after World War I and the depression of the 1930s. The invention of macroeconomics and new economic theories, such as Keynesianism, neoliberalism, and business cycle research, were attempts to make sense of the changing relation between national and world economies (Tooze 2001; Slobodian 2018). While Keynesianism and neoliberalism focused on markets and the monetary economy, business cycle research picked up on the material and technological changes too. Soviet economist Nikolai Kondratieff built an economic theory on the history of industrial revolutions, which he understood as initiating 'long waves' of economic growth. Joseph Schumpeter picked up Kondratieff's ideas in his work on business cycles, in which he associated each upswing with a new set of innovations and each downturn with the exhaustion of their profit potential (Hobsbawm 1989: 47). In this view, the upswing around the turn of the century was linked to marked innovations in the electrical, petroleum and chemical industries. One British economist even saw electrification and the related spread of automation as signs of a "second industrial revolution", one which would prove more conse-quential than the first (Jevons 1931).

Edwardian Technocracy

Taking into perspective later eras of Depression, such as that of the 1930s, simplistic descriptions of the period 1873 to 1896 as a 'Great Depression' have met criticism, instead it has been suggested it was more a specific problem for the Victorian economy of Britain. Prices had indeed fallen, and this was registered in falling profits for those who owned productive means. Such in-dustrialists, often with access to the press, were prone to raising the specter of depression in pursuit of sympathetic policies. Whether or not it was truly a depression, as it is understood in contemporary economics, some described it as such. This would, in contemporary parlance, involve a sustained fall in GDP which did not occur (Friedberg 1988: 24). But relative to the 'boom' of industrialism, which was most apparent in the early 1870s, even minor con-tractions in growth appeared significant. This was also a question of perspec-tive. As Britain had industrialized first, productivity rate increases tailed-off there first. Decline and supremacy were relative phenomena: as other coun-tries industrialized, learning from the prime mover's mistakes as well as its successes, their rates of productivity growth began to exceed those of Britain (Saul 1985: 23; Friedberg 1988: 24-26).

Little known today, a distinct energetic productivist movement emerged in Edwardian Britain in response to this perceived economic slump and a more wide-ranging belief in national decline. Faced with defeat in the Boer war, a conflict that had begun in 1899 and which had seen British soldiers disastrously deployed against the Transvaal and the Orange Free State, the collective belief in the country's natural supremacy had been shaken. In the words of foreign secretary Joseph Chamberlain, the nation was a "weary Titan" undergoing relative decline in contrast to rival powers, particularly Bismarck's Germany (Friedberg 1988: 116). In response, calls for greater 'efficiency' in all aspects of statecraft came from across the political spectrum, providing, in historian Gerald Searle's view, "a cohering ideology" (Searle 1971: xxvi): a shared belief that national renewal could be achieved via internal improvements to the components of the British empire rather than, as in past decades, territorial expansion and the pursuit of untrammeled trade. The perceived economic depression between 1873-1896 had further undermined the tenets of British liberalism, whilst the interventionist policies of Germany, from conscription to state-sponsored science, suggested that the rationalization of state functions rather than imperial expansion would be the new determinant of power.

Seeking to address this challenge, in 1902 a dining club called the 'Co-Efficients' convened in London. The event provided a forum for the leading figures in the British efficiency movement. Historian Robert Scally called it a "peculiar experiment in English politics", partly given its informal nature; "interesting little dinners" were overseen by Fabian socialists Beatrice and Sidney Webb, and attended by the science-fiction author H.G. Wells, the Hegelian philosopher and statesman Richard Burdon Haldane, and the geographer Halford Mackinder, amongst others (Scally 2015: 81-82). An indication of its influence is suggested by the fact that one member, Edward Grey, Foreign Secretary between 1905-1916, became a key figure in British foreign policy before and during WWI, and afterwards became president of the League of Nations. Historian Andreas Rose notes the club "provided the future foreign minister with not only a forum in which he could develop his thoughts but also a free lesson on the domestic problems that might accompany his proposed course of action" (Rose 2017: 87). Though it split in 1909, long before the war, the club provided a venue for discussing emerging concerns over Britain's relative decline, from the threat presented by an ascendant Germany to a potential alliance with Russia (Friedberg 1988: 86-87).

Diverse in political opinions, the group broadly coalesced under the twin banners of Imperialism and what journalist and Co-Efficient club member Leo Amery called its pro-interventionist "semi-socialism" (Scally 2015: 78). As Sidney Webb stated their aim had been high minded conversation that might lead to the development of a political program to address what was seen as "the pompous inefficiency of every branch of our public administration" (Searle 2002: 196). Through the advocacy of prominent Co-Efficients, moves toward the technical rationalization of state administration began to find a foothold in public life, particularly after WWI. Given its interstitial role, at least one historian characterized the group as an "Edwardian 'think tank'" (Polelle 1999: 71). Amid a more widespread energy productivist movement, the Co-Efficients provided a distinctly British iteration of such thinking.

The formation of the Co-Efficients had been partly prompted by a growing sense that the competitive dynamics of free trade had failed, for Britain at least. Supporters of the Tariff Reform movement had argued in response to Britain's perceived economic slump that higher taxes should be imposed on domestic and foreign trade to increase state revenue and better provide for the security and welfare of the recently enlarged electorate (Thompson 1997). The 1867 and 1884 Reform Acts had created an upswell of political demands from the working classes. Though diverse in opinions, a significant number of Co-Efficients saw increased tariffs as a means of increasing the capacity of the state to invest in interventionist efficiency-oriented policies: from technical education to scientific research to improve worker efficiency, for the benefit of industry and the Empire in general. The question was whether free trade could be balanced with this more technocratic and welfare-oriented vision of the state. Not least, geographer Halford Mackinder saw the origin of British decline in the nation having measured its prosperity according to the value of foreign trade. In his mind, the pursuit of "Money-power" served only as a measure of the rate at which the British Empire was divesting itself of its resources (Mackinder 1906). In its place, he believed the nation should strive toward increased "man-power", a measure of a population's potential "laboring and fighting power" (Mackinder 1905).

Mackinder's formulation of energetic productivism was distinguished by its focus on human physiology. At a lecture to the Compatriots Club, a more overtly Imperialist spin-off group from the Co-Efficients, he asked his audience "to turn for a while from thought of values, and even of wealth itself, to the output of human energy for which wealth affords but part of the fuel" (Kearns 2009: 55; Mackinder 1906: 21). He believed wealth measured in pecuniary terms was no indication of physiological power, nor did it confer levels of resource wealth, as via competition, war, and increased efficiency, the availability of resources could be dramatically increased. For Mackinder, the ultimate determinant of national power was the size and efficacy of its population rather than currency or resources. His point was that via competition, efficiency, or war one could dramatically increase resource availability, so the ultimate determinant of productive and martial power was the size and efficiency of a potentially working or fighting population. Mackinder was less interested in the "sources of human energy" (1906: 143), coal and oil or agricultural produce, than in the energetic capacities of human bodies such sources could support and improve.

How could such measurements of manpower be accounted for? Given his social Darwinist beliefs, he argued that it was not possible to simply count the number of people in a given state, as that would assume "all men are equally efficient" (ibid: 136). Comparing Britain to other nations revealed that a focus on money-power at the expense of other values had left the nation's population growing more slowly than almost all other European states and paling in comparison to Russia and America's abundant citizenry. Moreover, the conscription of soldiers during the Boer war had revealed a section of working people who had been rendered anemic, malnourished, weak, and poorly educated (Searle 1971: 65). Mackinder believed that if the state were to invest in this underclass's educational improvement, administer to their health, and improve the human stock through eugenic interventions, individual units of manpower could be increased, and Britain could re-assert itself against the stronger bodies of Wilhelmine Germany (Searle 1976). In this distinctly biopolitical formulation, the health and efficiency of working and fighting bodies became the focus of this particular form of late Imperial energetic productivism.

The idea that efficiency increases provided a means of restoring national competitiveness was central to Mackinder's geopolitical vision. From a geographical perspective, he believed the year 1900 had marked the beginning of a 'post-Columbian epoch', the end of an age of sea-power in which the earth had been circumnavigated and almost wholly mapped. This known planet was now "a closed political system" in which political attention had to shift from conflictual "territorial expansion to the struggle for relative efficiency" (Mackinder 1904: 422). The pursuit of efficiency, a goal that was relative rather than absolute, offered a new competitive domain within which the global balance of powers could be fought over. The goal was by no means equality but continual struggle to maintain a relative position against increasingly powerful rivals. Seen as a component of a more widespread energy productivist movement, Mackinder's aim was to improve the quantity and quality of physical manpower as means to reinvigorate a declining Empire.

What effect did such ideas have in practice, and were such ideas confined to imperialistic geographers? World War I was of great consequence in shifting the onus of productivity from human labor to electrical power. Another former Co-Efficient, Haldane, had been Secretary of State for War, and afterward led a Parliamentary committee to address the conservation of coal, as part of national reconstruction efforts. In this role, with the help of the acclaimed electrical engineer Charles Merz, Haldane would help promote electrification as a means of increasing both the power and efficiency of Britain. The Coal Committee's central argument was that "the question of the conservation of coal is the question of economy in the use of coal through supplying electricity" (Haldane and Merz 1918). Their final report proposed that the existing electricity industry, composed of 600 privately owned small-scale plants, should be replaced with a rationalized system that divided Britain into 16 regions, each with a "super" electrical power plant. Connections would create a vast "interconnected power distribution system" spanning the entire nation; this "gridiron" could act as a means of transporting power equivalent to that of a thousand of tons of coal at any interconnected point across the British Isles (Cochrane 1985).

In an extension of Mackinder's emphasis on efficiency led individual improvement, Haldane's report on coal conservation had called for national electrification on the basis that it would increase the productivity of British manpower. In a formulation we might expect more to have come from Vladimir Lenin, the Committee's final report stated: "It is only by largely increasing the amount of power used in industry (by two or more times) that the average output per head (and as a consequence the wages of the individual) can be increased" (Haldane and Merz 1918: 8). Haldane's investigation into the conservation of coal had concluded that the key to national wealth lay in "the greatest possible use of power", not in a figurative sense, nor in the purely physiological sense of Mackinder's pre-war formulations, but by efficiently transforming coal into a stream of electrons that could be used to augment the power of human labor. As it was, nationalized electricity would not emerge until 1948, but the report led to the establishment of a Central Electricity Board in 1925, which began a program of connecting existing small networks into a larger grid (Hannah 1979). Such interventionist and centralized planning proposals would have seemed almost unthinkable to a previous generation of diehard Victorian liberals.

Socialist Energetics

Energetic productivism in Russia has to be seen in the context of catching up with the Western industrial powers. In terms of the extent of industrializa-

tion and the development of institutions, pre-war Imperial Russia was closer
to Asia, the Middle Eastern or Latin America (Allen 2003: 3f, 16). The Tsarist
state had already embarked on a slow course of modernization in the 19th
century. It harbored imperial ambitions in Siberia and, like Britain, suffered
a painful defeat from a 'rising power' in the Russo-Japanese War in 1904-5.
By then, it had established six non-military technical schools, opened the oil
industry in Baku to foreign capital, and had begun constructing the Trans-
Siberian Railroad (Balzer 1980: 18; Barnett 2004: 29; Moser 2018). Supported
by the military and small technical societies, electrification slowly spread between 1880-1914, particularly around industrial centers (Cummins 1988: 41,
Coopersmith 1992: 45-59). These changes galvanized a small cadre of modern-
izers and technical intelligentsia.

World War I accelerated the dissolution of the Tsarist regime and provided
an important spark for the revolutions of 1917. The Bolsheviks inherited an
economy that was very unevenly industrialized, and many technicians and
engineers were ready to put their expertise at the service of the new state
(Bailes 1978: 19-43). The war experience also gave a new urgency to the idea
of the rational management of production based on the newest technologies.
Lenin had first been skeptical of scientific management, but after the war
approved of it: "The war taught us much [...]," he noted in 1918,

> "but especially the fact that those who have the best technology, organiza-
> tion, discipline and the best machines emerge on top; it is this the war has
> taught us, and it is a good thing it has taught us. It is essential to learn that
> without machines, without discipline, it is impossible to live in modern so-
> ciety. It is necessary to master the highest technology or be crushed" (Bailes
> 1978: 49; Bailes 1977: 376).

While not all Bolsheviks were prone to such technocratic faith, Lenin and a
number of Bolshevik engineers believed the latest technologies were necessary to the survival of the young socialist state. Until his death in 1923, Lenin
would continue to push for the inclusion of technical experts in the planning
institutions of the Soviet Union—a policy of which Stalin was very critical.

Lenin's illness and death sparked not only a power struggle within the
communist party, but also conflicts over the course of industrialization. These
include the well-known controversies around the 'retreat' to state capitalism
(the New Economic Policy) and the pace of industrial development as indi-
cated in the goals stated in the Five-Year-Plans (Erlich 1967; Carr 1979; Siegelbaum 1992: 82). Much lesser known is the conflict between Viacheslav Molo-

tov, Stalin's trusted industrial administrator, and Gleb M. Krzhizhanovskii, an old friend of Lenin, who headed both the state electrification commission (GOELRO) and the state planning commission (Gosplan) in the 1920s. Planning methods had always been contentious (Haumann 1974), but in the late 1920s, the institution of long-term planning was challenged as such, and Gosplan became a site of Stalin's struggle against the older Bolshevik intelligentsia.

Drawing on the experience with the first large-scale economic plan, GOELRO, Krzhizhanovskii and other engineers had developed a theory of energetic development—*energetika*—which emphasized electrification as the 'technical-economic basis' of socialism. Attacking the authority of the GOELRO and Gosplan engineers and planners, Molotov shifted the focus on the importance of technology in a general and favored rapid industrialization on the basis of mechanical engineering, not electrification (Flakserman 1964: 145-150; Davies 1996: 135-137). While this had only little influence on the level of electrification, it cut short the administrative careers of the *energetiki* and neutralized their critique of Stalin's energy policies. Having lost their positions at the center of economic planning, most of them found a new home in the Institute of Energetics of the 'bolshevized' Academy of Science.

Energetika is most closely associated with the life and work of Gleb M. Krzhizhanovskii, an early Bolshevik and engineer who had worked for the railroads and developed a peat-fired power station under the Tsarist regime. As a technically versed comrade in arms, he rose to public office after the Bolshevik revolution and headed the central administration of the power industry (*Glavelektro*). The idea for an all-Russian electrification plan can be traced back to conversations between him and Lenin (Cummins 1988: 66-68). Krzhizhanovskii was widely-read and very familiar with the Socialist discourse of the time, but he understood himself rather as an engineer and poet than as a theorist of the revolution. Lenin had to push him to reformulate the electrification plan in a less technical way and to strengthen its character as "a political or state plan" (Krzhizhanovskii 1936: 97). In his double role as head of GOELRO and head of Gosplan, Krzhizhanovskii tried to more explicitly link electrification to the problems of constructing a Socialist economy (Russ forthcoming).

This broader understanding is already apparent in some of Krzhizhanovskii's early remarks. By 1923, he had developed an idea of energetics that was anchored in, but no longer limited to, electrification. In a discussion on wages in Gosplan, a delegate asked why an increase in productivity preceded an increase in wages and how that time lag could be explained. This knowledge, he added, would surely be of the greatest importance for managing the self-consciousness (in that case, the acceptance of low wages) of the masses. Krzhizhanovskii replied that "the formula that gives the true perspective of economic development [*razvertyvanie*] and the right approach to its higher forms—is energetic." This formula, he pointed out, was not that of Taylorism or scientific management, nor was it the mechanization of labor as pursued in GOELRO. The formula came close to GOELRO's *method*: a method of material efficiency. He envisioned energetics as a "skeleton," which, once its construction was mastered, would in a "kind of automatism" realize the maximum production of labor with the smallest expenditure of energy (State Planning Commission 1923: 46f).

What Krzhizhanovskii and the other *energetiki* had in mind can be seen from their work on the reconstruction of economic regions (*raionirovanie*). In 1920, the All-Russian central executive committee (VZIK) formed an administrative committee to prepare a method of *raioniravonie* and make a proposal for the precise course of regional borders. As part of this work, a sub-commission within Gosplan was formed, which was headed by Ivan G. Aleksandrov, a GOELRO engineer and economist, and Krzhizhanovskii. Drawing on their work on regional power stations as part of GOELRO, they developed an understanding of economic regions as "combined production complexes" formed according to "energetic principles", self-sufficient, but open, economies (Krzhizhanovskii 1957; Karelin 2010: 15). Water power and long-distance transmission would allow the location of new branches of industries in underdeveloped areas. This concept of regionalism was explicitly contrasted with the uneven development of industry in capitalist countries: Socialist regions would be as autarkic as possible in terms of energy and would otherwise specialize in different industries according to locally available resources and climatic conditions.

Krzhizhanovskii understood his energetic plans as a distinctly Socialist realization of a productive potential that had developed under capitalism. He surmised that behind the historical form the power industry had taken in capitalist countries lurked the truth of energetic principles. This common point of reference both justified international comparisons and was actualized by them. In his first speech 'Electrification and the Planning Economy' after Lenin's death in 1924, Krzhizhanovskii emphasized electrification as a general technological development, referring to the commissions in Britain, France, and Bulgaria (1924: 3). Gosplan dedicated fifty pages of its bulletin to a discussion of the first World Power Conference (WPC)—an international conference on the power economy—to assess GOELRO against other countries' planned electrification. The report concluded that GOELRO was in line with the two basic principles of modern electrical development projects: concentration and interconnection. Capitalist countries, gloated the reporter, became aware that competition in electrical systems was detrimental because of the need for multiple investments in a parallel infrastructure (Kukel' 1925: 131-133). To the Soviet *energetiki*, the planned forms of economic organization in capitalist countries—trusts, syndicates, and institutions of the war economy—were evidence of a general economic development and as such deserved attention. They were truth in a wrong form: rational organization separated from the struggle to realize a Socialist order.

In Newcastle-upon-Tyne, the heart of the British coal industry, the engineer Charles Merz, already discussed in the previous section, had demonstrated as early as 1904 that the bigger the plant, and the greater the mix of load profiles, the greater the operating efficiency and profitability that could be achieved.[1] If not Merz's iteration in particular, this general model of electrical development, emphasizing economies of scale and the mix of different load profiles to increase profitability, had become widespread in the 1920s. In fact, the GOELRO system of large regional stations followed this model, brushing aside more radical approaches (Coopersmith 1992: 151). The *energetiki* interpreted this as a general turn to centralization as capitalist countries unconsciously following a form of technological development which would eventually usher them into socialism. The Soviet engineer Modest Rubinstein would later argue that socialism was a necessary precondition for the 'full development' of electrification (Rubinstein 1971: 189). British Conservatives thought much the same about its centralizing tendencies and argued Haldane's plans for centralized electrification was "jumping the first fence of socialism" (Hannah 1979: 330). In the words of Gosplan's American correspondent, electrification would be capitalism's last technological achievement.

When Stalin announced the building of socialism in one country in 1925, these comparisons took on a less emancipatory and more competitive form. Electrification would not only soothe internal disagreements but also mediate external conflict: Electrification was a weapon in an economic war. "The general situation is such," reflected Krzhizhanovskii (1925a: 12) under the impres-

---

1   Merz had co-authored Haldane's coal conservation report in 1918. For the role of Merz/Mclellans (1904) calculations, see Hughes (1993: 454).

sion of the first WPC and reflecting a sentiment similar to that of Mackinder's geography of efficiency, "that in the near future the center of the gravity of struggle shifts from military to economic conflicts." Not for a moment did he fall for the supposed peaceableness of the 'technocratic internationalism' championed by the British host, who pictured all nations advancing together by making use of the "marvelous resources of nature" (WPC 1925: viii). For Krzhizhanovskii, the WPC was a tool of the electrotechnical industry, which, accelerated by wartime industry, was desperately searching for new markets. He was convinced to live in a moment in which international conflict "expresses itself in the struggle for energetic resources." What he meant was not so much territorial struggle, but a race to develop one's territory: "If we look at what is done in America (sic), how they build their economic proposition, then you can see that this powerful state pervades itself with 'energetic rails' and grids, which become the backbone of its economy." (1925b: 11) The Soviet state had to do the same, but better, to win the economic war for the future (Coopersmith 1992: 251).

Krzhizhanovskii thought that it would be possible for a socialist country to catch up and even surpass capitalist countries. Only socialist countries could combine central planning with national ownership of power utilities and industries, so that the interests of producers and consumers were aligned, and electrification would operate as a rationalizing and socializing force. Even if the energy economy of capitalist countries—calculated in the physiologically centered amount of power produced per person—was still many times more powerful, their forces acted chaotically against each other, in a "complex polygon" (Krzhizhanovskii 1928: 35). When the metabolism of nature and society was rationally regulated, Krzhizhanovskii argued, the 'forces of nature' and human labor would come to work in parallel, as a single, rectified force. Through rational planning of the energy-equipment of labor, the Soviet Union would appropriate the energetic law of economic development and accomplish it. The struggle against and emancipation from the elements of nature was universal, and the Soviet Union should be judged in terms of the amount of natural power it was able to exploit (Krzhizhanovskii 1928: 18).

Krzhizhanovskii wrote his strongest papers on *energetika* in preparation of the first *pyatiletka* between 1925-1928. By that time, he felt ready to make "an energetic approach to economic problems" the basis of the first prospective plan (1925b: 10), and energy indeed had a prominent place in the plan (State Planning Commission 1930: 24-26). Scholars in the Communist Academy of Science picked up energetic ideas and began empirical studies, which, in turn, helped to make Krzhizhanovskii's thinking more specific. However, this was also the time when his influence in Gosplan was already waning. Stalin's path to securing state power made use of industrial policies in an instrumental way and cut short many alternative projects and approaches to planning (Shearer 1996: 12-13). He had long been sceptical of the technocratic engineers of Gosplan and was eager to demote them to less influential positions. The model of industrial development shifted from a focus on electrification to machine-building and Krzhizhanovskii's electrification plan for the Second Five-Year-Plan was quietly ignored by Stalin and Molotov (Bailes 1978: 185). In the perspective of this view on economic development, the output of electricity was now no more important than the output of tractors to catch up with capitalist countries. While material accounting continued to play a role in Soviet planning, there was no equally bold vision of a moneyless economy after 'energetika': the energetiki were, arguably, the last Soviet planners who believed they were building an economy in kind (Davies 1996: 463).

Epilogue

In 1933, the North American engineer Howard Scott argued in the nation's press that the mass unemployment and economic stagnation of that decade's economic depression had resulted from a collective failure to understand that "physical wealth is not measured in terms of labor, goods, or money, but in terms of energy" (Scott 1933). Measured in ergs, joules, and calories, energy was a unit in accordance with universal laws, a more precise indicator of wealth than dollars, whose value was relative to that of other currencies and subject to inflation. With no metrological consistency and no direct relation to the material world, dollars were "a purely arbitrary unit" (ibid). Seemingly unmoored from physical reality, Scott believed pecuniary economics had caused the dramatic imbalances to the US economy that were currently at work. Having risen unaccountably, prices seemed no longer to correlate with utility. Moreover, their value merely reflected the tenets of wasteful competition-driven transactions, obsolescence, and debt rather transactions that meet human needs. Simultaneously, technological advancement was undermining the human components of industrialism; productivity increases were no longer dependent on increased human labor, and this had created technological unemployment.

Scott's solution to economic depression had lain in physics, as he stated "the law of Conservation of Energy has a perfectly definite social implication"; economic stability could be achieved if society saved energy as they did dollars (ibid). As it was, energy went unaccounted for aside from its in terms of their monetary cost. What could be done? Scott's message was that the current ruling class of politicians, economists, and lawyers should be replaced by engineers and technicians who would manage the economy according to the principles of technological efficiency, in which the maximization of energy efficiency would be the goal rather than the pursuit of pecuniary wealth. Given the apparent failure of orthodox economics to solve the crisis, Scott's populist 'Technocracy Movement', the most prominent iteration of a more widely shared energetic productivism, enjoyed a brief period of populist credibility before orthodox economic thinking reasserted itself (Elsner 1967).

Scott's Technocracy movement has long been seen as an eccentric outlier in economic history, but we have presented two less well-known versions of energetic productivism that were central to state planning in Great Britain and the Soviet Union, and which both preceded this more well-known call for energy-driven development and exceeded it in consequence. Productivism with an accounting system based on labor, energetic prime movers, and resources, clearly contributed to more orthodox implementations of energo-materialist productivism at the beginning of the twentieth century, not least national electrification. Indeed, its advocates considered it more universal than later 'monetary' conceptions of the economy and a means to restore various perceived imbalances. With the League of Nations and the International Labor Organization poised to build an international statistical infrastructure, information on other countries was assembled from books, international conferences and economic journals and services. Energy constituted an energo-material and quantifiable entity that could be measured across all economic sectors, on the basis of which states could compare and compete (Guyol 1960).

Energy productivists engaged in an indirect form of competition. We have shown that, in close observation, they strive to outdo their competitors, Germany in the British case, and the capitalist world in the Soviet case, in maximizing the productivity of land, labor and resources by utilizing electrical power. It is notable that there was very little debate about the overarching goal of energy productivism. Their goal was not a shared norm, an idea of what society should be, but a shared understanding of how economic progress could be achieved. In other words, energy productivism implies a theory of history as a teleological process of technological progress, a view accepted across the political spectrum. Because this goal was not absolute but one enacted via the efficacy of technologies that are always relative in efficiency, energetic productivism could entail endless competition. Moreover, as the interwar period shows, this competition was only 'formally' peaceful. For all its focus on domestic economic reform, energy policies remained linked to questions of national security, access to strategic resources, and capacity for armed conflict. Competition over the provision of power never ceased to have a double meaning.

References

Allen, Robert C. (2003): Farm to Factory. A Reinterpretation of the Soviet Industrial Debate, Princeton: Princeton University Press.

Arvay, Janos (1994): "The Material Product System. A Retrospective." In: Zoltan Kennedy (ed.), The Accounts of Nations, Amsterdam: IOS Press, pp. 218-236.

Bailes, Kendall E. (1977): "Alexei Gastev and the Soviet Controversy over Taylorism, 1918-24." In: Soviet Studies 29/3, pp. 373–394.

Bailes, Kendall E. (1978): Technology and Society under Lenin and Stalin: Origins of the Soviet Technical Intelligentsia, 1917-1941, Princeton: Princeton University Press.

Balzer, Harvey D. (1980): "Educating Engineers: Economic Politics and Technical Training in Tsarist Russia." Ph.D., University of Pennsylvania.

Barnett, Vincent (2004): The Revolutionary Russian Economy, 1890-1940: Ideas, Debates and Alternatives, London: Routledge.

Breger, Herbert (1982): Die Natur als arbeitende Maschine: Zur Entstehung des Energiebegriffs in der Physik, 1840-1850, Frankfurt: Campus Verlag.

Cain, P. J. (2002): Hobson and Imperialism: Radicalism, New Liberalism, and Finance 1887-1938, Oxford: Oxford University Press.

Carr, Edward Hallett (1979): The Russian Revolution: from Lenin to Stalin, New York: Free Press.

Chandler, Alfred D. (2002): The Visible Hand: The Managerial Revolution in American Business, Cambridge, MA: Harvard University Press.

Cochrane, R. (1985): Power to the People: The Story of the National Grid, 1935-1985, Feltham: Newnes Books.

Coopersmith, Jonathan (1992): The Electrification of Russia, 1880-1926, Ithaca: Cornell University Press.

Cummins, Alex G. (1988): "The Road to NEP, the State Commission for the Electrification of Russia (GOELRO): A Study in Technology, Mobilization, and Economic Planning." Ph.D., University of Michigan.

Davies, Robert William (1996): Crisis and Progress in the Soviet Economy, 1931-1933, London: Macmillan.

Elsner Jr., Henry (1967): Technocrats: Prophets of Automation, Syracuse: Syracuse University Press.

Erlich, Alexander (1967): The Soviet Industrialisation Debate, 1924-1928. Cambridge, MA: Harvard University Press.

Flakserman, Iuri N. (1964): Gleb Maksimilianovich Krzhizhanovskii, Moscow: Izdatel'stvo Nauka.

Friedberg, Aaron (1988): The Weary Titan: Britain and the Experience of Relative Decline, 1895-1905, Princeton: Princeton University Press.

Friedrich, Brestislav/James, Jeremiah (2017): "From Berlin-Dahlem to the Fronts of World War 1: The Role of Fritz Haber and His Kaiser Wilhelm Institute in German Chemical Warfare." In: Bretislav Friedrich, Dieter Hoffmann, Jürgen Renn, Florian Schmaltz, Martin Wolf (eds.), One Hundred Years of Chemical Warfare: Research, Deployment, Consequences, Cham: Springer, pp. 25–45.

Garavini, Giuliano (2019): The Rise & Fall of OPEC in the Twentieth Century, Oxford: Oxford University Press.

Guyol, N. (1960): "Energy Consumption and Economic Development." In: Norton Ginsburg (ed.), Essays on Geography and Economic Development, Chicago: Chicago University Press.

Haldane, Richard B./Merz, Charles (1918): The Coal Conservation Committee, Final Report, London: HMSO.

Hannah, Leslie (1979): Electricity Before Nationalisation: A Study of the Development of the Electricity Supply Industry in Britain to 1948, London: Macmillan.

Hardach, Gerd (1981): The First World War, 1914-1918, Berkeley: University of California Press.

Haumann, Heiko (1974): Beginn der Planwirtschaft: Elektrifizierung, Wirtschaftsplanung und gesellschaftliche Entwicklung Sowjetrusslands, 1917-1921, Düsseldorf: Bertelsmann.

Hausman, William J./Hertner, Peter/Wilkins, Mira (2008): Global Electrification Multinational Enterprise and International Finance in the History of Light and Power, 1878-2007, Cambridge: Cambridge University Press.

Hays, Samuel P. (1999): *Conservation and the Gospel of Efficiency: The Progressive Conservation Movement, 1890-1920*. Pittsburgh: University of Pittsburgh Press.

Hobsbawm, Eric J. (1989): The Age of Empire, 1875-1914, New York: Vintage.

Hobson, John A. (1902): Imperialism: A Study, London: James Nisbet & co.

Hughes, Thomas P. (1993): Networks of Power: Electrification in Western Society, 1880-1930, Baltimore: JHU Press.

Jevons, Herbert (1931): 'The Second Industrial Revolution', In: The Economic Journal 41/161, pp. 1-18.

Karelin, E. G. (2010): "'Zapadnaia Oblast Gosplana': Iz Istorii Ekonomicheskogo Rayonirovaniya Strany v 1920-e Gody." In: Rossiiskaia Istoriia 2, pp. 15–18.

Kearns, Gerry (2009): Geopolitics and Empire: The Legacy of Halford Mackinder. Oxford: Oxford University Press.

Krzhizhanovskii, Gleb M. (1924): "Elektrifikaciia i Planovoe Khoziaistvo [Electrification and the Planning Economy]." In: Planovoe Khoziaistvo 2, pp. 3-9.

Krzhizhanovskii, Gleb M. (1925a): "Perspektivy Elektrifikaciia [Perspectives of Electrification]." In: Planovoe Khoziaistvo 2, pp. 3-21.

Krzhizhanovskii, Gleb M. (1925b): "K peresmotru plana GOELRO [On a revision of the GOELRO plan]." In: Planovoe Khoziaistvo 7, pp. 7–28.

Krzhizhanovskii, Gleb M. (1928): "Zadachi Energeticheskogo Khosiaistva [Tasks of the Energy Economy]." In: Planovoe Khosiaistvo 6, pp. 7–43.

Krzhizhanovski, Gleb M. (1936 [1931]): "Osnovy tekhniko-ekonomicheskoi rekonstrukcii SSSR [The basis of the technical-economic reconstruction of the USSR]." In: Gleb M. Krzhizhanovskii (ed.), Sochineniia III: Socialisticheskoe Stroitel'stvo, Moscow: Gosudarstvennoe energeticheskoe izdatel'stvo, pp. 298-316.

Krzhizhanovskii, Gleb M. (1957): Voprosy ekonomicheskogo raionirovaniia SSSR. Sbornik materialov i statei (1917-1929 gg.) [Problems of Soviet economic regionalisation, a collection of materials and articles], Moscow: Gosudarstvennoe izdatel'stvo politicheskoi literatury.

Kukel', S. A. (1925): "Pervaia vsemirnaya konferenciia energetiki v Londone [First World Power Conference in London]." In: Planovoe Khoziaistvo 1, pp. 123–152.

Livingstone, David (2008): The Geographical Tradition: Episodes in the History of a Contested Enterprise, Oxford: Blackwell.

Mackinder, Halford J. (1904): "The Geographical Pivot of History." In: The Geographical Journal 23/4, pp. 421-437.

Mackinder, Halford J. (1905): "Man-Power as a Measure of National and Imperial Strength." In: The National Review 44, pp. 136-143.

Mackinder, Halford J. (1906): Money-Power and Man-Power: the underlying principles rather than the statistics of tariff reform, London: Simpkin, Marshall & Co. Ltd.

Maier, Charles (1970): "Between Taylorism and Technocracy: European Ideologies and the Vision of Industrial Productivity in the 1920s." In: Journal of Contemporary History 5, pp. 27-61.

Maier, Charles (1988): In Search of Stability: Explorations in Historical Political Economy, Cambridge: Cambridge University Press.

McKinnon, Andrew (2010): "Energy and society: Herbert Spencer's 'energetic sociology' of social evolution and beyond." In: Journal of Classical Sociology 10/4, pp. 439—455.

Meer, Elisabeth van (2012): "The Transatlantic Pursuit of a World Engineering Federation: For the Profession, the Nation, and International Peace, 1918–48." In: Technology and Culture 53/1, pp. 120–145.

Michalka, Wolfgang (1997): "From War Economy to 'New Economy': World War I and the Conservative Debate About the 'Other' Modernity in Germany." In: Bernd Hüppauf (ed.), War, Violence and the Modern Condition, Berlin: De Gruyter, pp. 77–95.

Mirowski, Philip (1989): More Heat than Light: Economics as Social Physics, Physics as Nature's Economics, Cambridge: Cambridge University Press.

Mirowski, Philip (2002): Machine Dreams: economics becomes a cyborg science, Cambridge: Cambridge University Press.

Mommsen, Wolfgang J. (1990): Max Weber and German Politics, 1890-1920, Chicago: University of Chicago Press.

Moser, Nat (2018): Oil and the Economy of Russia: From the Late-Tsarist to the Post-Soviet Period, London: Routledge, Taylor & Francis Group.

Müller, Ernst (2020): "Energy." In: Forum Interdisziplinäre Begriffsgeschichte 9/1, pp. 29-39.

Mumford, Lewis (1934): Technics and Civilization, Chicago: University of Chicago Press.

Nef, John (1932): The Rise of the British Coal Industry, London: George Routledge.

Polelle, Mark (1999): Raising Cartographic Consciousness: The Social and Foreign Policy Vision of Geopolitics in the Twentieth Century, Lanham: Lexington Books.

Rabinbach, Anson (1992): The Human Motor: Energy, Fatigue, and the Origins of Modernity, Berkeley: University of California Press.

Rabinbach, Anson (2018): The Eclipse of the Utopias of Labor, New York: Fordham University Press.

Rose, Andreas (2017): Between Empire and Continent: British Foreign Policy before the First World War, New York: Berghahn Books.

Rubinstein, Modest (1971 [1931]): "Electrification as the Basis of Technical Reconstruction in the Soviet Union." Bukharin, N. et al, ed., Science at the Crossroads: Papers from the Second International Congress of the History of Science and Technology, 1931, London: Frank Cass & Co, pp. 115-145.

Russ, Daniela (2021 forthcoming): "The Ennoblement of Nature: Gleb M. Krzhizhanovskii's 'Energetika' and Socialist Industrialization." In: Historical Materialism.

Sampson, Anthony (1975): The Seven Sisters: The Great Oil Companies and the World They Made, London: Hodder and Stoughton.

Saul, S.B. (1985): The Myth of the Great Depression, 1873-1896, London: Macmillan.

Scally, Robert James (2015): The Origins of the Lloyd George Coalition: The Politics of Social Imperialism, 1900-1918, Princeton: Princeton University Press.

Schabas, Margaret (2005): The Natural Origins of Economics, Chicago: University of Chicago Press.

Scott, H. (1933): 'Technology Smashes the Price System." In: Harpers' Magazine 166, pp. 129-142.

Searle, Gerald (1971): The Quest for National Efficiency: A Study in British Political and Political Thought, 1899- 1914, Berkeley: University of California Press.

Searle, Gerald (1976): Eugenics and Politics in Britain, 1900-1914, Leyden: Noordhoff.

Searle, Gerald (2002): "'National Efficiency' and the 'Lessons' of the War." In: David Omissi/Andrew Thompson (eds.), The Impact of the South African War, London: Palgrave Macmillan, pp. 194-211.

Shearer, David R. (1996): Industry, State, and Society in Stalin's Russia, 1926-1934, Ithaca: Cornell University Press.

Siegelbaum, Lewis H. (1992): Soviet State and Society between Revolutions, 1918-1929, Cambridge: Cambridge University Press.

Slobodian, Quinn (2018): Globalists. The End of Empire and the Birth of Neoliberalism, Cambridge, MA: Harvard University Press.

Smith, Neil (2003): American Empire: Roosevelt's Geographer and the Prelude to Globalization, Berkeley: University of California Press.

Snow, Alpheus Henry (1919): "The Mandatary System under the Covenant of the League of Nations." In: Proceedings of the Academy of Political Science in the City of New York 8/3, pp. 68–79.

Solvay, Ernest (1900): Notes sur le productivisme et le comptabilisme, Bruxelles: H. Lamertin.

State Planning Commission (1923): "Plenum Gosplana [Gosplan plenum]." In: Planovoe Khoziaistvo 6–7, pp. 39–76.

State Planning Commission (1930): Pervyi Piatiletnii Plan Narodno-Khoziaistvennogo Stroitel'stva SSSR [First Five Year Plan of the National Economic Construction of the USSR], Moscow: Izdatel'stvo Planovoe Khoziaistva.

Strachey, John (1959): The End of Empire. London: Gollancz.

Thomas, William (2015): Rational Action: The Sciences of Policy in Britain and America, 1940-1969, Cambridge, MA: MIT Press.

Thompson, Andrew S. (1997): "Tariff Reform: An Imperial Strategy, 1903-1913." In: The Historical Journal 40/4, pp. 1033-1054.

Tooze, Adam (2001): Statistics and the German State, 1900-1945: The Making of Modern Economic Knowledge, Cambridge: Cambridge University Press.

Tooze, Adam (2015): The Deluge: The Great War, America and the Remaking of Global Order, 1916-1931, London: Penguin.

Turnbull, Thomas (2020): 'Toward histories of saving energy: Erich Walter Zimmermann and the struggle against "one-sided materialistic determinism."' In: Journal of Energy History/Revue d'Histoire de l'Énergie 1/4, unpaginated.

Tyrell, Ian (2015): Crisis of the Wasteful Nation: Empire in Theodore Roosevelt's America, Chicago: University of Chicago Press.

Underwood, Ted (1995): "Productivism and the Vogue for 'Energy' in Late Eighteenth-Century Britain." In: Studies in Romanticism 34/1, pp. 103-125.

Veblen, Thorstein (1975 [1921]): The Engineers and the Price System, New York: Augustus M. Kelly.

Wilkins, Mira (2009): The History of Foreign Investment in the United States, 1914-1945, Cambridge, MA: Harvard University Press.

Wise, M. Norton/Smith, Crosbie (1989a): "Work and Waste: Political Economy and Natural Philosophy in Nineteenth Century Britain (I)." In: *History of Science* 27/3, pp. 263–301.

Wise, M. Norton/Smith, Crosbie (1989b): "Work and Waste: Political Economy and Natural Philosophy in Nineteenth Century Britain (II)." In: *History of Science* 27/4, pp. 391–449.

Wise, M. Norton/Smith, Crosbie (1990): "Work and Waste: Political Economy and Natural Philosophy in Nineteenth Century Britain (III)." In: *History of Science* 28/3, pp. 221–261.

World Power Conference (1925): The Transactions of the First World Power Conference, London, June 30th to July 12th, 1924, London: P. Lund, Humphries & Co., Ltd.

Zimmermann, Erich (1933): World Resources and Industries: A Functional Appraisal of the Availability of Agricultural and Industrial Resources, New York: Harper & Brothers.

Competition and Emergent Technologies

Diplomacy and Artificial Intelligence in Global Political Competition

Didzis Kļaviņš

The arts of diplomacy have traditionally been associated with the balance of power, which is one of the founding principles of Realpolitik. By taking into account the fact that reconciliation has historically been necessary between conflicting parties, diplomats have been trusted with the role of mediators. This mediating function has promoted the establishment and development of Ministries of Foreign Affairs (MFAs) and representations, and also the association of diplomatic practice with the concept of co-operation. This commonplace view of diplomacy has enabled it to constantly establish and renew itself under different systems of world politics, from the early modern period to the present day (see Youssef in this volume). Although diplomacy as a process of communication and negotiation has been present wherever different and competing political entities have existed, and thus surrounded by continuous changes, it has been able to successfully adapt until now without changing its core. To paraphrase Iver B. Neumann (2013, 2015), old sites of diplomacy have assumed new characteristics, while new sites are physically and virtually emerging.[1]

The enormous growth in political interest and economic investment in artificial intelligence (AI) has the potential, this chapter argues, to produce fundamental changes in both the practice of diplomacy and the nature of inter-state competition. Although it may seem that AI is one of the neutral fields in which there is no increasing state competition, in practice this assumption is misleading. As AI can offer governments sustainable competitive

1   This work was supported by the European Regional Development Fund project 'Post-doctoral Research Aid', project title 'Comparative research on foreign ministries in Baltic States and Nordic Countries (2012–2015)', research application Nr. 1.1.1.2/VIAA/1/16/082 and research agreement Nr. 1.1.1.2/16/I/001.

advantages, rivalry encourages states and other political actors to use diplomatic capabilities to achieve their goals. Given that AI-powered technologies have great potential to rearrange winners and losers in global markets, and thus to affect the balance of power in world politics, it is unsurprising that they are becoming a major focus for diplomats and diplomatic institutions. Yet the nature of AI technology challenges traditional assumptions of how diplomacy should function. As AI interacts with a wide range of conventional foreign policy issues, it requires specific knowledge from diplomats, structural reorganizations, and process re-engineering in foreign ministries. "The imminent transformations of AI", observe Scott, Heumann and Lorenz,

> "intersect with conventional foreign policy issues in fundamental ways. At the highest level, it is the impact on the balance of global power. The potential that AI brings to advance national economic and security interests has triggered a heated competition among governments to gain a strategic advantage [...] it will not be enough to create a special office for AI" (2018: 7-9).

Given that large AI companies are already influencing the international agenda, this in turn requires greater involvement and expertise of diplomatic institutions in setting international framework conditions for AI.

The purpose of this contribution is to investigate how diplomacy, as an instrument of foreign policy, can adapt to the emergence of AI as a rapidly developing technology in an era of intensified global competition. It does not seek to offer a definitive conclusion concerning the relationship between diplomacy and competition. Rather, it aims to describe the complexity and interplay between diplomacy and competition in the race for dominance in the emergent technology of emerging artificial intelligence. It considers, first, how diplomacy has evolved and since the end of the Cold War, before evaluating its interactions with present-day state competition. It then pivots to consider the role of AI in reshaping the role of diplomacy in state competition and raises the question of whether AI can be considered a novel and qualitatively different arena for state competition, in contrast to more long-standing policy fields such as climate, trade and human rights.

The Transformation of Diplomacy

Traditional understandings of diplomacy have been related to its use as the primary instrument for the implementation of national foreign policies. In this case, diplomacy is associated with the MFA, which has played a vitally significant role in the central administrative hierarchy of many states for several centuries and continues to do so today. Since at least the turn of the 21st century, however, there has been a significant expansion in the variety of participants and political processes in the international system. Diplomacy must now be understood more broadly. It cannot be reduced just to what is practiced by MFAs but should instead be regarded as a part of a far more multifaceted international process. It is also important to take into account varied types and sub-types of diplomacy, which have proliferated since the beginning of the 21st century (Barston 2006; Constantinou et al. 2016; Cooper et al. 2013; Stanzel 2018).

It may often seem that diplomacy, understood as a mere instrument, has no decisive significance in world politics (Brown 2019; Cohen 2013; Tavares 2018). On this view, diplomats are actively involved in the preparation of visits, participates in high-level negotiations or fulfil other diplomatic duties, but their role is not determining (Singh 2002). This is to understate, however, the crucial enabling role that diplomacy plays in modern world politics. According to Sending, Pouloit and Neumann (2015: 1): "many global phenomena of our time, from international law to world order, through humanitarianism, global hierarchies, and public power, are made possible by evolving forms of diplomacy". Political, economic, safety and social issues are only the most visible fields which are promoted by diplomatic transformation. Given that diplomacy as a "master-institution" of international politics (Wight 1979: 113) has undergone major changes in the last thirty years, it is important to look at the main features of change in diplomacy.

Since the end of the Cold War, dynamic changes have been observed in diplomacy, which over many centuries has been convincingly associated with foreign policy implemented by the state and has been a vital component in the implementation of national interests. "To the degree that contemporary diplomacy is new," writes Iver B. Neumann (2015: 3),

> "it is not because of diplomacy's internal dynamics. Neither it is due to the emergence of new core tasks. Newness stems from change in the general political and social fields that surround diplomacy."

Globalization (Eisenstadt 2012), increasing competition and a "rapidly changing international environment" (Moses/Knutsen 2001: 357; Leijten 2019: 3) require us to review the significance of diplomacy in a wider pattern and context. New types and varieties of diplomacy that take place in different sites
are explicit confirmation of this (Cooper et al. 2013). Digital diplomacy (Bjola
2018; Bjola/Zaiotti 2021), science diplomacy (AWTI 2017; Melchor 2020; Miremadi 2016; Rüffin 2018; Soler 2020) and innovation diplomacy (Bound 2016;
Leijten 2016, 2017) are only a few examples that demonstrate the nature and
variety of diplomatic changes.

One way to understand and analyze rapid changes in diplomacy is through
the approach of James N. Rosenau (2009). In describing fundamental changes
in the international system, the author uses the term "turbulence". According
to Rosenau, this influences the very foundation of the international system
(ibid). The changes caused by turbulence are more rapid than normal political changes, and they do not take place via conventional forms of interaction in international policy. Moreover, "turbulence" is characterized by complexity and instability, as well as by its sometimes contradictory nature. Describing "turbulent" transformation, Rosenau has proposed the bifurcationist
paradigm that

> "focuses on two prime sets of tensions deemed to be unfold in world politics
> during the present era: one highlights tensions between change and conti-
> nuity and the other involves the tensions that flow from the clash of central-
> izing and decentralizing dynamics which shape the changes and sustain the
> continuities" (Rosenau 2006: 218).

In this context of the dynamics of change and statics of continuity researchers
such as Murat Gül (2009) have argued it even if it is still unclear whether global
turbulence is a permanent or a temporary condition, changes are transforming the parameters of world politics.

One example of the impact and dynamics of change is the MFA (Hocking
2007; Rana, 2004, 2007, 2011, 2013; Rana/Kurbalija 2007). The MFA has historically fulfilled the role of "gate-keeper" between international and domestic politics (Hocking/Spence 2002: 1-17). In conformity with national interests
and norms of activity developed over centuries, the MFA has been regarded as
an exclusive public administration institution, the monopoly status of which
in foreign affairs is not doubted. However, the situation has changed since
the end of the 20th century because the MFA, although still the leading public administration institution in foreign affairs, is forced to take the activities

of other institutions and participants into account (Constantinou et al. 2016; Hocking/Spence 2002; Kleiner 2008; Rana 2011). Moreover, the variety of new participants and subjects in foreign affairs has been promoted even more by globalization and processes related to information and communication technologies.

Nowadays, it is impossible to find any central administration institution which would be internationally isolated or closed (Greenstock 2013: 115). The MFAs are no exception. In response to external environmental changes, foreign services today are forced to restructure and expand their boundaries. Adapting Brian Hocking's theoretical reflections on images of diplomatic systems (2002), the MFA is a good example of a transition from the "gate-keeper" model to "boundary-spanner image". The new model is based on the assumption of a reformed MFA, which, by relinquishing its monopoly on foreign affairs, places itself at the center of international relations. Unlike a traditional ministry of foreign affairs where the "gate-keeper" approach dominates, the "boundary-spanner" delegates part of its functions to other participants, and serves as a service provider to all those who need support in the use of international mechanisms. In this case, we can talk about support mechanisms for other public administrations, as well as diverse support for representatives of different social groups, such non-governmental organizations (Hocking/Spence 2002: 1-17).

Speaking about the provision of support to other state institutions, it is important to discuss the use of the "whole-of-government approach" in the formation of international issues and managing of public administration (Christensen/Lægreid 2007). The types of support MFAs offer to other public institutions may be different, starting from the co-ordination of cross-institutional issues, to the servicing of all government institutions. They thereby act as the central component of a "national diplomatic system" (Hocking 2016: 74-75). The functions of the employees of diplomatic representatives have similarly broadened. In order to be able to establish a co-ordinated policy in host countries, the powers of activity of ambassadors of many countries have been broadened and they are fulfilling the role of the "national team leader" abroad (Rana 2011: 136).

Regardless of the size of the country or political regime, the role of the MFAs in the co-ordination of foreign policy has thereby increased. The ability to form the "whole-of-government approach" in foreign affairs by promoting the co-operation of all administrative institutions in the achievement of common political objectives is regarded as the essential factor in the modernization of the work of MFAs (Hocking et al. 2012). More attention is paid to the use of action policy instruments in practice and work outside the central body: for example, the creation of co-operation with diasporas and activities of commercial diplomacy (Birka/Kļaviņš 2020). By responding to varied agenda issues, more and more specialists are being employed in MFAs alongside diplomats of a classical type. Diplomacy embraces an even wider range of subjects which also means the acquisition of new and varied knowledge for diplomats or agents involved in the diplomatic process, such as the use of newest technologies in the formation of national branding, the applicability of artificial intelligence in the promotion of the competitiveness of the country or the creation of scientific diplomacy (Bjola 2019, 2020).

Diplomatic representations abroad are also becoming more varied and are forced to redirect their activity to specific work tasks and functions (Hocking et al. 2012). The number of mobile and joint embassies is accordingly growing. Diplomats are involved more actively in the creation of the national image by using innovative communication solutions (Bjola/Holmes 2015). More emphasis is also placed on a social networking and partnership-orientated approach, which helps the MFAs to create purposeful co-operation with nongovernmental actors (Hocking et al. 2012; Moses/Knutsen 2001; Rana 2011).

One of the features which characterizes the essence of diplomacy in the 21st century quite well is the use of modern means of communication in everyday circulation, which change the nature of diplomatic communication. Digital proficiency has become almost a must-have skill in many MFAs. Brian Hocking and Jan Melissen (2015) have rightly argued that it is necessary to keep in mind that "the use of websites and social networking sites like Facebook, Twitter and other online platforms for public diplomacy is just the tip of the larger digital iceberg" (Hocking/Melissen 2015: 30). During the COVID-19 pandemic even so-called Zoom diplomacy has become "the New Normal" for diplomats worldwide (Boehm 2020; Shapiro/Rakov 2020). These new means of communication—which generate vast quantities of information for diplomats to process—change the dynamics of diplomatic work, demanding faster responses and new principles for the selection of relevant information to communicate to other government agencies. With a view to establishing closer dialogue with society, many MFAs are seeking to reduce the time necessary to reach a co-ordinated position across government agencies, or to reach common decisions about policy (Rana 2011; Hocking et al. 2012, 2013).

Although it may seem that diplomacy has already experienced significant changes the trends of development of diplomacy and increasing competition in world politics (e.g. promoting and attracting Foreign Direct Investment) confirms that many large changes are still expected: the emergence of AI as a major policy field foremost among them.

If we view such changes from the perspective of conventional diplomacy, there is an issue regarding the readiness of each country and ability to adjust to such changes. Will MFAs be able to successfully adjust their practice to new types and formats of co-operation with other governmental and non-governmental actors? The rapid development of technologies and the financial possibilities of non-governmental players will continue to be a challenge for the foreign ministries of small countries. As MFAs play a crucial role in the changing "national diplomatic system" (Hocking 2013) and in implementing numerous foreign policy goals, small countries will be required to balance the "tous azimuts" foreign policy approach with their real capabilities. Insufficient financing and human resources may even cause encumbrances for the full functioning of the services of foreign affairs of these countries in competitive global politics. On the other hand, such challenges may also encourage small countries to explore and specialize in particular foreign policy niches. The next section describes how AI affects diplomacy, as well as the role of diplomacy in this growing international competition. To better answer these questions, it is first important to define what artificial intelligence is.

Artificial Intelligence and Competition

Analyzing the international challenges of AI transformation, Ben Scott, Stefan Heumann, and Philippe Lorenz (2018) describe three topical areas (economic disruption and opportunity; security and autonomous weapons systems; democracy and ethics) that require the engagement of diplomacy. These challenges also require a specific foreign policy toolbox, which includes policy making, public diplomacy, bilateral and multilateral engagement, actions through international and treaty organizations, conventions and partnerships, grant-making and information-gathering and analysis (Scott/Heumann/Lorenz 2018). All of these activities are likely to have a strongly competitive dimension. As Claudio Feijóo (2020:1) and others have noted, "many expect that the winners of the AI development race will dominate the coming decades economically and geopolitically, potentially exacerbating tensions between countries". Due to the expansion of big data, advanced algorithms and fast computing power, AI has become a highly demanded technology of the 21st century. While AI technologies and applications continue to evolve and shape many industries and sectors such as transportation, security and healthcare, the AI field in general "is shifting toward building intelligent systems that can collaborate effectively with people, including creative ways to develop interactive and scalable ways for people to teach robots" (One Hundred Year Study on Artificial Intelligence (AI100) 2016: 9). Conversational AI, large-scale machine learning, robotics, Internet of Thigs (IoT), deep learning, natural language processing, neuromorphic computing, reinforcement learning, computer vision, collaborative systems, algorithmic game theory, computational social choice, crowdsourcing and human computation are rapidly expanding areas of AI research (Yao 2020; One Hundred Year Study on Artificial Intelligence (AI100) 2016: 9). Although the manifestations of AI are different, they are united by a common goal—"to create computer software and/or hardware systems that exhibit thinking comparable to that of humans, in other words, to display characteristics usually associated with human intelligence" (Lucci/Kopec 2015: 6).

The competition for AI superiority has been ongoing for several years and is widely analyzed in the literature (Allen/Chan 2017; Cummings 2017; Drezner 2019; Feng 2019; Horowitz et al. 2018; Johnson 2019). There are several reasons for this, but the main ones are economic benefits because it can dramatically boost productivity. According to Bell, "one of the great promises of AI is its potential for improving quality of life" (Bell 2018). Michael C. Horowitz (2018: 39) also points out that "AI competition could feature actors across the globe developing AI capabilities, much like late-19th-century competition in steel and chemicals." The growing importance of AI is also evidenced by the strategies adopted by the superpowers and statements by the country leaders. As "artificial intelligence has become the new engine of economic development" (Cui 2020: 10), the State Council of the People's Republic of China released a roadmap in July 2017. In order to surpass its rivals technologically and become the world leader in AI by 2030, China has the aim of making the industry worth 1 trillion yuan ($150 billion) (The New York Times 2017). Moreover, Chinese President Xi Jinping has also "called for efforts to break new ground" in diplomacy (Chen 2018). In summer 2018, China's Foreign Ministry has already acknowledged that several prototypes of AI-powered diplomatic systems are under development in China. According to an article published in the South China Morning Post, "the programme draws on a huge amount of data, with information ranging from cocktail-party gossip to images taken by spy satellites, to contribute to strategies in Chinese diplomacy." (Chen 2018)

The Chinese Ministry of Foreign Affairs has already announced its plans to use AI technology to facilitate the work of diplomats in China's 'Belt and Road Initiative' (ibid). Given the limited availability of information on this issue and the general confidentiality of diplomacy, however, it is too early to judge and assess the impact of these AI solutions.

Meanwhile, in order to balance China's ambitions to accelerate dominance in AI and seek dominance in emerging technologies, US President Donald Trump signed the Executive Order 13859 on maintaining American leadership in AI in February 2019. As President Trump noted: "continued American leadership in Artificial Intelligence is of paramount importance to maintaining the economic and national security of the United States" (The White House 2019). China and the US are not the only frontrunners in AI international race. Russia has also stated that it wants to be involved in this great-power competition. Russian President Vladimir Putin has said AI offers "colossal opportunities and threats that are difficult to predict now" (The Associated Press 2017). Moreover, Putin has stated "the one who becomes the leader in this sphere will be the ruler of the world" (ibid). Not only China, US and Russia are competing with each other to develop nation AI strategies and gain a strategic advantage. In the face of growing global competition, more than 20 countries, including Argentina, Australia, Canada, Denmark, Finland, France, Germany, Italy, Japan, the Netherlands, Norway, Saudi Arabia, Sweden and United Kingdom, have launched AI initiatives and strategies (OECD 2019). Moreover, international organizations such as the European Union (EU), United Nations (UN), the Organisation for Economic Co-operation and Development (OECD) and even regional players such as the Nordic-Baltic region have published AI strategy documents.

According to Katharina Höne, a DiploFoundation researcher who analyses the interplay between diplomacy and AI:

"Countries are working on their competitive advantage in terms of AI. Very often, the sense of competition is in relation to US and China, the two countries that are seen as leading in the technology and have the capacity to make quick developments on AI research and application. Other countries are always looking at these two countries as guideposts, something to compare themselves to and as something to work in relation to" (Foster 2019).

AI technologies have already showed the potential to be politically and economically destabilizing. Russia's interference in America's 2016 presidential election (Hass/Balin 2019) and disputes over technologies are disrupting global trade (Lucas 2018; The New York Times 2019). Moreover, analyzing AI's ability to reshape the global order, Nicholas Wright has addressed the coming competition between liberal democracy and digital authoritarianism. According to Wright, the debate over the impacts of AI has been dominated by the worry that AI has the potential to exceed human intelligence. Moreover, there is also a belief that AI and machine can surpass humans in almost every area of society (Wright 2018). That being said, Wright believes that there is another aspect in which AI technologies and solutions promise to reshape the world. "By enabling governments to monitor, understand and control their citizens far more closely than ever before, AI will offer authoritarian countries a plausible alternative to liberal democracy, the first since the end of the Cold War" (ibid). One of the countries already building and operating such AI systems is China, thus participating in "a global competition with liberal democracy" (Wright 2019: 13). Depending on whether there is a democratic or authoritarian regime, the country's foreign policy, including diplomacy, is adapted to the political focus of its choice.

Competition can be minimal or even hard to detect, while at the same time it can be clear and even aggressive. In the context of the competitiveness of national or international organizations, the role of diplomacy can be difficult to discern because it employs conventional diplomatic practices to pursue foreign policy goals. In contrast, where states or international organizations have declared ambitious goals and formally expressed their commitment to compete with other political actors, this allows diplomacy to be pursued more vigorously. A rapid increase of financial and human resources in one of the foreign policy areas, frequent requests for meetings and new appointments of diplomats in the specific field indicates the strategy chosen by the country. The competition for AI superiority simultaneously has both a direct and indirect effect on diplomacy. Diplomats are directly involved in the preparation of negotiating themes, but also participate in negotiations between intergovernmental and international organizations. AI undoubtedly expands the scope of the agenda in diplomacy. Participating in negotiations or involving diplomats requires diplomats to be competent in dealing with AI issues. In order to ensure appropriate qualifications in AI matters, MFAs or international organizations choose to recruit specialists or train and better prepare career diplomats. Ongoing competition in the AI field also requires diplomats to develop new and in-depth forms of collaboration with new actors such as large corporations, specialized think-tanks or research centers focusing on AI.

As diplomacy is an integral component of foreign policy and is actively involved in international policy-making, the promise of AI as a public good and sustainable competitive advantages also indirectly influences diplomacy. In recent years, MFAs in many countries have been actively researching, developing and deploying AI-enabled technologies (Bjola 2019, 2020). That being said, the goals for the implementation of AI solutions are different for each country and are not always related to the competition aspect. They can be purely practical, for instance, to ensure a faster flow of information or to provide a more efficient service to the citizens (e.g. consular services). Authors such as Michael C. Horowitz, Gregory C. Allens, Edoardo Saravalle, Anthony Cho, Kara Frederik and Paul Sharre (2018: 11-12) believe that AI technologies have the potential to transform the practice of diplomacy by reducing language barriers between countries through language processing algorithms and identifying potential risks and vulnerabilities to diplomats and diplomatic missions by image collection, recognition and information sorting. In order to deliver and deploy AI solutions in diplomacy, Corneliu Bjola (2020) suggest that MFAS deploy the TIID (Task, Innovation, Integration, Deployment) framework as a conceptual roadmap. According to Bjola, "that combines considerations about what the objective is (task improvement), how to accomplish it (innovation), with what resources (physical/digital integration) and in what institutional configuration (deployment)" (Bjola 2020: 42).

In the context of AI, it is difficult for states to be isolated and to pursue a policy of neutrality. Through various forms of diplomacy, such as digital or economic diplomacy, or combinations thereof, countries are looking for ways to achieve their goals faster. As AI systems and solutions have profound impacts on geopolitical and economic power balances (Cummings et al. 2018), states and other political agents use diplomacy as part of their chosen strategies in international competition. There are several strategies of competition in AI in which diplomacy can play a role as a mediator. These include investments in technology, building military power, formal alliances, economic primacy, economic statecraft, informal partnerships, diplomacy to shape the international environment, information and public diplomacy campaigns, embedding influence in rules and institutions, lawfare, intelligence and clandestine activities. In order to achieve a competitive advantage over other international actors, countries can choose one or a combination of several means of competing (Mazarr et al. 2018: 24-27). Focusing on states' strategies for addressing competitive situation must not overlook the fact that diplomacy is a key foreign policy tool. If countries like China are pursuing an aggressive AI strategy, then other powers will be forced to compete. If the foreign policy goals are ambitious and the statements of the leading politicians are clear, then diplomacy is subordinated to these attitudes and all the possibilities available to the foreign services of these countries are used. As many researchers point out, this is a unique moment because countries need to decide quickly what to do next (Scott/Hemann/Lorenz 2018; DiploFoundation 2019; Oxford Insights 2019). Delayed action can create even more risks and threats for countries. At the same time, it is important to remember that without competition in the world, cooperation is unthinkable. Often, both manifestations are closely linked in terms of relations between countries. In the context of US-China competition, Ryan Hass and Zach Balin (2019) state the following: "AI will create both immense stress on the U.S.-China relationship as well as opportunities for potential collaboration". Hass and Balin also point out that one way to overcome the trend of global competition in the field of AI would be to identify areas where the US and China are mutually beneficial and where there is a clear risk of conflict (ibid). The authors also point out that both countries should not look at AI as a zero-sum game, but seek a new and more balanced approach. This would allow them "to build cooperation where interests are aligned, which would give both sides greater confidence in dealing with issues where they divide" (ibid). Knowing that AI-driven technologies are playing an increasingly important role in issues such as autonomous weapons, surveillance and censorship, like-minded liberal democracies will be forced not only to compete but to work even more closely together. These threats and potential risks will require governments and international organizations to invest more in their human and financial resources.

Conclusion

The terms of competition in world politics are not set by any one actor. Instead, they are created and developed under the influence of many actors. Like diplomacy itself, which has experienced considerable development since the end of the Cold War, competition itself is constantly evolving and difficult to capture.

Countries have different perceptions of innovation and AI rivalry, which strongly influence the evolution of their diplomatic practices and institutions. Great powers such as the US and China are ready for an aggressive competition in which diplomacy plays an important role. Using diplomacy, countries seek allies and try to persuade undecided political actors to support their priorities. Like-minded states, such as the Nordic and Baltic countries, do not, by contrast, pursue an explicit strategy of competition with one another. On the contrary, using regional co-operation formats such as the Council of the Baltic Sea States (Ozoliņa/Etzold 2020), NB-6 (Nordic-Baltic Six), NB-8 (Nordic-Baltic Eight) and the Baltic Council of Ministers, Northern European countries are looking for ways to become more integrated in the Baltic Sea region. The Nordic countries also aim to be at the forefront in the ongoing battle for democratic and rules-based cyberspace. As stated in the Nordic Foreign and Security Policy 2020, one of the goals of the Nordic countries "should also be to support the development of expertise and private initiatives within competitive fields, such as Artificial Intelligence (AI) and quantum computing to develop international credibility" (Bjarnason 2020: 19). Expertise in AI is also of great importance. As several authors points out, competition for highly qualified personnel in AI has also intensified in recent years (Cummings et al. 2018). A recent Chatham House Report states that "governments worldwide must invest in developing and retaining home-grown talent and expertise in AI if their countries are to be independent of the dominant AI expertise that is now typically concentrated in the US and China" (Cummings et al. 2018: vi).

States and other international actors may pursue foreign policies or strategies that are difficult to operationalize. New foreign policy initiatives, an increase in funded research, or an increase in the number of announcements in a particular area attest to the willingness of a political actor or agent to be a 'player' in this field of competition. It is important to note here that the competition over AI is not restricted to the US and China. Although the political, economic or social influence of these actors in world political processes may seem insignificant, small states can influence processes in world politics. There are many examples where small countries, with the support of public diplomacy or other types of diplomacy, have been able to significantly promote nation branding, attract more investment, and succeed in negotiations with multinational corporations, as well as create their own international framework conditions and address grand challenges. Denmark, which has the world's first 'Tech Ambassador' and has recently appointed a climate ambassador, is one of many such examples.

In line with foreign policy or international practice, diplomacy adapts and serves as a support tool in countries' efforts to make joint progress in the use of AI, while securing their own vital interests in this powerful set of emergent technologies. Diplomacy can also the competition for AI superiority or pursue less ambitious but competing goals in the AI field. In addition to traditional activities of national interest, MFAs are involved in building AI expertise as it could offer improved effectiveness, speed and augmentation (Bjola 2020: 42). As developments in AI are so dynamic and comprehensive, the race for AI superiority imposes new obligations on the actors involved. To paraphrase Joseph E. Stiglitz, who has previously stated that "designing a competition policy that works will be the most important part of the strategy for maintaining competitiveness in the market economy" (2002: 22), it is important for national governments to develop a long term AI strategies in which diplomacy can play a leading role as a mediator between the competing interests of states, civil society, and private sector actors.

References

Allen, Greg/Chan, Taniel (2017): Artificial Intelligence and National Security, Cambridge, MA: Belfer Center for Science and International Affairs.

AWTI (2017): STI Diplomacy: Advancing the Internationalization of Science, Technology and Innovation, The Hague: Advisory Council for Science, Technology and Innovation.

Barston, R. P. (2006): Modern Diplomacy, Essex: Pearson Education Limited.

Bell, Ganesh (2018): "Why countries need to work together on AI," World Economic Forum, September 16, (https://www.weforum.org/agenda/2018/09/learning-from-one-another-a-look-at-national-ai-policy-frameworks/).

Birka, Ieva/Kļaviņš, Didzis (2020): "Diaspora diplomacy: Nordic and Baltic perspective." In: Diaspora Studies 13/2, pp. 115-132.

Bjarnason, Björn: "Nordic Foreign and Security Policy 2020", July 15, 2020 (https://www.bjorn.is/greinar/nordic-foreign-and-security-policy-2020).

Bjola, Corneliu/Holmes, Marcus (eds.) (2015): Digital Diplomacy: Theory and Practice, New York: Routledge.

Bjola, Corneliu: "Diplomacy in the Digital Age", October 11, 2018 (http://www.realinstitutoelcano.org/wps/portal/rielcano_en).

Bjola, Corneliu: "Diplomacy in the Age of Artificial Intelligence", October 11, 2019 (http://www.realinstitutoelcano.org/wps/portal/rielcano_en).

Bjola, Corneliu (2020): "Diplomacy in the Age of Artificial Intelligence." In: EDA Working Paper. Abu Dhabi: Emirates Diplomatic Academy, pp. 1-47.

Bjola, Corneliu/Zaiotti, Ruben (eds.) (2021): Digital Diplomacy and International Organisations: Autonomy, Legitimacy and Contestation, Abingdon: Routledge.

Boehm, Peter M: "Is Zoom Diplomacy the New Normal? COVID-19 and the End of the Air Kiss", May 21, 2020 (https://policymagazine.ca/is-zoom-diplomacy-the-new-normal-covid-19-and-the-end-of-the-air-kiss/).

Bound, Kirsten (2016): "Innovating Together? The Age of Innovation Diplomacy?" In: Soumitra Dutta/Bruno Lanvin/Sacha Wunsch-Vincent (eds.), The Global Innovation Index 2016: Winning with Global Innovation, Beijing, China and Geneva Switzerland: World Intellectual Property Organization; New Delhi, India: Confederation of Indian Industry, pp. 91-95.

Brown, Stephen: "Diplomacy, disrupted", November 14, 2019 (https://www.politico.eu/article/diplomacy-disrupted-foreign-policy-improvised/).

Chen, Stephen: "Artificial intelligence, immune to fear or favor, is helping to make China's foreign policy", July 30, 2018 (https://www.scmp.com/news/china/society).

Christensen, Tom/Lægreid, Per (2007): "The Whole-of-Government Approach to Public Sector Reform." In: Public Administration Review 67/6, pp. 1059-1066.

Cohen, Roger: "Diplomacy is Dead", January 21, 2013 (https://www.nytimes.com/2013/01/22/opinion/global/roger-cohen-diplomacy-is-dead.html).

Constantinou, Costas M./Kerr, Pauline/Sharp, Paul (eds.) (2016): The SAGE Handbook of Diplomacy, London: SAGE.

Cooper, Andrew F./Heine, Jorge/Thakur, Ramesh (eds.) (2013): The Oxford Handbook of Modern Diplomacy, Oxford: Oxford University Press.

Cui, Yadong (2020): Artificial Intelligence and Judicial Modernization, Singapore: Springer Nature Singapore.

Cummings, M. L. (2017): Artificial Intelligence and the Future of Warfare, London: The Royal Institute of International Affairs.

Cummings, M. L./Roff, Heather M./Cukier, Kenneth/Parakilas, Jacob/Bryce, Hannah (2018): Artificial Intelligence and International Affairs: Disruption Anticipated, Chatham House Report, London: The Royal Institute of International Affairs.

DiploFoundation (2019): Mapping the Challenges and Opportunities of Artificial Intelligence for the Conduct of Diplomacy, Geneva: DiploFoundation.

Drezner, Daniel W. (2019): "Technological change and international relations." In: International Relations 33/2, pp. 286-303.

Eisenstadt, Shmuel N. (2012): "Contemporary Globalization, New Intercivilizational Visions and Hegemonies: Transformation of Nation-States." In: Georg Peter/Reuß-Markus Krauße (eds.), Selbstbeobachtung der modernen Gesellschaft und die neuen Grenzen des Sozialen, Wiesbaden: Springer VS, pp. 21-29.

Feijóo, Claudio/Kwon, Youngsun/Bauer, Johannes M./Bohlin, Erik/Howell, Bronwyn/Jain, Rekha/Potgieter, Petrus/Vu, Khuong/Whalley, Jason/Xia, Jun (2020): "Harnessing artificial intelligence (AI) to increase wellbeing for all: The case for a new technology diplomacy." In: Telecommunications Policy 44/6, pp. 1-14.

Feng, Shuai (2019): "Toward a Transformed and Unequal World: The AI Revolution and the New International System." In: China Quarterly of International Strategic Studies 5/2, pp. 267-287.

Foster, Kendrick: "AI and Diplomacy: Interview with Katharina Höne", April 15, 2019 (https://harvardpolitics.com/category/interviews/).

Greenstock, Jeremy (2013): "The Bureaucracy: Ministry of Foreign Affairs, Foreign Service, and Other Government Departments." In: Andrew F. Cooper/Jorge Heine/Ramesh Thakur (eds.), The Oxford Handbook of Modern Diplomacy, Oxford: Oxford University Press, pp. 106-121.

Gül, Murat (2009): "The concept of change and James N. Rosenau: Still international relations?" In: African Journal of Political Science and International Relations 3/5, pp. 199-207.

Hass, Ryan/Balin, Zach: "US-China relations in the age of artificial intelligence", January 10, 2019 (https://www.brookings.edu/series/a-blueprint-for-the-future-of-ai/).

Hocking, Brian (2002): "Introduction: Gatekeepers and Boundary-Spanners—Thinking about Foreign Ministries in the European Union." In: Brian Hocking/David Spence (eds), Foreign Ministries in the European Union: Integrating Diplomats, New York: Palgrave Macmillan, pp. 1-17.

Hocking, Brian (2007): Adapting foreign ministries to a changing world: a question of credentials, Bangkok: Ministry of Foreign Affairs, Kingdom of Thailand, DiploFoundation.

Hocking, Brian (2013): "The Ministry of Foreign Affairs and the National Diplomatic System." In: Pauline Kerr/Geoffrey Wiseman (eds.), Diplomacy in a Globalizing World, Oxford: Oxford University Press, pp. 123-140.

Hocking, Brian (2016): "Diplomacy and Foreign Policy." In: Costas M. Constantinou/Pauline Kerr/Paul Sharp (eds.), The SAGE Handbook of Diplomacy, London: SAGE, pp. 67-78.

Hocking, Brian/Melissen, Jan (2015): Diplomacy in the Digital Age, Clingendael Report, The Hague: Clingendael Institute.

Hocking, Brian/Melissen, Jan/Riordan, Shaun/Sharp, Paul (2012): Futures for Diplomacy: Integrative Diplomacy in the 21st Century, No.1 of Clingendael Report, The Hague: Clingendael Institute.

Hocking, Brian/Melissen, Jan/Riordan, Shaun/Sharp, Paul (2013): Whither Foreign Ministries in a Post-Western World, No. 20 of Clingendael Policy Brief, The Hague: Clingendael Institute.

Horowitz, Michael C. (2018): "Artificial Intelligence, International Competition, and the Balance of Power." In: Texas National Security Review 1/3, pp. 36-57.

Horowitz, Michael C./Allen, Gregory C./Saravalle, Edoardo/Cho, Anthony/Frederick, Kara/Scharre, Paul: "Artificial Intelligence and International Security", July 10, 2018 (https://www.cnas.org/publications/reports/artificial-intelligence-and-international-security).

Johnson, James (2019): "Artificial intelligence & future warfare: implications for international security." In: Defense & Security Analysis 35/2, pp. 147-169.

Kleiner, Juergen (2008): "The Inertia of Diplomacy." In: Diplomacy & Statecraft 19/2, pp. 321-349.

Leijten, Jos: "Is there something like innovation diplomacy?", September 12, 2016 (https://www.el-csid.eu/single-post/2016/09/12/blognote5).

Leijten, Jos (2017): "Exploring the future of innovation diplomacy." In: European Journal of Futures Research 5/20, pp. 1-13.

Leijten, Jos (2019): "Innovation policy and international relations: directions for EU diplomacy." In: European Journal of Futures Research 7/4, pp. 1-21.

Lucas, Louise: "US-China tech wars threaten global sector disruption", May 8, 2018 (https://www.ft.com/louise-lucas).

Lucci, Stephen/Kopec, Danny (2015): Artificial Intelligence in the 21st Century: A Living Introduction, Dulles: Mercury Learning and Information.

Mazarr, Michael J./Blake, Jonathan S./Casey, Abigail/McDonald, Tim/Pezard, Stephanie/Spirtas, Michael (eds.) (2018): Understanding the Emerging Era of International Competition: Theoretical and Historical Perspectives, Santa Monica: RAND Corporation.

Melchor, Lorenzo (2020): "What Is a Science Diplomat?" In: The Hague Journal of Diplomacy 15, pp. 409-423.

Miremadi, Tahereh (2016): "A Model for Science and Technology Diplomacy: How to Align the Rationales of Foreign Policy and Science." In: SSRN, pp. 1-34.

Moses, Jonathon W./Knutsen, Torbjørn (2001): "Inside Out: Globalization and the Reorganization of Foreign Affairs Ministries." In: Cooperation and Conflict 36/4, pp. 355-380.

Neumann, Iver B. (2013): Diplomatic Sites: A Critical Enquiry, London: Hurst and Company.

Neumann, Iver B. (2015): "Sited diplomacy." In: Jason Dittmer/Fiona Mc-Connell (eds.), Diplomatic Cultures and International Politics: Translations, Spaces and Alternatives, Routledge New Diplomacy Studies, London: Routledge, pp. 79-92.

OECD (2019): Artificial Intelligence in Society, Paris: OECD Publishing.

One Hundred Year Study on Artificial Intelligence (AI100): "Artificial Intelligence and Life in 2030", August 1, 2016 (https://ai100.stanford.edu/).

Oxford Insights: "Government Artificial Intelligence Readiness Index 2019", May 21, 2019 (https://www.oxfordinsights.com/ai-readiness2019).

Ozoliņa, Žaneta/Etzold, Tobias (eds.): "Reflection Paper on the Vilnius Declaration—A Vision for the Baltic Sea Region by 2020", July 1, 2020 (https://cbss.org/publications/reflection-paper-on-the-vilnius-declaration-a-vision-for-the-baltic-sea-region-by-2020/).

Rana, Kishan S. (2004): Performance Management in Foreign Ministries, No. 4 of Discussion Papers in Diplomacy, The Hague: Clingendael Institute.

Rana, Kishan S. (2007): Bilateral Diplomacy, Malta: DiploFoundation.

Rana, Kishan S. (2011): 21st Century Diplomacy: A practitioner's guide, London: Continuum.

Rana, Kishan S. (2013): The Contemporary Embassy: Paths to Diplomatic Excellence, Hampshire: Palgrave Macmillan.

Rana, Kishan S./Kurbalija, Jovan (eds.) (2007): Foreign Ministries: Managing Diplomatic Networks and Optimizing Value, Malta: DiploFoundation.

Rosenau, James N. (2006): The Study of World Politics, Vol. 1: Theoretical and Methodological Challenges, New York: Routledge.

Rosenau, James N. (2009): "Turbulence in World Politics: A Theory of Change and Continuity." In: Richard W. Mansbach/Edward Rhodes (eds.), Global Politics in a Changing World, Belmont: Wadsworth Publishing, pp. 13-17.

Rüffin, Nicolas (2018): "Case study. Science and Innovation Diplomacy Agencies at the nexus of research, economics, and politics." In: EL-CSID Working Paper 10/10, Brussels: Institute for European Studies at the Vrije Universiteit Brussel, pp. 1-20.

Scott, Ben/Heumann, Stefan/Lorenz, Philippe (2018): Artificial Intelligence and Foreign Policy, Berlin: Stiftung Neue Verantwortung.

Sending, Ole Jacob/Pouliot, Vincent/Neumann, Iver B. (eds.) (2015): Diplomacy and the Making of World Politics, Cambridge: Cambridge University Press.

Shapiro, Daniel B./Rakov, Daniel: "Will Zoomplomacy Last?", May 18, 2020 (https://foreignpolicy.com/2020/05/18/will-zoomplomacy-last/).

Singh, Naunihal (2002): Diplomacy for the 21st Century, New Delhi: Mittal Publications.

Soler, Marga Gual/Oni, Tolullah: "Here's how 'science diplomacy' can help us contain COVID-19", May 5, 2020 (https://www.weforum.org/agenda/2020/05/here-s-how-science-diplomacy-can-help-us-contain-covid-19/).

Stanzel, Volker V. (ed.) (2018): New Realities in Foreign Affairs: Diplomacy in the 21st Century, Berlin: Stiftung Wissenschaft und Politik German Institute for International and Security Affairs.

Stiglitz, Joseph E. (2002): "Competition and Competitiveness in a New Economy." In: Heinz Handler/Christina Burger (eds.), Competition and Competitiveness in a New Economy, Vienna: Austrian Ministry for Economic Affairs and Labor, Economic Policy Center, pp. 11-22.

Tavares, Rodrigo: "International diplomacy needs an overhaul to stay relevant. Here's why", May 2, 2018 (https://www.weforum.org/agenda/2018/05/international-diplomacy-needs-an-overhaul-to-stay-relevant-here-s-why/).

The Associated Press: "Putin: Leader in artificial intelligence will rule world", September 1, 2017 (https://apnews.com/bb5628f2a7424a10b3e38b07f4eb90d4).

The New York Times: "Beijing Wants A.I. to Be Made in China by 2030", July 20, 2017 (https://www.nytimes.com/2017/07/20/business/china-artificial-intelligence.html).

The New York Times: "How Disputes Over Big Tech Are Disrupting Global Trade", December 5, 2019 (https://www.nytimes.com/section/business/dealbook).

The White House: "Artificial Intelligence for the American People", February 11, 2019 (https://www.whitehouse.gov/ai/executive-order-ai/).

Wight, Martin (1979): Power Politics, London: Royal Institute of International Affairs.

Wright, Nicholas: "How Artificial Intelligence will reshape the global order: The coming competition between digital authoritarianism and liberal democracy", July 10, 2018 (https://www.foreignaffairs.com/articles/world/2018-07-10/how-artificial-intelligence-will-reshape-global-order).

Wright, Nicholas (ed.) (2019): Artificial Intelligence, China, Russia, and the Global Order, Maxwell: Air University Press.

Yao, Mariya: "What are Important AI & Machine Learning Trends for 2020", January 22, 2020 (https://www.forbes.com/sites/mariyayao/2020/01/22/what-are--important-ai--machine-learning-trends-for-2020/#567036fe2323).

Small, Smart, Powerful?
Small States and the Competition
for Cybertech Superiority in the Digital Age

Madeleine Myatt

"Size matters in international relations," claim Steinsson and Thorhallsson (2017: 1). But does it still matter in the digital age, and on the new terrain of cyberspace? Scholars have long believed that larger states are better equipped for state competition due the size of their populations, economies militaries. This basic assumption needs to be reviewed in light of new theories concerning the competitive advantage conferred by the adoption of digital and emerging technologies. The growing interconnectedness of world society through the internet and other information and communication technologies (ICTs) has created new realities for national and international politics. The digital transformation of public services (e.g. e-Government, e-Voting, e-public-procurement), critical infrastructures (e.g. IT/telecommunication, energy, water, health, public transport), the increasing digitalization of the business world, new forms of digital communication and the strategic value of huge amounts of data and its processing on a daily basis have a transformative impact on national and global affairs (see also Kļaviņš in this volume). They have also created new opportunities for small states to attempt to shape the emergent field of cybertechnology and cyber-power.[1]

To be sure, cyber power is not primarily a field of small powers. Persistent notions of an US/China "Digital or Tech Cold War" (Segal 2020), the emphasis on the use and misuse of digital tech supremacy, and the maintenance of traditional adversary concepts in the cyber domain, keep the spirit of 'great power' competition alive. Larger states are able to shape regulations,

1   I would like to thank the editors for their comments and input throughout the writing process.

norms and processes of technical standardization in ways that reinforce their competitive advantage. At the same time, however, hacking attacks, cyber espionage, disinformation campaigns, electoral interference, surveillance, and different forms of cyber intelligence operations are carried out by big and small states alongside non-state actors (including through the use of proxies). Indeed, small states like Israel, Singapore and Estonia are considered—although for different reasons—as "leading nations" in cyber security and digitalization.

The traditional correlation of size with power is therefore newly contested in the digital age. The following contribution explores how small states influence cyber security politics on the world political stage from a strategic point of view, aiming to describe the strategies Nordic countries, in particular Finland and Estonia, have adopted over the past years in cyber security politics. It further selectively addresses the translation of their strategic approach to digitalization and cybersecurity and highlights the relation of size and power in cyber affairs. The question of how far "cyber power" transcends traditional ways of understanding power is also addressed, and related to the old IR discussion on the relation of size and power (cf. e.g., Alesina/Spolaore 2003, Katzenstein 2015 [1985], 2003). The idea of cyber power rests—in distinction to a more traditional view of power—on an asymmetric notion of efficiency related to the increasing role of decentralized data and information flows, technological supply and services (Areng 2014: 1, Nye 2010). Understanding cyber-power requires a perspective which emphasizes the role of technological innovation and linked strategies of nation branding, specialization and norm shaping. Since cyber is an inherently public-private system, it also requires us to recognize the importance of effective modes of organizing relations between states and the (often transnational) private sector actors who own and operate critical technologies.

The two small states examined here, Estonia and Finland, provide interesting insights into how 'small states' make use of their digital transformation and the linked cybersecurity discourse to strive for a 'leading nation' status. 'Leading' refers to their strategic and quick digital technology adoption; their building of expertise in digital and cyber affairs based on an increasing investment in cybersecurity capacity building to develop best-practice blueprints; their strong regional cooperation, with its associated benefits for knowledge and technology transfer; and their visible striving for core hosting positions in the form of hubs of digital/cyber expertise and/or administrative coordination units within International Organisations (IOs). These expertise hubs which not only organize cooperation but also serve as discourse arenas which (re-) produce cybersecurity politics. What is more, Estonia and Finland are particularly engaged in cybersecurity regulation, cyber norms, standard setting, the use of emerging technologies as tools and as topics in international affairs, and the fostering of digitalization more generally (domestically, regionally and internationally). Norm-entrepreneurship, a well-known strategy of the Nordic countries, involves promoting interests and shaping, shifting and setting agendas to foster the development and implementation of new norms (cf. Finnemore/Sikkink 1998; Ingebritsen 2002). This strategy and tool to exert influence on decision-making processes has been extensively addressed by scholarship on the EU (Björkdahl 2008, Ingbritsen 2002, Kronsell 2002). Theoretical scholarship on norm diffusion focuses predominantly on the role of normative non-state actors and IOs as platforms. Here, by contrast, light is shed on norm entrepreneurship as a foreign policy tool (Davies/True 2017:1-2; for Norm-Entrepreneurship in Scandinavia States, Ingebritsen 2002).

The contribution at hand analyzes if and how digital technological innovation and the strategic orientation towards cyber security help small states like Finland and Estonia to gain influence and recognition as 'authorities' in global cyber politics. The chapter begins by providing a brief overview of the different attempts to conceptualize small states in the discipline of International Relations. It then offers an equally short discussion on the advantages and disadvantages of being 'small', in order to conceptualize and evaluate the role and choices of small states in influencing world politics in general and pursuing their goals in cyber (security) politics. The chapter then turns to the conceptualization of cyber-power, and in particular the question of how some states come to be recognized as 'authorities' in cyber (security politics). Using Ole J. Sending's adapted field-theoretical lens (2017), it will be shown how states become 'authorities' in cyber-security through an ongoing competition over expertise and technological leadership between different actors. Finally, the strategies of Estonia and Finland, will be discussed in greater detail, including their translation into concrete practices.

Mapping Power, Smallness & Competition in IR: Concepts, Perceptions and Shifts

It is a common view that small states lack significant influence in great power competition (Long 2017a: 186). In a (neo-)realist lens the concept of a 'small states' is closely linked to power, which is defined as a state's ability to influence outcomes (Browning 2006: 671). From this point of view, power manifests itself in a materially measurable form: population (sometimes understood as 'human capital'), GDP, arsenals of weapons, and armed forces personnel. These indicators are collected, compared, interrelated, and interpreted. In a processed form they are used to define 'smallness' as a relatively small amount of power. 'Smallness' becomes synonymous with 'weakness' in common narratives and political rhetoric.

In recent years, researchers have presented alternative, multifaceted analytical frameworks which compare 'size' from a more complex perspective. The six-size framework of Baldur Thorhallsson (2006) differentiates between a fixed size (population and territory), sovereignty size (e.g. degree of control over territory and borders), political size (military and administrative capabilities, domestic cohesion, foreign policy consensus), economic size (GDP, market size, and development), perceptual size (internal and external recognition), and preference size (the ideas, ambitions, and priorities of domestic elites regarding their role in the international system).

In spite of this additional complexity, however, neo-realist analysis of small states retains a focus on raw military strength and its distribution in what is taken to be an anarchic world political system. This assumption has implications for the interrelations between 'large' and 'small powers'. The freedom and scope of action of small states is considered to be dependent on larger powers in form of their goodwill, strategic interests and the hierarchical network of relations between small states and larger powers. They are classified as a category of states according to the interests (and identities) attributed to them in relation to a theoretical understanding of the logic of anarchy and the balance of power. In that respect, smallness is considered to entail a certain degree of vulnerability and a strategic security problem (Vital 1971: 8–9; Keohane 1969: 299; Knudsen 1996: 3-20; Knudsen 2002: 184, Archer et. al. 2014; cf. Thorhallsson 2018).

Liberal IR theory challenges this neorealist view of small states by focusing on the role and value of institutions and interdependence. Although scholars following this tradition often tend to stick to the established dichotomous lens of a simultaneity of small/weak and large/powerful as a descriptive category, an alternative view of power has been introduced, stressing that it "cannot be considered a homogenous, highly interchangeable commodity." (Keohane/Nye 1973: 160). A driving force for this development was the acknowledgement of an increasing interdependence on the international stage. This also changed perceptions of the strategic and practical options remain for smaller states with limited capacities under these circumstances. Emphasizing interdependence and the emerging complexity of world politics, Keohane and Nye argue that the context in which power is exercised must be taken into account. They point to the different dynamics and logics of issue areas and the specific forms power can take in each of these (Keohane/Nye 1977: 91–98).

This perspective is reflected in studies of small states to a great extent. For instance, empirical research on the strategic behavioral characteristics of small states has highlighted, alongside their tendency to build alliances (including by 'free-riding' on larger powers [Moghaddam 2017: 310-312]), that small states also seek to foster cooperation through a strong commitment to multilateralism and an international rule-based system, and a certain degree of specialization and concentration of specific issue areas which allow particular small states to occupy a particular niches in world politics (Tarp/Bach Hansen 2013).

The neoliberal argument rests on the assumption that small states rely on and benefit from multilateral organizations more than larger ones (Neumann/Gstöhl 2006: 3-36). It also relies on the assumption that we have witnessed a 'multilateralization' of international politics over time, with an impact on actor constellations striving for multilateral cooperation (see also: Tarp/ Bach Hansen 2013: 6-7). This view of the evolution of the international political architecture has been challenged recently with the rise of populist nationalism around the globe. But it is associated not just with the popular legitimacy of international institutions. The shift in world politics towards multipolarity and 'fragmented authority' goes along with an increasing awareness for the global nature of issues like climate change, sustainability and development, terrorism, cybersecurity, pandemics, digitalization and state building process in post-conflict areas (ibid: 7). These new issue areas have created windows of opportunity for non-state actors, and also for small states to influence global politics through international organizations and institutions.

Multilateral institutions serve as vehicles to influence policies. They provide 'horizontal' discourse arenas with a participatory framework which includes codes of conduct, dispute settlement mechanisms and voting rules. Within these arenas, small states benefit from the access to information and expertise exchange (research bodies), best practice learning, and opportunities to shape the definition, implementation and monitoring of norms, rules, and codes in various issue areas (cf. Karns/Mingst 2004, Steinsson/Thorhallsson 2017: 13-14). Small states can also gain influence by occupying core institutional positions in the administrative system of international organizations (on this sort of 'network power', see Boyashov in this volume).

Research has shown that small states pursue a variety of strategies in international organizations: direct and indirect forms of lobbying (incl. influencing on the national level (cf. Keohane 1971, Mearsheimer/Walt 2009); the use of 'normative appeals' underlining the legitimacy of/ drawing on international institutions (Steinsson/Thorhallsson 2017: 9); and influencing institutional structures and policy processes, through high-level policy processes and decision making through strategic alliances as well as institutional priorities, and operational practices in international institutions (Tarp/Bach Hansen 2013). In sum, the use of this so-called soft-power toolkit plays a significant role alongside strategic and rational behavior.

A 'good reputation' and the internal and external recognition of the former is an essential element of Nye's concept of "soft power", coined in the late 1980s (cf. Nye 1990, 1999, 2002, 2004, 2006). Contrasting 'soft' with 'hard power', Nye emphasized states' ability to shape the long-term attitudes and preferences of other actors, in particular through civil society such as companies, universities, churches and charitable foundations (Nye 2004). The small states' forms of power have in common that they are not 'tested' on the battleground but depend on symbolic recognition. Liina Areng observes that small states compete over resources, markets, and attention, as well. "In this battle," she concludes, "a small state's success depends on its self-perceptions and the ability to portrait itself to others" (2014: 4). In other words, in order to influence policies and exert power in a certain field, small states have to compete for recognition as both effective and trustworthy actors in international organizations, and effective "experts" in relative policy fields. It is their success in these respects that have allowed small states such as Finland and Estonia to become recognized authorities in the field of cyber-security.

Understanding the ways in which small states have gained positions of recognized authority in a highly technical field such as cyber-security requires us to go beyond both neo-realist understandings of small states in opposition to 'great powers', and neoliberal understandings of small states as effective utilizers of 'soft power' and international organizations. It requires, instead, a more sustained look at the "politics of expertise" (Sending 2017) that structure the competition for authority in global policy fields. Sending's work employs a Bourdieuean field-theoretical lens to observe the competitive dynamics and logics for authority in the realm of global politics (for a more general view on Bourdieu in IR, cf. Adler-Nissen 2012). It offers a fruitful route to capturing the role of expertise for small states in order to be recognized as authorities in world politics (Sending 2017: 11; cf. Müller/Freistein this volume).

Sending's work emphasizes the competition of actors for authority within policy fields. Authoritative actors decide 'what is to be governed, how and why' (ibid.). They define and determine the 'rules of the game'. This field-theoretical understanding of authority brings in a more comprehensive analytical view on the power of small and big states. It does so by pointing out that the construction and evolution of authority is fundamentally shaped by its relational dimension in the form of recognition and misrecognition (Sending 2017:12-13). For Sending, the emergence of authority on the world political stage rests on an ongoing competition for recognition in more or less distinctive issue areas of world politics (Sending 2017: 13f.) Therefore, it is important to analyze the interplay between the definition process of issues, performed governance practices, the social organization of issue areas and authority claims. For the given context and the focus on cyber and digital affairs, this also means taking a closer look at the role of knowledge and knowledge production in the Bourdieusian tradition (Bourdieu 1971, 1991, 2000). In this sense, 'knowledge' contains more than what we today would subsume under expertise. It also entails a social dimension closely linked to the Bourdieusian concept of *habitus*. It involves knowledge about how to do things, how to act and how to engage in the social sphere.

Scholars have long emphasized the role of expertise as a fundamental source of authority for various actors (e.g. the idea of epistemic communities: Adler/Haas 1992, Cross 2013, Haas 1992, or more generally: Antoniades 2003, Hall/Biersteker 2002, Price 2003). However, the development of a recognized expertise on specific issues has rarely been studied as a source of authority (see also Sending 2017: 15-18). Expertise, and the recognition as a 'leading nation' in the digital age, play a key role in small states' efforts to shape the emergent policy field of cyberspace. There are several examples of states subsumed under the 'small' label which can be discussed as being 'smart' due to their relative success in creating a brand and a recognizable blue-print for a digital or information society, in occupying specific issue areas, and in expanding their influence through the cultivation of expertise. Alongside Estonia and Finland, we might also mention Denmark, Israel and Singapore. Before considering specific cases of small states gaining authority in the field of cybersecurity policy, however, it is necessary to describe the contours of this emergent policy field in more detail.

The Coming of the Digital Age and the Cyber Domain— a New Window of Opportunity

The digital age brings several new opportunities for small states to increase their international standing. The emergence and distribution of ICTs has led to the evolution of a domain of global cyber politics, focused on topics such as internet governance, cybersecurity and cyber norms. This new field entails the development of new issue areas, which accelerate the need for international collaboration and force existing institutions to adapt. As well as being a new issue area within world politics, moreover, ICTs are transforming the ways in which world politics functions, reducing the relevance of geographical distance, and offering new means of communication, participation and observation (see Kļaviņš in this volume).

The emergence of cyber politics as both a major field *within* world politics and a transformational agent *for* world politics has significant implications. First, the cyber space is a challenge to the sovereignty of states. It is a highly integrated feature of everyday life, omnipresent in the social, political and economic sphere. Yet it is also based on the global and decentered interconnectivity, enabling a free and quick flow of data and information across national borders and jurisdictions. The everyday lives of citizens of all states are thereby implicated in transnational networks of communication that are far harder to monitor or control than older telegraph, telephone or postal infrastructures. Against this background, the relevance of borders in relation to cyberspace and cybersecurity issues needs to be addressed (Hare 2018: 1-2). In 2016, NATO and others recognized 'cyber' as an operational domain (NATO 2016). As Forrest Hare (2018: 14-15) highlights 'merely mediums in which we interact, do not have borders' but that does not mean that they do not play a role because borders 'define boundaries of sovereignty.' Second, cyberspace changes the relation between public and private actors. The sheer fact that most of the internet and ICT-infrastructure is privately owned, and that enabling technologies and emerging technological solutions are offered and distributed by private and often globally acting tech companies, requires states to acknowledge these companies as significant political interlocutors. This has boosted the evolution of new forms of 'tech diplomacy' and public/private relations. The former is best illustrated by Denmark's appointment of the first tech ambassador, approaching Silicon Valley and other tech hubs around the globe directly (Danish Ministry of Foreign Affairs 2017). This Danish foreign policy flagship aims to open up a direct diplomatic post to represent Danish interests before companies like the 'Big Five' tech giants and to promote its tech agenda (incl. norms and values) internationally. The latter manifests itself the huge number of different forms of public/private collaboration to tackle cybersecurity issues. One recent example, the launched collaboration between the UK Government's National Cyber Security Centre (NCSC) and Microsoft for its 2021 Cyber Accelerator programme, aiming to encourage start-ups to support UK cybersecurity efforts (Yates-Roberts 2020). The contractual public private partnership (cPPP) on threat intelligence between the U.S. Department of Homeland Security, the Infrastructure Security Agency (CISA) and U.S company FireEye is another example.

Third, cyber space constitutes a new security challenge. Digitalization and emerging technologies are subject to a high pace of technical innovation and progress. The latter creates new issue areas such as certification, standardization and the need for norms and regulation. Policy action, however, mostly lags behind technological progress. Further, the vulnerabilities, and potential misuse, of the cyber domain create the need for new security and defense frameworks, or at least the modernization of existing ones (see Miadzvetskaya in this volume). Size, in its conventional sense, plays a minor role in the weaponization of digital technologies. Cyber operations such as cyber espionage, hacking attacks, system infiltration and manipulation have been carried out by small and large states alike, including Iran, North Korea, Israel, the US, the UK, China and Russia (incl. state-sponsored activities by using proxies). It seems that there really is a new way to become powerful.

Following Nye's concept of hard and soft power (1990), recent scholarship has focused on power in the digital age. Christopher Walker's essay "The Authoritarian Threat: The Hijacking of 'Soft Power'" (2016) discusses the visibility of a global trend which refers to the use of cutting-edge information technology by authoritarian regimes in order to penetrate, control and influence democracies. This is a recent and urgent matter of concern for western democracies and their institutions, as they face the challenge of being increasingly confronted with authoritarian influence from within (ibid.). Walker argues that this trend is supported and accelerated by the pervasion of digital technology, the evolution of the internet as the backbone structure of the digital age, and the transformation of the media landscape. The projection of authoritarian influence involves efforts in the form of censorship as well as the manipulation of data and content, often in the scope of disinformation campaigns to fuel friction and distrust in democratic institutions (ibid.). The International Forum for Democracy Studies published a report on these phe-

nomena and coined a term for states pursuing this strategy—"sharp power."
(NED 2017) The report examines Chinese and Russian influence in four young
democracies in Latin America and Central Europe. According to the report,
"sharp powers" pursue the strategy to "pierce, penetrate, or perforate" the political and information environments of targeted countries (ibid.:10).

Power in world politics is both a capacity to act and a goal of action which
cannot be simply reduced to the use of force. Power in cyberspace means the
ability both to produce (in-)security *in* cyberspace and (in)security *through* cyberspace. Cybersecurity appears as a complex and dynamic configuration of
state and non-state actors, institutions and clashing jurisdictions (Choucri
et.al. 2012: 16; Choucri/Clark 2018). As Lior Tabanski (2016: 54) highlights:

> "Cyber power is not limited to information, but cuts across the other facets,
> elements and instruments of power, often referred to as Diplomatic, Infor-
> mational, Military, and Economic (DIME). Cyber connects these elements in
> new ways to produce preferred outcomes within and outside cyberspace."

Nye points out that "the barriers to entry in the cyber domain are so low that
non-state actors and small states can play significant roles at low levels of
cost," which will lead to more competition and contestation (Nye 2010: 4).
Most importantly, power can shift even to non-traditional actors, who have
developed important cyberspace capabilities over time. Nye calls this transition of power from state to non-state actors "power diffusion" (ibid.: 1-2). The
cybersecurity technology toolkit offers new and, generally speaking, afford-
able instruments to pursue political interests' via ICTs and IT-based applications (incl. open-source technologies).

Nye's conceptualization of cyber power and his insight that there are now
"different actors sharing the stage" urges political scientists to broaden their
perspective (ibid.: 3). Namely, they should focus on the disruptions caused by
the ongoing competition for power, authority and ownership in cybersecurity.
Relations in cybersecurity transcend distinctions of the public and private, the
global and local. They can be observed as a dynamic web which is competitive,
conflictual as well as cooperative and sometimes highly coordinated.

Capturing and visualizing "cyber power" by drawing on easily quantifiable
technology projections, such as networking and system architecture, cryptog-
raphy, malware or military commands is not sufficient. Conceptualizing cyber
power and translating such a concept into practice requires a more comprehensive view and an understanding of the underlying variables, fundamental
for the employment of practices, tools and technologies for wielding power

in cyberspace (cf. Klimburg 2011, Rowland et. al. 2014, Inkster 2017, Bebber 2017). To speak of cyber power in relation to geopolitical competition is to mainly focus on the role of states and their ability to "coordinate and employ" respective tools and practices "on the political, strategic, operational, and tactical levels" (Bebber 2017: 426). That does not mean that non-state actors cannot be powerful in cyberspace; something that is often underlined by the use of proxies in state-sponsored hostile cyber activities (on hacking, see Nissenbaum 2004).

Moreover, impactful cyber-attacks are not just reducible to a respective code. Strategic orchestration, planning, preparation and intelligence gathering play a key role. To attack an adversary at the right time and the right place requires a profound contextual knowledge, encompassing user patterns and internal workflows, system vulnerabilities, and even cultural inducing factors. One prime example of this is the 2016 Bangladesh Bank cyber heist, in which alleged state-sponsored hackers used the Swift messaging system to capture $81 million by exploiting security loopholes and drawing on deep insights in relevant context factors. The SolarWinds supply chain attack, disclosed in December 2020, is another good example of a timely, orchestrated attack. Conceptualizing cyber power more comprehensively also means focusing on the role of designing an effective relationship between ends, ways and means in potentially competitive or adversarial dynamic relations (Tabanski 2016: 54).

Identifying strategic ends is important before focusing on the means and ways used in relation to cyber and the digital realm. Because of the extensive penetration of the cyber realm into all aspects of modern life, it also means uncovering the vision and overarching idea of a given national society in relation to cyberspace.

Table 1: The different Levels of Strategy

Level	Geographic Scale	Temporal Scope	Type of Ends	Type of Power (Means)
Grand Strategy	Global	Long-term (decades)	Highest political ends	All
Strategy	All theatres of War and Conflict	Mid-term (years)	Overall military victory	Military, informational, economic
Operations	One particular theatre of war	Short term (weeks to month)	Campaign Victory	Military, Informational
Tactics	Battlefield	Very short term (minutes to days	Achievement of tactical objectives	Military
Technology	Home front, academia, industry	Variable time horizon	Competitive advantage over enemies	Technical Expertise

Source: Based on William C. Martel (2015: 30), see also: Tabansky 2016: 55.

As technological change is rapid in cyberspace, cyber power also depends on the stability and strength of internal affairs in order to be successful in external affairs. The status of the digital or information society of a country plays a significant role the recognition of that country as an authority in cyberspace. The manner in which a country deals with the digital transformation is also measured by its contacts with its citizens: both through the conduct of elections and other forms of democratic participation, and the management and security of the data generated by citizens' interactions with welfare or identity services. In this sense, digitalization impacts the way people of a society experience and practice citizenship today (e.g. Allen/Light 2015, on youth engagement: Bennett 2008). The increasing diffusion of ICTs in public management and the distribution of public goods is beneficial for small states because it reduces costs and offers the potential to increase efficiency (Areng 2014: 2-3, Kattel et. al. 2011: 61-81).

The Nordic countries are well known for developing concepts and strategies by investing in tech-diplomacy relations with major tech actors to ensure knowledge and technology transfer as well as reinforcing digital approaches to citizenship. As an educational approach 'Digital Citizenship' normally focuses on developing a high level of knowledge and skills to effectively use digital technologies for communication, social and political participation, including the creation, distribution, and consumption of digital content. It can also extend to introducing emerging technologies like Artificial Intelligence (AI). This approach further includes the distribution of a fundamental understanding of concepts like cybersecurity, privacy, copyright and creative credit regulation, digital footprints, digital and information literacy, netiquette, and codes of conduct.

In order to benefit from and create an image as a blue-print digital society, the innovation system of a country serves further as an important cornerstone. Hence, it is important to take education, science and research into account. Core indicators for the latter are R&D spending (Anderson/Hearn 1996), education, cyber security industry relations and structures, technology export rates as well as transnational network building with view to research collaboration and tech diplomacy (cf. also: Tabansky 2016: 56-59). Even a short analytical view on the figures of R&D spending show that many small states focus on the development of their innovation system (OECD 2020). Furthermore, in order to weigh the power potential of states in the domain, it is also important to engage with principle of internal strength and stability from an institutional point of view, namely, the structure and level of cooperation of ministries in cyber politics (whole-of-government approach and/ or whole-of-society approach).

The relevance of creating a brand of a 'digital and innovative' self- and external perception in order to be recognized through the lens of expertise and a cyber power image, points further to another element of a comprehensive cyber power conceptualization: norm-entrepreneurship. As previously outlined, studies on small states underline the relevance of trying to influence institutional structures and policy processes, high-level policy processes and decision making, institutional priorities and operational practices in international institutions. Hence, being powerful in the cyber domain is also linked to the ability to shape and influence the cyber norm discourse, including technological certification and standardization. This is a strategy which especially small states are well-known for, at least in terms of stimulating and fostering attempts at regulation and standardization. In order to add empirical insights from the reality of small states in the field of global cyber politics, concrete examples, practices and strategies in relation to the cyber domain will be discussed in the following section.

The Evolution of Small State Authority in Global Cyber Politics

Small states are sometimes seen as particularly vulnerable to the perils of the digital age. One line of argumentation in the policy discourse on cyber power argues that small states are more likely to be exposed to cyber-attacks because of their relatively small size of their population, their human resource capacity, limited domestic IT capability, and the resources available for funding cyber security. This argumentation clearly follows in (neo-)realist footsteps.

As I have shown above, however, other scholars highlight the structural advantages of small countries, their efficiency and the adaptability of their domestic specialization. Scholarship on small states emphasizes their governance and bureaucracy structures, which are seen as better organized, with shorter communication channels within and between public agencies and less political distance between local and national governments (cf. Areng 2014:3-4; Kattel et. al. 2011). Moreover, the digital infrastructure and the state of a digital society plays a key role. Namely, internet and ICT-access, deployment of wireless technology and networks (incl. investment in 5G), the application and technical state of digital solutions on the governmental level as well as public management, norms and regulations, fostering digital competences among the population. This points, last but not least, to the important role of cyber capacity building measurements.

In this view, it is not the size of a population, its density or distribution that counts most. Instead, the innovation potential, the coherence of cybersecurity strategies and practices, the effectiveness of public-private relations, norm entrepreneurship and multilateral engagement, and the digital resilience of society—based on a high degree of digital and cybersecurity capacities and capabilities—appear to be relevant sources of power in cyberspace.

The following section discusses the cyber power strategies of small states in greater detail, examining the interaction between domestic strategies for maximizing cyber preparedness and innovation potential, and the pursuit of external influence through international organizations, nation branding, and regional cooperation.

Creating a Nation Brand, Finding Niches and Influencing Institutional Priorities

The Nordic countries are seen as a prime example—both as a region and as individual countries—for being 'smart, small and powerful' in cyberspace. They regularly achieve high positions in rankings on digital and cyber matters. When it comes to the use of ICT or e-governance, they are considerably above the EU average (EUROSTAT 2021). Indicators like the World Economic Forum's Network Readiness Index have listed Sweden, Denmark and Finland in the top 10 for the past several years.

Table 2: Network Readiness Index, Top 10 2019

Rank	Country/Economy	Score (Total)	Technology	People	Governance	Impact
1	Sweden	82,65	82,28	78,17	87,43	82,73
2	Singapore	82,13	78,45	73,55	88,19	88,33
3	Netherlands	81,78	84,34	74,40	88,01	80,37
4	Norway	81,30	77,69	76,00	90,30	81,20
5	Switzerland	81,08	83,47	79,54	87,28	80,27
6	Denmark	81,08	77,22	79,54	87,28	80,27
7	Finland	80,34	78,66	75,28	88,15	79,27
8	The United States	80,32	87,32	73,59	88,74	71,65
9	Germany	78,23	77,51	72,6	83,94	78,87
10	United Kingdom	77,73	78,16	69,81	88,32	74,62

Source: World Economic Forum, Network Readiness Index 2019 (WEF 2019)

Estonia has been one of the first countries to prioritize the development of a comprehensive digital and ICT strategy. This strategy has been consequently followed and implemented by adapting its institutional structure accordingly and investing in the development of cyber capacities and capabilities. The slogan "We have built a digital society and we can show you how", carried on Estonia's "E-Estonia" website, expresses Estonia's nation brand as a role model for the construction of an "efficient, secure, and transparent" digital "ecosystem"—an e-state (E-Estonia 2020). The small country with a population of 1.3 million has the highest level of e-governmental structures with 99% of state services online and 99% of the population in possession of an electronic ID. Estonia possesses an e-resident system and has established an e-voting system. Image branding constantly underlines how well Estonia has done in international rankings (#2 Internet Freedom Index, #1 entrepreneurial activity (World Economic Forum), #1 digital health index (Bertelsmann Foundation). In sum, Estonia remains an interesting and relevant case to study, as it stands like no other for coping with its comparable small size by increasing its "functional size" through emphasizing "the transformative power of ICTs and innovation" (Areng 2014: 7-8).

Estonia's ambitious e-resident project (which started in 2014) is particularly relevant in this context. This project aims not only to provide e-services to Estonian residents, but to foster investment and get hold of global expertise. Instead of tapping only the IT expertise of Estonia's native population, the e-residency gathers a "borderless digital society" of "global citizens" (E-Estonia 2020). Estonia's image campaign puts forward the idea of a digital fraternity of allied states. With a rising significance of data, which is detached from a nation's territory, data flows become more and more constitutive for a country. The "Data-Embassy" project predominantly stands for this idea in form of exploring options to duplicate vital national databases in highly secure servers abroad, provided through transnational public/private partnerships. The project intends to ensure the digital survival of the state, even if it loses sovereignty over its territory. "Estonia is on its way to becoming a 'country without borders'" (OECD 2018: 5), writes the OECD, and highlights that "the data embassy is one of several Estonian programs that blurs the lines of national borders and sovereign identity in a digital world" (OECD 2018).

Despite and because of Estonia's efforts and achievements in digitalization, it has become a target of cyber-attacks and has experienced a glimpse of what cyberwar can look like. In 2007, Estonia's critical services and digital infrastructure were subjected to severe cyberattacks. It is today believed that they have originated in Russia and were meant as coercive punishment for Estonia's decision to relocate a Soviet military monument. This experience had a fundamental impact on the state's domestic, regional, and international political agenda in terms of prioritizing cybersecurity and fostering security collaboration in the cyber domain. The chain of incidents created furthermore a new awareness on the world political stage, namely the acknowledgement that cyber operations have become an indispensable element of modern, hybrid conflicts. In this sense, cyber means can enhance traditional means or can be a "stand-alone capability that can give substantial asymmetric advantage

to states that are considered weaker in terms of traditional combat power"
(Areng 2014:6).

Estonia has accordingly taken on the role of a constant and active player
in creating awareness for cyber related issues, especially by pushing cybersecurity and the establishment of cyber norms. The country is hence a prime
example for showing off the "ability of militarily aligned small states to function as norm entrepreneurs to increase their own state interests" in the cyber
realm (cf. Crandall/Allan 2015: 346). The country plays a leading role in shaping
and accelerating the cyber policy discourse, particularly in the NATO and the
EU. Estonia's leading role in the development of NATO's first cyber defense
policy in 2008, and its numerous contributions of fostering EU initiatives in
ICT security, are just a few examples of this. Against this background, it is not
surprising that Estonia introduced its 2017 presidency of the Council of the
EU under the label of the "digital presidency" (Patriocolo 2017). Many of the
themes pushed and implemented during the presidency aimed at digitalization: progression on the taxation of the digital economy and the free movement of data, approval of an ecommerce VAT package, and an agreement on
further steps to develop 5G networks across Europe.

Beside Estonia, Finland is usually named as a digital forerunner in Europe. The two countries have a close cross-border relationship especially in
digital affairs based on their rather early jump on the digital bandwagon.
With respective roots in the late 1990s, Finland and Estonia evaluated their
cross-border relationship in advance of Estonia's EU accession in 2004. The
final report "Finland and Estonia in the EU" highlighted cross-border cooperation, information society and energy cooperation as common priorities with
respective synergy effects ever since (Sirviö 2019).

In many respects, Finland is the stereotype of a small state in the neorealist understanding. It has a rather small population of just above 5.5 million,
limited military capabilities, and natural resources. Its territory of 338,455
km² is small from a global, but large from a European perspective. Finland's
geopolitical position next to Russia and the former Soviet Union shaped its external and self-perception and has an ongoing impact on its politics. Against
the background of having a relatively long border with Russia as well as the
previous experience of the rise, expansion and fall of the former Soviet Union,
the country preserved a threat narrative which is still powerful. Hence, it is
not surprising that besides fostering the digital transformation of the Finnish
society and a brand as an innovative tech-nation (e.g the AI governmental

project and the AI online citizen education program 'Elements of AI'[2]), Finland occupied the issue of hybrid warfare in the digital age. As well as making hybrid threats and hybrid warfare a central national political issue, the country took advantage of the contemporary discourse on disinformation, fake news, manipulation and electoral interference through digital means by state and non-state adversaries including cyber espionage and cyber-attacks, to address the role of security relevant grey-zone practices on the world political stage by framing and distributing a concept of 'hybrid warfare' and fostering institutionalization in the respective policy field. Finland's EU Council Presidency, running under the program slogan "Sustainable Europe—Sustainable Future" highlights that in a complex and unpredictable world, innovation is needed, but EU common norms and values are increasingly challenged, online and offline. The digital age and interconnectivity through the cyber domain create a paradox, namely, more connectivity goes along with more vulnerabilities which can be exploited by adversaries. Hence, strengthening the capacities and capabilities to prevent and respond to hybrid threats, including fostering closer NATO/EU relations, was one of the main priorities during Finland's presidency.

Hosting the Hybrid Centre of Excellence for Countering Hybrid Threats (Hybrid CoE9), is not only relevant in order to emphasize the respective genesis of the issue at hand and its interrelation with the evolution of future technologies. The organizational structure of Hybrid CoE is interesting as well in order to capture the relational dimensions of recognition. Hybrid CoE, established in April 2017 based on a collaboration of originally nine participating states (Finland, Sweden, the United Kingdom, Latvia, Lithuania, Poland, France, Germany and the United States), joined by Estonia, Norway and Spain in July 2017, the Netherlands, Italy, Denmark, Czech Republic, Austria, Canada, Romania, and Cyprus during 2018 and Greece, Hungary, Luxembourg, Montenegro, Portugal, Slovenia, and Turkey in 2019, takes on the space of organized transnational political forum.

Finland, which holds the secretariat that manages the center's administration, general functions, and external relations, including the organization of cooperation and liaison with participating states, the EU and the NATO, therefore plays a key role in shaping the center and its transnational discourse arena of practitioners and academic experts. The secretariat moreover coordinates all the relevant activities of the three communities of interest (COI):

---

2   See for more information https://www.elementsofai.com/ (last access: 02/09/2020).

(1) hybrid influencing, (2) strategy and defense, and (3) vulnerabilities and re-silience and the work of linked expert pools, consisting of academics and prac-titioners of participating member states and IOs. A lot of the organizational and social practices in use clearly reflect and the gatekeeper and management role of Finland, incorporate the dynamics of recognition and misrecognition as a central constitutional element of constructing authority.

Regional Cooperation, Using Institutional Institutions as Platforms and Influencing Institutional Structures

Regional collaboration forms between Baltic and Nordic states in different policy areas has a long tradition, resting on strong political and cultural ties, and is recently omnipresent in the policy fields of digitalization and cyber-security. This long tradition is especially embodied through the 'Nordic co-operation' which establishes constant collaboration forms between Denmark, Finland, Iceland, Norway, and Sweden as well as the Faroe Islands, Green-land and the Åland Islands. Institutionalized through the Nordic Council of Ministers (inter-governmental format) and the Nordic Council (inter-parlia-mentary format), it claims to be "one of the most extensive forms of regional co-operation anywhere in the world", seeking to raise "a strong Nordic voice in the world and an in European and international forums. The values shared by the Nordic countries help make the region one of the most innovative and competitive in the world." (NORDEN 2020)

Nordic cooperation can be seen as an attempt to build a regional brand, resting on the attribute ensemble of green, sustainable, innovative, smart and technologically advanced. This set of attributions is moreover used for indi-vidual nation branding attempts. Noticeable in this context, it seems that the Nordic countries follow a niche strategy which enables to create country spe-cific external visibility in a specific digital tech niche in line with the engage-ment in IOs (e.g. Finland: Hybrid Warfare & AI applications, Estonia: Cyber-security, Denmark: Introducing new ways of Tech.-Diplomacy & Big Data).

This strategy is extended through the Nordic states' visible striving for oc-cupying hosting and gatekeeper positions in the shape of central positions in the bureaucracy networks or in form of hubs of digital/cyber expertise (cen-ters of excellence) within IOs or in strong relation to multiple IOs. States like Estonia (NATO Cooperative Cyber Defense Centre of Excellence (CCD COE), Finland (Hybrid Centre of Excellence (Hybrid CoE)) or Denmark make use of the asymmetric toolbox of 'cyber power' to gain leverage in the international security realm, especially by obtaining those strategic positions in addition their national and joint regional attempt to create digital and cyber resilient societies. These expertise hubs which not only organize cooperation and knowledge production, but also serve as discourse arenas which (re-)produce security politics, the involved imaginaries of (cyber) security and insecurity and their visualization.

Furthermore, small states are often very keen to place their nationals in high-ranking positions in IOs (Nordic countries in the UN system, see: Thorhallsson 2012). This pattern is also observable in the context of global cyber as well as digital politics. One example is the Estonian/Brussels revolving door effect with view on staff and personal is remarkable, as former Estonian government and ministry officials increasingly take over key position in the context of the EU Digital Single Market. Similar attempts to establish respective modes of organization, aiming to support the development of sustainable and common ICT-security and regional competitive advantages, are already discussed on a higher political level.

Norm entrepreneurship: being small, smart, and powerful through shaping and influencing cyber norm building

Another important element of cyber power is the ability to influence and shape norms and regulation in relation to cyberspace and cyber security in particular. This involves the enhancement of international normative power by taking on an active role in the adaptation and development of new norms of state behavior for cyberspace. Shaping technical certification and standardization can similarly be perceived as an example of exercising smart power in the cyberage. Therefore, it is no surprise that some small states are explicitly engaged in the global cyber norm forums like the United Nations Group of Governmental Experts (UN GGE) and the UN-mandated Open-Ended Working Group on Developments in the Field of ICTs in the Context of International Security (OEWG), in launching and playing a key role in initiatives like the 'Freedom Online Coalition' (e.g. Finland & UKs collaboration on dis-& misinformation) or participating in multi-stakeholder formats like Global Commission on the Stability of Cyberspace (GCSC).

The NATO Cooperative Cyber Defense Centre of Excellence (CCD COE) in Tallinn, and the engagement of Estonia but also other small member states in its activities, is another example. The CCD COE serves a key driver for technical capability and epistemic authority on cyber related issues (Hansen/Nissenbaum 2009). The latter entails e.g., the ongoing legal analysis of the applicability of international law to cyber conflict, which led to the publication of the Tallinn Manual on the International Law Applicable to Cyber Warfare.

The pursuit of norm entrepreneurship in cyberspace is not restricted to the Nordic states. One of the small states which not only regionally, but also on the global level, advanced recently as a cyber norm entrepreneur with a respective standing is Singapore. Singapore has sought to foster cybersecurity collaboration under the ASEAN umbrella, and collaborated recently with the UN in order to develop a checklist for cyber security norm implementation for countries. The cybersecurity norm implementation checklist continues efforts to encourage the adoption of the eleven voluntary, non-binding norms for responsible behavior in cyberspace which have been proposed by the UN GGE in 2015 (UN GGE 2015).

Conclusion

There is little doubt about the fact that the digital age brings several new opportunities for small states to gain competitive advantages in the light of power politics on the world political stage. The internet and ICTs make it possible for small states to be highly connected by providing new channels of communication and information exchange, creating new opportunities to develop and shape their own ideas of a digital society, especially if their authority and expertise are recognized by others. Moreover, one could argue that the size and density of their digital footprints, which heavily rely on intangible goods, is disproportionately large. Even those voices who are in favor of emphasizing military power must admit that dependencies on digital infrastructure creates new issues, routines and vulnerabilities which cannot be addressed with conventional military means. The digitization of defense technology and increasing pervasion of open-source "dual-use" items increase the complexity of world affairs. Hence, a sheer focus on resource-based and compulsory power appears to be insufficient to assess the power of small states in the digital age. In this sense, the latter may specialize in less conventional ways and means, drawing on institutional, structural, and productive facets of power or non-traditional forms of compulsory power (Long 2017a: 200-201).

Cyber power or "the ability of states to project power in and through cyberspace" (Bebber 2017: 426) is more than a quantifiable technological toolkit and resources. It rests on a set of structural and domestic variables and resources like the innovation system and technology industry, human capital, strategic culture and thinking, the adaption and diffusion of ICTs on the social, political and economic level, the structure of political institutions (incl. inter-agency cooperation), public/private relations, the ability to integrate cyber capabilities and capacities (vertically & horizontally), the digital infrastructure (virtual and physical, e.g., fibre, cable, wireless, social networks), but also the ability to shift and shape global cyber norms and technical standards ore being integrated in international cooperative networks (ibid.: 427-429, for global cyber norms cf. Finnemore/Hollis 2016).

Furthermore, it is important to recognize that the possession of cyber power capabilities and capacities is just one aspect. Translating them into practice and orchestrating these efforts strategically is also fundamental. The comparison of cases of small but powerful states in cyberspace show that countries like Finland, Estonia, Israel or Singapore deploy and manifest their cyber power quite differently. Israel's cyber start-up nation is well-known and recognized on the world political stage for its innovative cyber tech industry, strategic behavior and offensive cyber security and defense capabilities, showed off regularly in—from time to time —controversial cyber operations (cf. Tabansky/Ben Israel 2015). Singapore in contrast is also recognized as an advanced cyber tech nation but recently occupied a strong visibility as normative force based on the recognition that cyber norm and standard-setting are power tools.

Both of these additional examples lead us further to the third important implication. Cyber powers have to be recognized as such, which brings us back to Ole J. Sending's instructive approach. This usefully highlights that authority is not given, nor inscribed into a specific set of actors, but rather induced by the ongoing competition for recognition as an 'authority' capable of determining what is to be governed, by whom and for what purpose (Sending 2017: 3-11). This also points to the relational dimension of power based on processes of recognition and misrecognition. This relational dimension, although not observed through a field-theoretical lens, has also been picked up by scholars of "small states studies". Tom Long (2017b: 163-165) for instance, defines power as an asymmetrical relationship to capture the agency of states.

Countries like Estonia and Finland represent prime examples of a coping strategy with its comparable small size label by increasing its "functional size" through emphasizing "the transformative power of ICT and innovation" (Areng 2014: 7-8) into a competitive advantage in the continuous competition for recognition as an authoritative actor. In this sense, the initial question, if the triad of being "small", "smart" and "powerful" is a suitable way to address the relative role of size in contemporary world politics, can be answered in the affirmative. But it is not without limitations. One example is the so-called digital divide and the ability to invest, adapt, foster and secure ICTs and an evolving digital infrastructure. Size is not irrelevant in world and global cyber politics. This is *inter alia* visible in the US/China global tech power competition. But in the cyber age, we should nonetheless consider a reformulation of a famous IR remark (Wendt 1992; 2013): "size and power are what states make out of them".

References

Adler-Nissen, Rebecca (2012): "Why International Relations Theory Needs Bourdieu", E-International Relations, October 23 (https://www.e-ir.info /2012/10/23/why-international-relations-theory-needs-bourdieu/).

Adler, Emanuel/Haas, Peter M. (1992): "Conclusion. Epistemic Communities, World Order, and the Creation of a Reflective Research Program." In: International Organization 46/1, pp. 367-390.

Alesina, Alberto/Spolaore, Enrico (2003): The Size of Nations, Cambridge, MA: The MIT Press.

Allen, Danielle/Light, Jennifer S. (2015): From Voice to Influence: Understanding Citizenship in a Digital Age, Chicago: University of Chicago Press.

Anderson, Robert H./Hearn, Anthony C. (1996): An Exploration of Cyberspace Security R&D Investment Strategies for DARPA: 'The Day After...in Cyberspace II', Santa Monica: RAND Corporation.

Andreas Antoniades (2003): "Epistemic Communities, Epistemes and the Construction of (World) Politics." In: Global Society 17/1, pp. 21-38.

Archer, C./Bailes, A.J.K./Wivel, A. (2014): Small States and International Security. Europe and Beyond, Milton Park: Taylor & Francis.

Areng, Liina (2014): "Lilliputian States in Digital Affairs and Cyber Security", The NATO Cooperative Cyber Defense Centre of Excellence Archive, Tallinn Paper Series 4, (https://ccdcoe.org/uploads/2018/10/TP_04.pdf).

Bebber, Robert (2017): "Cyber Power and Cyber Effectiveness: An Analytic Framework." In: Comparative Strategy 36/5, pp. 426-436.

Bennett, W. L. (2008): "Changing Citizenship in the Digital Age." In: W. L. Bennett (ed.), Civic life online: Learning how digital media can engage youth, Cambridge, MA: MIT Press, pp. 1-24.

Bourdieu, Pierre (1971): "Systems of Education and Systems of Thought." In: M. F. D. Young (ed.), Knowledge and Control, New Directions in the Sociology of Education, London: Macmillan.

Bourdieu, Pierre (2000): Pascalian Mediations, Cambridge: Polity.

Bourdieu, Pierre/Thompson, John B. (1991): Language and Symbolic Power, Cambridge: Polity.

Browning, Christopher S. (2006): "Small, Smart and Salient? Rethinking Identity in the Small States Literature." In: Cambridge Review of International Affairs 19/4, pp. 669-684.

Choucri, Nazli/Clark, David (2018): International Relations in the Cyber Age. The Co-Evolution Dilemma, Cambridge, MA: The MIT Press.

Choucri, Nazli/Elbait, Gihan Daw/Madnick, Stuart (2012): "What is Cybersecurity? Explorations in Automated Knowledge Generation." In: MIT Political Science Working Paper 2012/30, pp. 1-27.

Claudia Patricolo (2017): "Estonia: Europe's Little Technological Giant", Emerging Europe, December 14 (https://emerging-europe.com/intelligence/estonia-europes-little-technological-giant/).

Crandall, Matthew/Allan, Collin (2015): "Small States and Big Ideas: Estonia's Battle for Cybersecurity Norms." In: Contemporary Security Policy 36/2, pp. 346-368.

Cross, Maia (2013): "Rethinking Epistemic Communities Twenty Years Later." In: Review of International Studies 39/1, pp. 137-160.

Danish Ministry of Foreign Affairs (2017): "Denmark names first ever tech ambassador", Ministry of Foreign Affairs of Denmark (https://um.dk/en/news/newsdisplaypage/?newsid=60eaf005-9f87-46f8-922a-1cf20c5b527a).

Davies, Sara/True, Jacqui (2017): "Norm Entrepreneurship in Foreign Policy: William Hague and the Prevention of Sexual Violence in Conflict." In: Foreign Policy Analysis 13/3, pp. 701-721.

E-Estonia (2020): "E-Identity", E-Estonia Website (https://e-estonia.com/solutions/e-identity/e-residency/).

Eurostat (2021): "Individuals using the internet for interacting with public authorities", Eurostat, January 26 (http://appsso.eurostat.ec.europa.eu/nui/show.do?dataset=isoc_bde15ei&lang=en).

Finnemore, Martha/Sikkink, Kathryn (1998): "International Norm Dynamics and Political Change." In: International Organization 52/4, pp. 887-917.

Haas, Peter M. (1992): "Introduction. Epistemic Communities and International Policy Coordination." In: International Organization 46/1, pp. 1-35.

Hall, Rodney Bruce/Biersteker, Thomas J. (eds.) (2002): The Emergence of Private Authority in Global Governance, Cambridge: Cambridge University Press.

Hansen, Lene/Nissenbaum, Helen (2009): "Digital Disaster, Cyber Security and the Copenhagen School." In: International Studies Quarterly 53/4, pp. 1155-1175.

Hare, Forrest (2018): "Borders in Cyberspace: Can Sovereignty Adapt to the Challenges of Cyber Security?", The NATO Cooperative Cyber Defense Centre of Excellence Archive, October 6 (https://ccdcoe.org/uploads/201 8/10/06_HARE_Borders-in-Cyberspace.pdf).

Ingebritsen, Christine (2002): "Norm Entrepreneurs: Scandinavia's Role World Politics." In: Cooperation and Conflict 37/1, pp. 11-23.

Ingebritsen, Christine/Neumann, Iver B./Gstöhl, Siegline (2012): Small States in International Relations, Seattle: University of Washington Press.

Inkster, Nigel (2017): "Measuring Military Cyber Power." In: Survival 59/4, pp. 27-34.

Karns, Margaret P./Mingst, Karen A. (2004): International Organizations: The Politics and Processes of Global Governance, Boulder: Lynne Rienner Publishers Inc.

Kattel R./Randma-Liiv, T./Kalvet, T. (2011): "Small States, Innovation and Administrative Capacity." In: V. Bekkers/J. Edelenbos/B. Steijn (eds.), Innovation in the Public Sector, IIAS Series: Governance and Public Management, London: Palgrave Macmillan, pp.61-81.

Katzenstein, Peter J. (1985): Small States in World Markets: Industrial Policy in Europe; Ithaca: Cornell University Press.

Katzenstein, Peter J. (2003). "Small States and Small States Revisited." In: New Political Economy, 8/1, pp.9- 30.

Katzenstein, Peter J. (2015): Small States in World Markets. Industrial Policy in Europe, Ithaca: Cornell University Press.

Keohane, Robert O. (1969): "Lilliputians' Dilemmas. Small States in International Politics." In: International Organization 23/2, pp. 291-310.

Keohane, Robert O. (1971): "The Big Influence of Small Allies." In: Foreign Policy 2, pp. 161-182.

Keohane, Robert O./Nye, Joseph S. (1973): "Power and Interdependence." In: Survival 15/4, pp. 158-165.

Keohane, Robert O./Nye, Joseph S. (1977): Power and Interdependence: World Politics in Transition, London: Little.

Klimburg, Alexander (2011): "Mobilizing Cyber Power." In: Survival 53/1, pp. 43-60.

Knudsen, Olav (2002): "Small States, Latent and Extant: Towards a General Perspective." In: Journal of International Relations and Development 5/2, pp. 182-198.

Knudsen, Olav F. (1996): "Analysing Small State Security: The Role of External Factors." In: Werner Bauwens/Armand Cleese/Olav F. Knudsen (eds.): Small States and the Security Challenge in the New Europe, London and Washington: Brassey's.

Kronsell, Annica (2002): "Can Small States Influence EU Norms? Insights from Sweden's Participation in the Field of Environmental Politics." In: Scandinavian Studies 74/3, pp. 287-304.

Long, Tom (2017a): "Small States, Great Power? Gaining Influence Through Intrinsic, Derivative, and Collective Power." In: International Studies Review 19, pp. 185-205.

Long, Tom (2017b): "It's not Size that Matters, it's the Relationship: from 'Small States' to Asymmetry." In: International Politics 54/2, pp. 144-160.

Martel, William C. (2015): Grand Strategy in Theory and Practice: The Need for an Effective American Foreign Policy, Cambridge: Cambridge University Press.

Mearsheimer, John J./Walt, Stephen M. (2009): "Is It Love or The Lobby? Explaining America's Special Relationship with Israel." In: Security Studies 18/1, pp. 58-78.

Moghaddam, Fathali M. (2017): The SAGE Encyclopedia of Political Behavior, Thousand Oaks: SAGE.

NATO (2016): "Fact Sheet on Cyber Defense", North Atlantic Treaty Association (https://www.nato.int/nato_static_fl2014/assets/pdf/pdf_2016_07/20 160627_1607-factsheet-cyber-defense-eng.pdf).

NED (2017): "Sharp Power: Rising Authoritarian Influence", National Endowment for Democracy, December 5 (https://www.ned.org/sharp-power-rising-authoritarian-influence-forum-report/).

Neumann, Iver. B./Gstöhl, Sieglinde (2006): "Introduction: Lilliputians in Gulliver's world?" In: Christine Ingebritsen /Iver B. Neumann/Siegline Gstöhl/Jessica Beyer (eds.), Small States in International Relations, Seattle: University of Washington Press, pp. 3-36.

Nissenbaum, Helen (2004): "Hackers and the Contested Ontology of Cyberspace." In: New Media & Society 6/2, pp. 195-217.

NORDEN (2020): "Official Nordic Co-Operation", Nordic Co-Operation Website (https://www.norden.org/en/information/official-nordic-co-operation).

Nye, Joseph S. (1990): "Soft Power." In: Foreign Policy 80, pp. 153-171.

Nye, Joseph S. (1999): "Redefining the National Interest." In: Foreign Affairs 78/4, pp. 22-35.

Nye, Joseph S. (2002): The Paradox of American Power: Why the World's only Superpower can't go it Alone, Oxford: Oxford University Press.

Nye, Joseph S. (2004): Soft Power. The Means to Success in World Politics, New York: Public Affairs.

Nye, Joseph S. (2010): "Cyber Power", Harvard Kennedy School, Belfer Center for Science and International Affairs (https://www.belfercenter.org/sites/default/files/legacy/files/cyber-power.pdf).

OECD (2018): "Case Study: The first Data Embassy." In: Embracing Innovation in Government: Global Trends 2018, p. 42-44 (https://www.oecd.org/gov/innovative-government/Estonia-case-study-UAE-report-2018.pdf).

OECD (2020): "Gross domestic spending on R&D (indicator)", OECDilibary (https://www.oecd-ilibrary.org/industry-and-services/gross-domestic-spending-on-r-d/indicator/english_d8b068b4-en).

Price, Richard M. (2003): "Transnational Civil Society and Advocacy in World Politics." In: World Politics 55, pp. 579-606.

Rowland, Jill/Rice, Mason/Shenoi, Sujeet (2014): "The Anatomy of a Cyber Power." In: International Journal of Critical Infrastructure Protection 7/1, pp. 3-11.

Segal, Adam (2020): "The Coming Tech Cold War with China: Beijing is Already Countering Washington's Policy", Foreign Affairs, September 9 (https://www.foreignaffairs.com/articles/north-amrica/2020-09-09/coming-tech-cold-war-china).

Sending, Ole Jacob (2017): The Politics of Expertise. Competing for Authority in Global Governance, Michigan: University of Michigan Press.

Sirviö, Ville (2019): "Estonia and Finland—Digital forerunners in cross-border cooperation", The University of Turku, the Pan-European Institute, October 30 (https://sites.utu.fi/bre/estonia-and-finland-digital-forerunners-in-cross-border-cooperation/).

Steinsson, Sverrir /Baldur Thorhallsson (2017): "Small State Foreign Policy." In: Oxford Research Encyclopedia of Politics, Oxford: Oxford University Press.

Tabansky, Lior (2016): "Towards a Theory of Cyber Power: The Israeli Experience with Innovation and Strategy." In: Proceedings of the 8th International Conference on Cyber Conflict, NATO Cooperative Cyber Defense Centre of Excellence, 51-63.

Tabansky, Lior/Ben-Israel, Isaac (2015): Cybersecurity in Israel, New York: Springer.

Tarp, Maria Nilaus/Bach Hansen, Jens Ole (2013): "Size and Influence. How Small States Influence Policy-Making in Multilateral Arenas." In: DIIS Working Paper 2013/II, unpaginated.

Thorhallsson, Baldur (2012): "Small States in the UN Security Council: Means of Influence?" In: The Hague Journal of Diplomacy 7/2, pp. 135-160.

Thorhallsson, Baldur (2018): Small States and Shelter Theory: Iceland's External Affairs, Milton: Routledge.

UN GGE (2015): Groups of Governmental Experts on Developments in the Field of Information and Telecommunications in the Context of International Security, United Nations Group of Governmental Experts, Report A/70/174 (https://www.un.org/ga/search/view_doc.asp?symbol=A/70/174).

Vital, David (1971): The Survival of Small States: Studies in Small Power/Great Power Conflict, Oxford: Oxford University Press.

Walker, Christopher (2016): "The Authoritarian Threat: The Hijacking of 'Soft Power'." In: Journal of Democracy 27/1, pp. 49-63.

Wendt, Alexander (1992): "Anarchy is What States Make of it: The Social Construction of Power Politics." In: International Organization 46/2, pp. 391-425.

Wendt, Alexander (2013): "Anarchy is What States Make of it." In: Richard K. Betts (ed.): Conflict after the Cold War: Arguments on Causes of War and Peace, Boston: Pearson.

World Economic Forum (2019) Network Readiness Index 2019 (https://networkreadinessindex.org/2019/).

Yates-Roberts, Elly (2020): "NCSC and Microsoft partner for UK cybersecurity accelerator", TechRecord, November 5 (https://www.technologyrecord.com/Article/ncsc-and-microsoft-partner-for-uk-cybersecurity-accelerator-116960).

Between Strategic Autonomy and International Norm-setting
The EU's Emergent "Cyber-Sanctions" Regime

Yuliya Miadzvetskaya

Today's world is characterized by an increased strategic competition and rising threats to multilateralism and a rules-based order. In this fast evolving environment, the EU has shifted from its traditional 'values-based' approach in foreign policy to a 'principled pragmatism'. This holds that the European Union should solidify relations with countries with shared values, while also engaging strategically with rivals. The EU's goal is to protect its strategic interests in a world marked by the US-China rivalry, a more uncertain relationship with the US, and Russia's growing ambitions in their shared neighborhood.

The present chapter examines some aspects of the EU's efforts to secure its autonomy in an emergent terrain for international competition: cyberspace. The analysis will begin with an explanation of the broader context for the EU's approach to cybersecurity, which should be understood as part of the Union's longstanding pursuit of 'strategic autonomy' in an increasingly competitive geopolitical environment. It then offers a description of deterrence theory and its application to cyberspace, before turning to the development of the EU 'Cyber Diplomacy' toolbox and targeted restrictive measures in response to cyberattacks. It will then seek to assess the deterrence potential of restrictive measures on the basis of some generic attributes of the concept of deterrence, identified in rich theoretic contributions on deterrence theory and cyberspace. It concludes that while sanctions might appear to be ineffective and non-aligned with the operational characteristics of the cyber domain, their potential for establishing good practices should not be discarded. They should instead be used as a vehicle for promoting and informing the international discourse on the norms of responsible state behavior in cyberspace.

Strategic Autonomy in Cyberspace

EU policymakers increasingly believe that the EU has to take a greater respon-sibility for its cybersecurity challenges if it wishes to overcome its traditional dependence on the NATO and the US in the military domain. The EU's ability to engage with partners whenever possible and act autonomously whenever necessary will increase the EU's credibility at the international stage.

"Building greater resilience and strategic autonomy" are accordingly listed as EU cybersecurity strategy aims (European Commission 2017: 2). A stronger EU cyber 'actorness' requires the elimination of cyber threats that under-mine the EU's strategic independence. The concept of 'strategic autonomy', however, is vaguely defined, and is at times used interchangeably with self-sufficiency or sovereignty (Franke/Varma 2019). Furthermore, all the Member States can project their own understanding into this concept, which makes it even more difficult to establish common definitions.

The term 'strategic autonomy' is thought to have come into the EU discourse from French defense policy circles, where it has long been in use (Timmers 2019). Strategic autonomy is mentioned in a 1994 French white pa-per on defense (République Francaise 1994). The French president, Emmanuel Macron, is a strong advocate of strategic autonomy and even referred to "Europe's autonomous operating capabilities" in his 2017 Sorbonne speech on the future of the European Union (Macron 2017). Defense cooperation is one of the domains where France could potentially assert European leadership over Germany, in particular with the UK leaving the EU.

Strategic autonomy is often associated with a closer, more efficient se-curity cooperation between member states; one that would enable the EU to take decisions with regard to its own future independently from other global players (Brustlein 2017: 27). It also relates, however, to the EU's economic and cyber resilience, which consists in deciding on its own trade policy and rein-forcing its digital sovereignty. For these purposes, the European Council has recently invited the Commission to identify and decrease economic depen-dencies on external actors by diversifying production and supply chains as well as fostering production and investment in Europe (2020a). However, not all the EU Member States share the same enthusiasm for the catchphrase of 'strategic autonomy'; some view this initiative as a "protectionism in disguise" (Tamma 2017).

The EU has undertaken several initiatives for fostering its strategic au-tonomy and increasing its competitiveness in the cyber domain. They can be divided into three main areas: resilience, defense and deterrence building in cyberspace. These are the three core elements of the EU 2017 cybersecurity strategy.

Resilience encompasses "the capacity to withstand, recover from, and adapt to external shocks" (Dupont 2019: 2). It implies the establishment of solid structures capable of responding to cyber-attacks in the Member States and at the EU's institutional level. In this regard, the European Union Agency for Cybersecurity (ENISA) plays a crucial role in fostering EU cyber resilience and supports the implementation of the Directive on security of network and information systems (European Parliament and Council 2016). In addition, an EU cybersecurity certification framework was set up by the Cybersecurity Act (European Parliament and Council 2019) to strengthen resilience of ICT products and services.

When it comes to defense, the European Defense Fund (EDF) was established in 2017 to support cooperation between Member States, industry, research centers, and universities. The Coordinated Annual Review on Defense (CARD) has been operating on a trial basis since 2017. It monitors the defense plans of member states in order to ensure a greater coherence in defense spending (van Reybroeck 2019). In 2017, the decision was adopted to establish the Permanent Structured Cooperation on security and defense (PESCO), as laid down in Articles 42(6) and 46 of the Treaty on the EU (TEU).

Aspects of economic policymaking have also been linked to the strategic autonomy agenda. Concerned about investments in European high-tech and infrastructure, the EU rolled out a regulation for the screening of foreign direct investments on the grounds of security or public order in 2019. Here, the EU followed the US lead on the protection of sensitive domains from foreign control. The US introduced oversight over foreign investments via the 2018 Foreign Investment Risk Review Modernization Act (FIRRMA). This legal framework controls key US technologies, such as semiconductors, telecommunications, robotics and AI (Zable 2020).

Alongside these new initiatives in the fields of defense and foreign policy, the EU has also sought to establish elements of 'strategic autonomy' in the cyber domain. Over the past decade, widespread cyberattacks, remote controlled weaponry and the hyped concept of 'cyberwars' and 'cyberwarfare' posed a need for strategies to deter their use. Deterrence has long been a part of mainstream foreign policy discussions. But it is now applied in the cyber domain, as prominently as it is on land and in the air, sea and space. While the EU is just in the beginning of establishing its cyber deterrence strategies, the US, benefitting from a less fragmented decision-making and better cyber capabilities, was already more effective in applying sanctions or criminal charges against government-sponsored hackers (Department of Justice 2018a). For instance, in 2016, the US imposed sanctions against nine Russian parties, including two Russian Federal Security Services, the Main Intelligence Directorate (GRU) and Federal Security Service (FSB), over their alleged elections interference (White House 2016a). A North Korean programmer was accused by the US Department of Justice of involvement in several cyber-operations, including the WannaCry attack (White House 2016b). In October 2018, the US charged seven Russian GRU officers with compromising computer networks used by various sporting and anti-doping organizations, a US nuclear power company, the Netherlands-based Organization for the Prohibition of Chemical Weapons (OPCW) and the Switzerland-based Spiez laboratory (Department of Justice 2018b). In July 2020 the US announced an indictment against Chinese nationals for computer intrusion campaigns (Soesanto 2020). The US "cyber sanctions" program was in place for five years. Several Russian, Iranian and North Korean entities were put on the US Department of the Treasury's Office of Foreign Assets Control (OFAC) "cyber sanctions" list.

Deterrence also made its way into the EU discourse, with the EU's acknowledgement of the threats that cyberattacks pose to critical infrastructures, democratic processes and international stability. The EU uses alternative non-military instruments of deterrence and coercion so as to position itself as a force for peace. Deterrence is mentioned in the 2017 Communication "Resilience, Deterrence and Defense: Building strong cybersecurity for the EU" and constitutes one of the cornerstones of the EU cybersecurity policy (European Commission 2017). Deterrence is crucial for addressing new cybersecurity risks and discouraging potential perpetrators. The latter is done by the use of (or the threat of the use of) criminal and political measures in response to cyberattacks. In contrast to individual Member States, the EU's greater reach as a bloc allows it to influence the cost-benefit calculus of malicious actors and thus contribute to the maintenance of the status quo.

The EU deterrence toolbox was recently expanded with several instruments of influence, including sanctions and traditional 'name and shame' practices. The US was the first country to add sanctions to its existing deterrent tools (White House 2015). Following the US example, the EU introduced a legal framework in May 2019, which provides for restrictive measures in response to cyberattacks. Incorporating sanctions as a deterrence measure is

intended to strengthen the EU's capacity to respond to malicious cyber enabled activities, which undermine its economic, political and security interests (European Commission 2017). This framework also strengthens the EU's
position internationally since it allows it to signal an unacceptable behavior
in cyberspace.

At the end of July 2020, the EU imposed its first 'cyber sanctions'. The EU
emulated to a large extent the US sanctions and listed Russian, Chinese, and
North Korean entities and individuals which have already been sanctioned
by the US (European Council 2020b). The symmetry between the EU and US
sanctions signifies both sides' readiness to act as a bloc on cybersecurity issues in order to have a stronger position in the big power competition to set a
framework of responsible state behavior in cyberspace and sanction destructive, disruptive and destabilizing cyber-activities.

Deterrence in Cyberspace

Deterrence is identified as one of the main strategies for preventing cyberattacks. It can be understood as a form of coercion entailing a manipulation
of an adversary's estimation of the cost-benefit calculation. Deterrence also
refers to the use of a threat "explicit or not" by one party, with the objective
of persuading another party to change behavior or maintain the status quo
(Quackenbush 2011: 741). The concept of mutually assured destruction, which
creates the looming threat of mutual annihilation in the case of one party
launching an attack on another, represents maybe the most famous example
of nuclear deterrence (Crosston 2011).

Deterrence has become a widely used concept in cybersecurity discourse.
The term "(cyber)deterrence" was coined by Professor James Derian in a 1994
issue of *Wired Magazine*, which examined the potential deterrent effect of network technologies on the physical environment. Many scholars agreed that
the conventional concept of deterrence, as applied to the kinetic environment,
is difficult to transpose to the unique nature of cyberspace for a wide range
of reasons (Libicki 2009: 3). Libicki (ibid: 40-41) laid out some major elements
that would differentiate (cyber)deterrence from nuclear deterrence. First, the
logic of deterrence in cyberspace is undermined by the difficulty of ascribing
responsibility for attacks (on which more below). Secondly, it is difficult to
clearly communicate the threshold of an action leading to a reprisal (Libicki
2017). It is one thing to assess an attack that blows up a refinery; it is another

to assess a cyberattack that damages the refinery control system (Libicki 2009: 52). Furthermore, it is not clear what the threshold of response should be and how further escalation can be avoided (ibid.).

Critics of the application of deterrence theory in the cyber realm argue that there are "fundamental inconsistencies between the theory and the nature of cyber conflicts and cyberspace" (Taddeo 2018: 340). While some scholars insist on the need to reformulate and extend classic deterrence thinking to the cyber domain (Nye 2017) others call for a sharp break from the deterrence-centric paradigm (Harknett/Nye 2017). For instance, Fischerkeller and Harknett (2017) criticized deterrence for its strategic inertia in creating behavioral effects, which exacerbates, in their opinion, the absence of US leadership in shaping the parameters of acceptable behavior in cyberspace. They propose, instead, to replace a strategy of operational restraint and reaction with persistent engagement in advancing US interests. In other words, this would mean a shift from threat-based approach to capabilities-based strategy; from what threatens the US to what the US can do to proactively shape cyberspace. In 2018 the US Cyber Command and the National Security Agency (NSA) announced a strategy based on "persistent engagement" and "defend forward" (The Economist 2020). This can be understood as a return to pre-emption: not so much 'striking back' as 'striking first'.

Across this literature, denial and retaliation are commonly identified as two types of deterrence strategies. Denial is the defensive aspect of deterrence, whereas punishment is the offensive one. Deterrence by denial focuses on preventing an attack from occurring and denying an enemy an ability to cause damage. In contrast, deterrence by retaliation implies the threat of coercive measures to change behavior (Taddeo 2018). Cyber-sanctions offer a 'third way' of shaping cyberspace between passive deterrence and a US-style 'striking first' approach. The deterrent potential of cyber-sanctions could be leveraged as a means of regulating cyberspace and setting norms of responsible state behavior in cyberspace.

Deterrence by denial is difficult in cyberspace, since many vulnerabilities are not known until they are exploited by malicious actors. Sometimes knowledge of vulnerabilities is kept secret as a form of bargaining. As Thomas Schelling has observed, "the power to hurt is most successful when held in reserve" (2008: 3). Furthermore, potential perpetrators are many and diffuse. Consequently, no system in the world would be fully defended against infiltration attempts. What counts in this context is the resilience of the system and its "capacity to withstand, recover from, and adapt to external shocks"

(Dupont 2019: 2). 'Deterrence by denial' in the US discourse echoes 'resilience' in EU official documents. Resilience, as described in the EU 2013 Cybersecurity Strategy (European Commission 2013), aims at strengthening prevention and early warning mechanisms with regard to cyberattacks. This is deemed crucial for the maintenance of a well-functioning internal market.

As an illustration, Estonia represents one of the most prominent examples of deterrence by denial. After being targeted by the first (allegedly) State-sponsored distributed denial-of-service (DDoS) attack, Estonia launched an initiative called the "Data Embassy", with the objective of backing-up data storage facilities outside its borders (Sierzputowski 2019: 227; see also Myatt in this volume). In 2017 an Estonian data embassy was finally established in Luxembourg in order to ensure national digital continuity and service functionality "no matter what" (ibid.). 'Physical' embassies enjoy a wide range of immunities under the Vienna Convention on diplomatic relations. Estonia is setting the tone by bringing the same concept to the cyber world.

The key elements of deterrence theory were described by Morgan (2003: 8). They involve the assumption of a conflict, the assumption of rationality, the concept of a retaliatory threat, the concept of unacceptable damage, the notion of credibility, and the notion of deterrence stability. Taddeo discusses how ineffective those elements are when applied to a (cyber)conflict (2018: 340). She does so by suggesting the minimalist model of international deterrence (DM) defined according to the deterrence theory. The minimalist model of international deterrence (DM) includes three core elements: the attribution of responsibility for attack, deterrence strategies, and the capability of the defender to signal credible threats to potential attackers (Taddeo 2018: 340). For the purposes of this study, we will assess how sanctions in response to cyberattacks fit into the logic of deterrence by combining the elements of the Minimalist model of international deterrence and the deterrence attributes identified by Morgan (2003). The next section will provide an analysis of the development of a Framework for a Joint EU Diplomatic Response to Malicious Cyber Activities or the "EU Cyber Diplomacy Toolbox". Particular attention will be paid to restrictive measures as a deterrence instrument of the EU Cyber Diplomacy.

Restrictive Measures as a Deterrence Instrument in EU Cyber Diplomacy

The EU sanctions regime is designed to strengthen the EU's leadership in setting up a set of rules for regulating cyberspace. The efficiency and challenges of restrictive measures[1] from political, human rights and attribution perspectives have been examined elsewhere. This work will not repeat them but will instead explore restrictive measures as a concrete practical example of (cyber)deterrence tools available to the EU.

The EU's development of collective responses to cyberattacks has rested on a recognition that the multiplication of cyberattacks and their destructive character required a different response, beyond the conventional defense of networks and resilience-building paradigm. For the first time, the possibility of a joint EU diplomatic response to cyberattacks was mentioned in the Council conclusions on Cyber Diplomacy in February 2015 (European Council 2015). In 2016, the Dutch Presidency submitted a 'non-paper'[2] on "Developing a joint EU diplomatic response against coercive cyber operation", which argues that cyber diplomacy is one of the tools to influence a rational cost-benefit analysis of State and non-State actors by increasing the costs of coercive cyber operations and establishing a deterrent effect (European Presidency 2016).

While the resilience and security of networks are essential for preventing and mitigating the consequences of cyber operations, a broader response and a comprehensive use of a multitude of policy instruments were held to be required. The use of cyber diplomacy tools was identified as an appropriate means to deter state and non-state actors from carrying out cyberattacks for politico-military purposes. A common and comprehensive approach to cyber diplomacy can also contribute to the "mitigation of cybersecurity threats, conflict prevention and greater stability in international relations through the use of diplomatic and legal instruments" (European Council 2015).

The Council confirmed the added value of the Joint EU Diplomatic Response to Malicious Cyber Activities in the conclusions of June 2017. These conclusions endorsed that the EU must clearly signal the likely consequences of an EU response to cyber operations so as to influence the behavior of potential aggressors (European Council 2017a). In October 2017, the Council put for-

---

1   Sanctions and restrictive measures will be used interchangeably in this chapter. Restrictive measures refer to asset freezes and visa bans with regard to listed individuals.

2   Informal document issued to facilitate negotiations.

ward the implementing guidelines for the Framework development (2017b). The measures presented therein refer to a range of diplomatic actions to be undertaken by the EU and Member States. They include preventive, cooperative and stability measures, EU support to Member States' lawful responses, and restrictive measures within the CFSP. The above-mentioned measures could be used "either independently, sequentially or in parallel" as part of a comprehensive EU approach (ibid.).

Preventive measures encompass EU-supported 'Confidence Building Measures', including initiatives in third countries through the European Neighbourhood Instrument (ENI) or any other relevant financing instruments. They also include awareness-raising on EU policies, such as EU-led political and thematic dialogues, particularly cyber or security dialogues. Cooperative measures refer to EU-led political and thematic dialogues or EU-diplomatic *démarches* to facilitate the peaceful resolution of an ongoing incident. Stability measures are understood as statements expressing concern or condemning general cyber trends on behalf of the EU, for instance statements by High Representative of the EU; EU Council Conclusions or démarches by the EU delegations as a way to signal the likely consequences of a malicious cyber activity.

Possible EU support to Member States' lawful responses refer to non-forcible and proportionate countermeasures to compel or convince an attacker to change their behavior. In grave instances, cyberattacks could amount to a use of force or an armed attack within the meaning of Article 51 of the Charter of the United Nations. In this case, Article 42(7) TEU (the "Defense Clause") may be invoked by an attacked Member State to ask the EU for aid and assistance.

Restrictive measures, in turn, are usually meant to bring about a change in behavior and can include, *inter alia*, travel bans and the freezing of funds or economic resources. Sanctions of this nature constitute a central instrument of the EU Common Foreign and Security Policy (CFSP). Restrictive measures have as their objective the maintenance and restoration of international peace and security, the fight against terrorism and the proliferation of weapons of mass destruction, the upholding of respect for human rights, democracy and the rule of law. The EU is the second most active user of restrictive measures, surpassed only by the US (Russell 2018).

Sanctions have an inherently preventive character and are not necessarily adopted in response to a breach of an international obligation (Ruys 2016). For instance, the UN Security Council does not need to establish a violation of international law for their enactment, but must find a "threat to the peace, a breach of the peace or an act of aggression" in the meaning of Article 39 UN Charter (Kelsen 1948: 789). Generally, sanctions pursue three purposes, namely:

a) to coerce or change behavior
b) to constrain access to resources needed to engage in proscribed activities, or
c) to signal and stigmatize (van den Herik 2014: 433).

In June 2017, the European Council identified restrictive measures as a suitable foreign policy instrument in order to mitigate cyber threats and change the behavior of aggressors in the long term (2017a: 5). Since sanctions represent a traditionally contentious topic, discussions of the EU's capacity to deter cyberattacks through political measures were slow moving. The European Council (2018a) stressed the need to move forward in the work on attribution of cyberattacks and the practical use of the cyber diplomacy toolbox in its conclusions of June 2018. In October of the same year, the European Council (2018b) endorsed the objective to strengthen EU resilience against cyber-attacks and to conclude negotiations on all cybersecurity proposals before the end of the legislature. However, work was progressing slowly since many questions remained as to how the sanctions should be deployed and whether they would work at all.

The 2019 European Parliament elections, deemed 'Europe's most hackable', hastened the adoption of the new "cyber sanctions" framework, which came into being on the 17th of May—just a couple of days before EU citizens headed to polls. The new sanctions regime was introduced based on the traditional two-step approach. First the CFSP decision, which sets out the overall sanctions framework, is adopted by the Council on the basis of Article 29 TEU. Then the CFSP decision is implemented by the accompanying regulation on the basis of Article 215 TFEU.

When viewed from the perspective of international law, sanctions, if defined by the objective of a measure, can possibly amount to retorsion measures. Retorsion measures are measures of unfriendliness vis-à-vis another state but are intrinsically legal (Ruys 2016). They do not necessarily constitute a response to an internationally wrongful act, contrary to countermeasures, which are taken in response to a violation of an international obligation. Countermeasures are law enforcement measures meant to induce a

State to comply with its obligations. They are not punitive; they are by nature temporary and limited to a non-performance of an international obligation.

Sanctions, mentioned in the Cyber Diplomacy Toolbox, are targeted measures and they do not lead to the attribution of responsibility to a State. Nevertheless, Member States are free to make their own determinations with respect to the attribution of cyberattacks. It is thus incorrect to compare targeted sanctions under the EU's restrictive measures to either retorsion measures or countermeasures. First of all, both retorsion measures and countermeasures are taken in inter-state relationships, whereas the EU "cyber sanctions" framework applies to non-State actors and does not entail an attribution of State responsibility. Secondly, countermeasures constitute a response to a prior internationally wrongful act, which is not true for EU sanctions in response to cyberattacks. Thirdly, it is not established yet whether a cyber-operation amounts to a violation of an international legal obligation and, thus, triggers a state responsibility, as suggested by the authors of Tallinn Manual in Rule 14 (Schmitt 2017).[3] Fourthly, there is no general consensus on the application of countermeasures in cyberspace. The international legal framework was not designed to accommodate violations caused by cyberattacks; and persistent attempt to apply international law to cyber threats is sometimes compared to fitting square pegs into round holes (Anderson 2016: 141).

Restrictive Measures as a (Cyber)deterrence Instrument

How effective, then, are restrictive measures as a response to cyberattacks? The present section will assess the deterrence potential of restrictive measures on the basis of some generic attributes of the deterrence identified in rich theoretic contributions by Morgan (2003) and Taddeo (2018). First, we will analyze what constitutes a conflict in cyberspace from the deterrence perspective and what type of threat triggers the activation of the EU "cyber sanctions" framework. Secondly, we will explore the limits of the assumption of rationality when applied to restrictive measures in response to malicious cyber activities. Thirdly, we will analyze the EU's potential for making a deterrent

---

3   According to Rule 14: "A State bears international responsibility for a cyber-related act that is attributable to the State and that constitutes a breach of an international legal obligation."

declaration and signal clear consequences to potential attackers through re-course to restrictive measures.

The Assumption of a Conflict

The assumption of a conflict constitutes one of the main elements of deter-rence. Accordingly, the nature and intensity of a conflict will have a significant impact on the deterrence strategy. No one questions the destructive potential of cyberattacks. As an illustration, Michael Hayden, the former Central Intel-ligence Agency (CIA) and National Security Agency (NSA) director, compared the computer virus StuxNet to a new weapon (Greenberg 2017). According to Estonia's ex-president Toomas Hendrik Ilves, there is no need for missiles to destroy the infrastructure of a rival state, since everything can be orches-trated online (Sierzputowski 2019: 226). To some extent, this cyberwar sce-nario partly materialized in Ukraine in 2015, when an unprecedented hack of Ukraine's electricity grid caused an electricity blackout. The WannaCry and NotPetya attacks similarly demonstrated the extent of the damage to people and infrastructure that malicious cyber-enabled operations can inflict.

As per the 2019 European Council Decision on cyber sanctions, restrictive measures can be taken in response to performed and attempted cyberattacks of a "significant effect". It seems, however, disproportionate for the Council to suggest the use of sanctions as a response to an attempted, but deterred attack with a potentially significant effect. It is also unclear what the yard-stick is for measuring the significance of an attempted attack. Uncertainty is particularly dangerous in a situation where damage prediction is crucial for successful deterrence and compliance with the principle of proportional-ity. The Council decision provides a list of criteria relevant for the assessment of an attack's impact. Among them, it mentions "the scope, scale, impact or severity of disruption caused" (2019). To perform such an assessment, an im-portant cooperation effort on behalf of Member States will be required. Fur-thermore, the Council mentions as relevant assessment criteria "the number of natural or legal persons, entities or bodies" affected by a cyber-attack as well as "the amount of economic loss and the amount or nature of data stolen" (ibid.). Measuring the impact of a cross-border cyber-incident is a complex task. There is a traditional reluctance to share data concerning the destruc-tive effect of cyber operations on economic and societal activities, essential services, critical state functions and public order or public safety. More guid-ance is required with regard to the calculus applied. Will it require setting up a specialized body empowered to perform such assessment? Or will it be performed by the EU Intelligence Analysis Centre (INTCEN)[4] or the Horizontal Working Party (HWP) on Cyber Issues within the Council of the EU?

The activation of the adopted framework is foreseen in response to a cyberattack which constitutes an 'external threat' not only to the Union or its Member States, but also to third States or international organizations. The Council provides several illustrations of cyberattacks which constitute external threats. Such attacks entail damage to critical infrastructures or services—such as energy or transport; or the disturbance of critical State functions, such as the storage or processing of classified information. The notion of 'threat' is difficult to square with the existing terminology. It is unclear what threshold of an attack the Council refers to. Three interrelated thresholds are applied in international law and include: the threat or use of force; armed attack; and the threat to peace, breach of peace, and act of aggression (Delerue 2020: 276). In the EU Treaties, the reference to "threat" is made on two occasions. First, it is made in the context of "Solidarity Clause" (Art. 222(1)(a) and (4) TFEU), which conventionally refers to terrorist attacks. Pursuant to "Solidarity Clause", the European Council shall ensure the regular assessment of the threats facing the Union. The second reference to a "threat" is made under Article 347 TFEU, which provides for cooperation between Member States in order to alleviate the disturbing impact of measures taken in the event of a serious international tension constituting a threat of war.

It is not surprising that the EU does not try to align its vocabulary with the existing international legal framework. Instead, the Council introduces a new concept of "an external threat". This "escapism" from the international legal framework can be interpreted in a number of ways. First, while the EU accepts the application of international law in cyberspace, it has still not unveiled its views as to the interpretation of international legal rules. Second, the EU is traditionally known for its effort to preserve the autonomy of its legal order. Govaere (2018) compares the EU legal order to the autonomous EU balloon, which needs to be shielded from puncturing by international law interference. Thirdly, American exceptionalism or "New Sovereigntism", which has fuelled US foreign policy in recent years, has undermined transatlantic trust and the value of international law commitments (Spiro 2004). Some recent examples of the resistance of the US to the force of international law include the decision to leave the World Health Organization (WHO), and the

---

4   INTCEN is a network of security services of Member States.

Open Skies Treaties, alongside its withdrawal from the 1987 Intermediate-Range Nuclear Forces (INF) Treaty between the United States and Russia and from the Iran nuclear agreement.

We should also note the emphasis the European Council puts on the external origin of a cyberattack. This is defined on multiple levels:

a) the attack(s) are carried out from outside the Union;
b) the attack(s) use infrastructure outside the Union;
c) the attack(s) are carried out by any natural or legal person, entity or body established or operating outside the Union; or
d) are carried out with the support, at the direction or under the control of any natural or legal person, entity or body operating outside the Union.

The reliance on an external element seems unfit for the operational characteristics of cyberspace. It is technically possible to escape the qualification as "external". Different deception techniques via 'spoofing' and 'false flags' may be displayed in order to pretend that an attack originates within the EU territory. Establishing a link between a perpetrator and any natural or legal person, entity or body supporting, directing or controlling the performance of the operation in question is a difficult matter.

The Assumption of Rationality

Deterrence aims to convince another actor not to attack by threatening unacceptable damage; or by altering their calculations with respect to risks, response and reward (Nye 2017: 45). Rationality is therefore intrinsic to deterrence theory building. It entails forecasting the impact of expectations about benefits and costs on the adversary's behavior. However, the conventional assumption of rationality is usually ineffective in cyberspace. Some cyberattacks are opportunistic; the perpetrators are diffuse; and the costs of engaging in malicious cyber activities are often limited.

The EU Cyber Diplomacy Toolbox presumes a rational challenger as well. Restrictive measures are adopted with the objective of influencing the behavior of potential aggressors over the long term. The type of measures chosen by the EU points out to their mostly economic character: travel bans and the freezing of funds and other economic resources of natural or legal persons, entities or bodies that are responsible for (attempted) cyber-attacks. To constitute an efficient deterrent tool, the measure should be able to influence a cost-benefit analysis of perpetrator. The deterrent effect of sanctions would currently be meaningless where a perpetrator did not have any economic resources in the territory of the EU. EU restrictive measures, in contrast to American secondary sanctions, do not have an extraterritorial reach and apply to EU-based entities solely. Against this background, one could claim that the EU should not keep its expectations too high with regard to the dissuasive effect of its sanctions.

As follows from the implementation guidelines for the Framework on a Joint EU Diplomatic Response to Malicious Cyber Activities (2017b: 4), restrictive measures in response to cyberattacks must conform to the principle of utility in a sense that they need to be "proportionate to the scope, scale, duration, intensity, complexity, sophistication and impact" of an aggressive behavior in cyberspace. In general, sanctions are not punitive measures and have a preventive character. This view was confirmed by the European Court of Justice (ECJ) in the seminal Kadi II judgement (ECJ 2013: §130). In a similar vein, the International Law Commission (ILC) rejects the idea of "punitive damages" (ILC 2001). It stresses that countermeasures must be proportionate to the original wrongful act(s), temporary, and should be aimed at inducing the State to comply with the law. The principle of proportionality is also enshrined in Article 51 of the Articles on State responsibility. The ICJ expressed in the Gabčíkovo-Nagymaros case with respect to the proportionality requirement that the effects of a countermeasure must be commensurate with the injury suffered (ICJ 1997: §85). The authors of Tallinn Manual codified this in Rule 23, which reads as follows: "Countermeasures, whether cyber in nature or not, must be proportionate to the injury to which they respond" (Schmitt 2017).

It follows that a restrictive measure shall be adjusted to the damage suffered. However, determining the impact, value and type of damage of a cyberattack is not an easy exercise. It can be a serious hurdle to guarantee that a restrictive measure is proportionate to a performed cyber-operation. Estimation failures are dangerous and can trigger further escalation. Furthermore, restrictive measures, when targeted, are limited as to the number of options available. They entail either travel bans or the freezing of funds. There is not much flexibility for the EU as to the selection of scalable deterrence tools.

Deterrent Declaration and Credibility

Signaling credible threats is one of the elements of the minimalist model of international deterrence suggested by Taddeo (2018). It refers to the capacity of deterring an attacker through the prospective (signaled) threat of coercive measures. Deploying an appropriate deterrence strategy and clearly conveying a coercive message is crucial for an effective retaliation. There should be a clear understanding of what is acceptable and what are red lines.

Efficient deterrent declaration presupposes a number of elements. The deterrent declaration must be loud and clear so the target cannot misread it; it should be clearly mentioned in national policy, and be consistently echoed in the words and actions. For instance, NATO has already declared that a cyberattack could lead the alliance to invoke its Article 5 collective defense clause. This Statement aims to have a deterrent effect. Implicit or explicit threats of restrictive measures constitute another example of deterrent declarations.

The deterrent effect of the EU framework on restrictive measures is weakened by complexities of attribution and by political divisions within the EU. The ambiguities of cyberspace do not simply reflect the traditional challenges that are present in other domains, but are particularly exacerbated by operational features of the cyber realm (Roscini 2015). As it has been noticed "the Internet is one big masquerade ball" where the possibility of spoofing and masking IP addresses makes more difficult the identification of a computer or computers used to carry out a cyber-operation (Roscini 2015: 234). Contrary to the Cold War bipolar world, today's cyberspace is characterized by the unprecedented rise of active and sophisticated non-state actors. Since much ink has been spilled debating the contentious issue of political, legal and technical attribution, this contribution will limit itself to reaffirming the persistence of human-machine gap and of the challenge of establishing a sufficient legal nexus between non-state actors and a non-EU state.

Moreover, the EU often does not have one common stance on the issue of attribution. Unlike a few member states, which have publicly attributed cyberattacks, the EU has not taken any act of attribution or follow-up with regard to potential perpetrators. The question of collective attribution of cyber-attacks by the EU was passed over in silence on multiple occasions. While the UK and Denmark attributed the NotPetya cyberattack to the GRU (Russian Military Intelligence) and some Member States issued statements of support, the April 2018 Council conclusions were limited to a formal "condemnation of the malicious use of information and communications technologies (ICTs)"

(European Council 2018c). The same discrepancies became obvious at the institutional and governmental levels with respect to the attacks on the offices of the Organisation for the Prohibition of Chemical Weapons (OPCW) in The Hague.

The Decision of the European Council (2019) on cyber sanctions highlights that targeted sanctions should not be viewed as the attribution of responsibility to a state. Nevertheless, this delimitation between individual perpetrators and states remains rather artificial. The practice shows that a majority of cyberattacks with substantial consequences, such as StuxNet, WannaCry and NotPetya, were orchestrated at the request and with the support of governments.

The credibility of EU cyber sanctions is currently being tested by cyberattacks on Georgia and the German Parliament. In October 2019, Georgia was targeted with a number of cyberattacks undermining the websites and servers of several governmental agencies, including that of the President of Georgia, courts of Georgia, NGOs, local governments and various organizations. In February 2020, the Georgian Foreign Ministry Stated that the Russian General Staff Main Intelligence Directorate (GRU) carried out a "widespread, disruptive cyber-attack" (Agenda.ge 2020). The EU along with its Member States condemned the cyberattack and reaffirmed its willingness to continue to assist Georgia in increasing its cyber resilience (EU High Representative, 2020). In contrast to some Member States (Netherlands, Latvia, UK) and other partners (US, New Zealand), the EU did not attribute this cyberattack to Russia. Some commenters (Nakashidze 2020) were wrong in assuming that the general statement of condemnation constituted an act of attribution. The EU's reaction to a cyberattack on Georgia was passive despite the fact that the EU has the possibility of applying restrictive measures even in response to a cyberattack on a third country, pursuant to Article 1(5) of the Council Decision (2019). In the case of Georgia this could be justified by its special status as an associated partner. Georgia and the EU have an ambitious Association Agreement in place, which has as an objective the full integration of Georgia into the EU single market.

The cyberattack on German Parliament was another test of the deterrent effect of the 'cyber-sanctions'. In the present case, the perpetrator is known; and Germany considered triggering the framework. As this chapter was being written, the EU imposed sanctions against two Russian military intelligence officers and "military unit 26165", also known as "APT28", "Fancy Bear", and believed to be behind the breach of the German *Bundestag* in 2015 (European Council 2020c).

The Role of Restrictive Measures in Shaping Responsible State Behavior

While they may seem ineffective at first glance, restrictive measures nonetheless have a significant signaling potential. It will be argued in this section that they can serve as an instrument for cultivating a culture of compliance and responsibility in the cyber domain. This is in line with the European Union's objectives as outlined in the Lisbon Treaty, which expressly states in Article 3(5) that the Union "shall contribute to [...] the development of international law, including respect for the principles of the United Nations Charter". In addition, Article 21 of the Treaty commits the EU's action at the international scene should aim at safeguarding its security, consolidating principles of international law, strengthening international security, and promoting an international system based on stronger multilateral cooperation and good global governance. The EU also committed to strongly "uphold that existing international law is applicable to cyberspace" (European Council 2019). Sanctions have an important role to play in framing a normative framework by targeting, signaling and deterring a state's behavior when it crosses red lines.

Respect for international law and norms of responsible state behavior legitimize the actions of a state as a good global actor. Nevertheless, the questions remain as to the adequacy of the existing international legal framework when applied to cyberspace. Whereas some states, including Russia, favor the negotiation of new legal norms others led by the US find the existing legal norms sufficient (Korzak 2015).

In the seminal 2013 report of the UNGGE (United Nations Group of Governmental Experts on Information Security), participating states agreed that international law regulates the cyber domain and forms one of the key pillars of stability in cyberspace. However, there is no common understanding of how international law should apply in cyberspace. The problem is compounded by a persistent general disagreement over the potential use of the right to self-defense and the law of armed conflicts in cyberspace (Delerue 2019: 297). In the 2016-2017 discussions over a new report of the UNGGE, Russia and Cuba opposed equating the malicious use of ICTs to the concept of "armed conflict" under Article 51 of the UN Charter. Remaining divergences in views on international norms caused the failure of the 2017 UNGGE to concur on a final report.

In 2018, two separate processes were established under the auspices of the UN. Russia sponsored the resolution, which provided for the establishment of an Open-Ended Working Group (OEWG) open to any UN Member. The other resolution under the leadership of the US provided for a new Group of Governmental Experts (GGE) with a smaller membership. While Russia and the US presented the two resolutions as mutually exclusive, many countries voted for both of them (Delerue 2020: 210). Embarking in two overlapping discussions is a difficult endeavour, likely to aggravate the present lack of consensus.

Since it is not clear what international legal rules apply to cyber-operations, attribution in this context is reduced to a purely political condemnation without pointing to a specific legal obligation, let alone legal consequences for a wrongful act. A decision to attribute a cyber-operation to another state is often linked to broader policy objectives and is dependent on concrete instruments available in response to such malicious activities. Finnemore and Hollis (2020) explore the implications of cybersecurity accusations, which include three elements: attribution, exposure and condemnation. As a reminder, in accordance with Articles on State Responsibility, the state is responsible for the conduct of its organs, persons or entities exercising elements of governmental authority or those who act under its instructions, directions or control. The principle of due diligence can also serve for the establishment of indirect responsibility in the cyber realm (Chircop 2018, Buchan 2016). Cybersecurity accusations can be made with the objective of deterrence, aid, defense, and contribution to the emergence of new norms and international law (Finnemore/Hollis 2020).

Recent attributions of cyberattacks against Georgia were striking for their omission of an allegedly breached rule of international law. The omission of reference to rules of international law stems from a disagreement as to whether a breach of sovereignty constitutes a rule, which triggers state responsibility or just a principle of international law (Roguski 2020). One can also observe 'gray' area status of cyberattacks, which fall below the threshold of an armed attack, use of force or an internationally wrongful act.

Are restrictive measures capable of filling in the void? Can sanctions compensate the vacuum stemming from the as-yet unclear international legal framework? Would deterrence via sanctions be an efficient way of promoting and clarifying the norms of responsible state behavior? These questions cannot yet be answered, but they are worth reflecting upon. Even more so, for the EU, which is fundamentally committed to the development of international law. When conventional discussions reach a deadlock, someone needs to think outside the box. Restrictive measures constitute a tool which allow exposure and help to establish the bar for the assessment of what is acceptable in cyberspace. Only through signaling and communicating can the international community succeed in establishing the rules for cyberspace, whether through the codification of customary international law or through a treaty. Against this backdrop, sanctions represent a valuable tool to shape and promote responsible state behavior, even in the absence of a consensus on the interpretation of rules of international law in cyberspace.

Conclusions

The EU is committed to a rules-based international order. This commitment translates into an aspiration to shape, transform and adapt the existing system to a new cyber domain. EU cyber-sanctions, despite their limited strategic effectiveness, could serve as an instrument for cultivating a culture of compliance and responsibility in the cyber domain. Sanctions have an important role to play in framing a normative framework by targeting, signaling and deterring a state's behavior when this crosses red lines. Thus, EU sanctions could help to jump-start a necessary progress of agreeing international law frameworks for cyberspace that is currently stalled at the UN level.

EU cyber-sanctions are designed as deterrence measures for strengthening the EU's leadership in setting up a set of rules for regulating cyberspace. Along with the US, the EU emerges as a significant global actor establishing standards for itself and aligning approaches with other strategic partners. In this context, cyber deterrence via sanctions regime offers a norm-setting a 'third way' between passive deterrence and US-style 'striking first' approach in cyberspace. The development of the cyber diplomacy toolbox is indispensable for the EU if it wants to learn "the language of power" in the competitive cyber domain (Kribbe 2020).

References

Agenda.ge (2020): "Georgia accuses Russia of widespread cyberattack", Agenda.ge, February 20 (https://agenda.ge/en/news/2020/535).

Anderson, T. (2016): "Fitting a Virtual Peg into a Round Hole: Cyber Reprisals." In: Arizona Journal of International & Comparative Law 34/1, pp. 136-157.

Brustlein C. (2017): "Entry Operations and the Future of Strategic Autonomy." In: Focus Stratégique N° 70 bis, p. 27.

Buchan, R. (2016): "Cyberspace, Non-State Actors and the Obligation to Prevent Transboundary Harm." In: Journal of Conflict and Security Law 21/3, pp. 429-453.

Chircop, L. (2018): "A Due Diligence Standard of Attribution in Cyberspace." In: International and Comparative Law Quarterly 63/3, pp. 643-668.

Crosston, M. D. (2011): "World Gone Cyber MAD: How 'Mutually Assured Debilitation' Is the Best Hope for Cyber Deterrence." In: Strategic Studies Quarterly 5/1, pp. 100-116.

Delerue, F. (2019): "International Cooperation on the International Law Applicable to Cyber Operations." In: European Foreign Affairs Review 24/2, pp. 203-216.

Delerue, F. (2020): Cyber Operations and International Law, Cambridge: Cambridge University Press.

Department of Justice (2018a): "North Korean Regime-Backed Programmer Charged With Conspiracy to Conduct Multiple Cyber Attacks and Intrusions", The United States Department of Justice Press Release, September 6 (https://www.justice.gov/opa/pr/north-korean-regime-backed-pro grammer-charged-conspiracy-conduct-multiple-cyber-attacks-and).

Department of Justice (2018b): "U.S. Charges Russian GRU Officers with International Hacking and Related Influence and Disinformation Operations", The United States Department of Justice Press Release, October 4 (https://www.justice.gov/opa/pr/us-charges-russian-gru-officers-inter national-hacking-and-related-influence-and).

Derian, J. (1994): "Cyberdeterrence", January 9 (https://www.wired.com/1994/ 09/cyber-deter).

Dupont, B. (2019): "The Cyber-Resilience of Financial Institutions: Significance and Applicability." In: Journal of Cybersecurity 5/1, pp. 1-17.

ECJ (2013): "Cases C-584/10 P, C-593/10 P and C-595/10 P", European Court of Justice, Commission and United Kingdom v Kadi, Judgment of the Court (Grand Chamber).

EUGS (2016): Shared Vision, Common Action: A Stronger Europe, A Global Strategy for the European Union's Foreign and Security Policy, Brussels: European Union.

European Commission (2013): "Cybersecurity Strategy of the European Union: An Open, Safe and Secure Cyberspace", European Commission Joint Communication JOIN/2013/01, Brussels.

European Commission (2017): "Communication 'Resilience, Deterrence and Defense: Building strong cybersecurity for the EU'", European Commission Joint Communication JOIN/2017/0450, Brussels.

European Council (2015): "Conclusions on Cyber Diplomacy", European Council Report 6122/15, Brussels.

European Council (2017a): "Conclusions on a Framework for a Joint EU Diplomatic Response to Malicious Cyber Activities ('Cyber Diplomacy Toolbox')", European Council Report 10474/17, Brussels.

European Council (2017b): "Draft implementing guidelines for the Framework on a Joint EU Diplomatic Response to Malicious Cyber Activities", European Council Report 13007/17, Brussels.

European Council (2018a): "Conclusions", European Council Conclusions June 28 (https://www.consilium.europa.eu/en/press/press-releases/2018/06/2 9/20180628-euco-conclusions-final).

European Council (2018b): "Conclusions", European Council Conclusions, October 18 (https://www.consilium.europa.eu/en/press/press-releases/2018 /10/18/20181018-european-council-conslusions).

European Council (2018c): "Conclusions on malicious cyber activities—approval", European Council Report 7925/18, Brussels.

European Council (2019): "Decision (CFSP) 2019/797 concerning restrictive measures against cyberattacks threatening the Union or its Member States," European Council Decision OJ L 129I, Brussels, pp. 1-12.

European Council (2020a): "Special meeting of the European Council, Conclusions", European Council Report EUCO 13/20, Brussels.

European Council (2020b): "Decision (CFSP) 2020/1127 amending Decision (CFSP) 2019/797 concerning restrictive measures against cyber-attacks threatening the Union or its Member States", European Council Decision OJ L 246/12, Brussels.

European Council (2020c): "Decision (CFSP) 2020/1537 amending Decision (CFSP) 2019/797 concerning restrictive measures against cyber-attacks threatening the Union or its Member States", European Council Decisions OJ L 351I, Brussels, pp. 5-7.

European Council (2020d): "Declaration by the High Representative on behalf of the European Union—call to promote and conduct responsible behavior in cyberspace", 21 February 2020 (https://www.consilium.europ

a.eu/en/press/press-releases/2020/02/21/declaration-by-the-high-repres
entative-on-behalf-of-the-european-union-call-to-promote-and-conduc
t-responsible-behavior-in-cyberspace/).

European Parliament and Council (2016): "Directive (EU) 2016/1148 concerning
measures for a high common level of security of network and information
systems across the Union", European Parliament and Council Directive OJ
L 194, Brussels, pp. 1-30.

European Parliament and Council (2019): "Regulation (EU) 2019/881 on
ENISA (the European Union Agency for Cybersecurity) and on in-
formation and communications technology cybersecurity certification
and repealing Regulation (EU) No 526/2013) (Text with EEA relevance)
PE/86/2018/REV/1", European Parliament and Council Regulation OJ L 151,
Brussels, pp. 15-69.

European Presidency (2016): "Non-paper: Developing a joint EU diplomatic
response against coercive cyber operations", Non-Paper of the European
Presidency 5797/6/16 REV 6, Brussels.

Finnemore, M. B./Hollis, D. (2020): "Beyond naming and shaming: accusations and international law in cybersecurity." In: European Journal of International Law, 2020 forthcoming (https://ssrn.com/abstract=3347958).

Fischerkeller, M. P./Harknett, R. J. (2017): "Deterrence Is Not a Credible Strategy for Cyberspace." In: Orbis 61/3, pp. 381-393.

Franke, U./Varma, T. (2019): "Independence play: Europe's pursuit of strategic
autonomy", July 18 (https://www.ecfr.eu/specials/scorecard/independenc
e_play_europes_pursuit_of_strategic_autonomy).

Govaere, I. (2018): "Interconnecting Legal Systems and the Autonomous EU
Legal Order: A Balloon Dynamic." In: Research Papers in Law 2/2018, unpaginated.

Greenberg, A. (2017): "How an Entire Nation Became Russia's Test Lab for Cyberwar", June 20 (https://www.wired.com/story/russian-hackers-attack-
ukraine/).

Harknett, R. J./Nye, J. S. (2017): "Is Deterrence Possible in Cyberspace?" In:
International Security 42/2, pp. 196-199.

ICJ (1997): "The Gabcíkovo-Nagymaros Project (Hungary/Slovakia)", Judgment, International Court of Justice Reports, p. 7.

ILC (2001): "Draft articles on Responsibility of States for Internationally
Wrongful Acts, with Commentaries." In: Yearbook of the International
Law Commission 2/2, pp. 31-143.

Kelsen, H. (1948): "Collective Security and Collective Self-Defense Under the Charter of the United Nations." In: The American Journal of International Law 42/4, pp. 783-796.

Korzak, E. (2015): "International Law and the UN GGE Report on Information Security", December 2 (https://www.justsecurity.org/28062/international-law-gge-report-information-security/).

Kribbe, H. (2020): "No more Mr. Nice Europe", October 13 (https://www.politico.eu/article/no-more-mr-nice-europe-eu-foreign-policy).

Libicki, M. C. (2009): Cyberdeterrence and Cyberwar, Santa Monica: RAND.

Libicki, M. C. (2017): "It Takes More than Offensive Capability to Have an Effective Cyberdeterrence Posture", Testimony before the House Armed Services Committee, March 1 (https://www.rand.org/content/dam/rand/pubs/testimonies/CT400/CT465/RAND_CT465.pdf).

Macron, E. (2017): Speech on a New Initiative for Europe, 26 September 2016 (https://www.elysee.fr/emmanuel-macron/2017/09/26/president-macron-gives-speech-on-new-initiative-for-europe.en)

Morgan, P. (2003): Deterrence Now, Cambridge: Cambridge University Press.

Nakashidze, G. (2020): "Cyberattack against Georgia and International Response: emerging normative paradigm of 'responsible state behavior in cyberspace'?", Feburary 28 (https://www.ejiltalk.org/cyberattack-against-georgia-and-international-response-emerging-normative-paradigm-of-responsible-State-behavior-in-cyberspace/).

Nye, J. S. (2017): "Deterrence and Dissuasion in Cyberspace." In: International Security 41/3, pp. 44-71.

Roguski, P. (2020): "Russian Cyber Attacks Against Georgia, Public Attributions and Sovereignty in Cyberspace", March 6 (https://www.justsecurity.org/69019/russian-cyberattacks-against-georgia-public-attributions-and-sovereignty-in-cyberspace).

Roscini, M. (2015): "Evidentiary Issues in International Disputes Related to State Responsibility for Cyber Operations." In: Texas International Law Journal 50, pp. 233-273.

Russell, M. (2018): EU sanctions: A key foreign and security policy instrument, Brussels: European Parliamentary Research Service.

Ruys, T. (2016): 'Sanctions, Retorsions and Countermeasures: Concepts and International Legal Framework." In: Larissa van den Herik (ed.), Research Handbook on UN Sanctions and International Law, Cheltenham: Edward Elgar Publishing, pp. 19-51.

Sierzputowski, B. (2019): "The Data Embassy under Public International Law." In: International&ComparativeLawQuarterly 68/1, pp. 225-242.

Schelling, T. C. (2008): Arms and Influence, New Haven: Yale University Press.

Schmitt, M. (2017): The Tallinn Manual 2.0, Cambridge: Cambridge University Press.

Soesanto, S. (2020): "Europe's Incertitude in Cyberspace", August 3 (https://www.lawfareblog.com/europes-incertitude-cyberspace).

Spiro, P. J. (2004): "What Happened to the 'New Sovereigntism'?" In: Foreign Affairs, July 28 (https://www.foreignaffairs.com/articles/united-States/2004-07-28/what-happened-new-sovereigntism).

Taddeo, M. (2018): "The Limits of Deterrence Theory in Cyberspace." In: Philosophy & Technology 31/3, pp. 339-355.

Tamma, P. (2017): "Europe wants 'strategic autonomy'—it just has to decide what that means", Politico, October 15 (https://www.politico.eu/article/europe-trade-wants-strategic-autonomy-decide-what-means).

Timmers, P. (2019): "Strategic Autonomy and Cybersecurity", Policy in Focus (https://eucyberdirect.eu/wp-content/uploads/2019/05/paul-timmers-strategic-autonomy-may-2019-eucyberdirect.pdf).

The Economist (2020): "America rethinks its strategy in the Wild West of cyberspace", May 28 (https://www.economist.com/united-States/2020/05/28/america-rethinks-its-strategy-in-the-wild-west-of-cyberspace).

Quackenbush, S. L. (2011): "Deterrence Theory: Where Do We Stand?" In: Review of International Studies 37, pp. 741-762.

Van den Herik, L. J. (2014): "Peripheral Hegemony in the Quest to Ensure Security Council Accountability for Its Individualized UN Sanctions Regimes." In: Journal of Conflict and Security Law 19/3, pp. 427-449.

Van Reybroeck, R. (2019): "What's in the CARDs?" In: Egmont Security Policy Brief 103, pp. 1-7.

White House (2015): "Blocking the Property of Certain Persons Engaging in Significant Malicious Cyber-Enabled Activities", Executive Order 13694, US Federal Register 80/63, pp. 18077-18079.

White House (2016a): "Taking Additional Steps to Address the National Emergency with Respect to Significant Malicious Cyber-Enabled Activities", Executive Order 13757, US Federal Register 82/1, pp. 1-3.

White House (2016b): "Statement by the President on Actions in Response to Russian Malicious Cyber Activity and Harassment", Office of the Press Secretary, December 29 (https://obamawhitehouse.archives.gov/the-pres

s-office/2016/12/29/statement-president-actions-response-russian-malic
ious-cyber-activity).

République Francaise (1994): Livre blanc sur la defense, Paris: La documenta-
tion francaise.

Zable, S. (2018): "The Foreign Investment Risk Review Modernization Act of
2018", Law Fare Blog, August 2 (https://www.lawfareblog.com/foreign-in
vestment-risk-review-modernization-act-2018).

Afterword

Competition During Covid-19

Heidi Tworek

Ranking failed during Covid-19. Autumn 2019 saw the release of the first World Health Preparedness Report, accompanied predictably with a Global Health Security Index (Global Health Security Index 2019). Compiled by the Johns Hopkins University's Bloomberg School of Public Policy, the Nuclear Threat Initiative, and the Economist Intelligence Unit, the Global Health Security Index offers a classic example of a ranking produced by "rationalised third-parties" (Werron 2015), which collect information and collate it into a plausible index. Like most indices, it created numerical values for multiple parameters and combined them to rank nation-states on their preparedness to address an epidemic. The report ran over 300 pages and contained more than 50 pages detailing its methodology.

The Global Health Security Index has now become infamous for having no predictive power whatsoever. The index had ranked the United States and the United Kingdom as the first and second most prepared countries for a pandemic. When one economist compared the index with fatalities per capita in January 2021 (Milanovic 2021), he found that there was no correlation between a country's rank on the index and its performance during Covid-19. As of January 2021, the United States' fatality rate was 145th out of 153 countries, while the UK was in 149th place. One of the most striking aspects of this crisis is how ranking discourse so poorly anticipated nations' performance during the crisis. The Index had done what rankings are supposed to do: "To aggregate a variety of dimensions into one ranking position, rankings translate qualities into quantities" (Brankovic et al. 2018: 274f.). And yet those quantifications bore no resemblance to the reality that unfolded mere months later.

While commentators have lambasted the Index for its poor choice of measurements, the report's subtitle highlights the paradoxical nature of such indices: "Building Collective Action and Accountability." An index that created national competition through ranking was supposed to generate collaboration. And yet, during this crisis, national comparison and competition have dominated, much to the detriment of most of the world's population.

This volume asks when competition becomes "a globally relevant political category" (Russ/Stafford this volume). The Covid-19 pandemic offers a telling and tragic example of how competition can exacerbate systemic risks and ultimately undermine recovery. Competition has remained all too relevant, whether through statistics around cases and deaths or, more recently, vaccines. Even more strikingly, Covid-19 follows an older pattern where the nation-state is used as the default unit of "competitive comparisons" (Steinmetz 2019). The chapters in this volume highlight other crucial questions—what is the political power behind units of comparison? What do comparisons of deaths or cases of Covid omit? What is the development against which countries are measured and how does that translate into political or economic power? Finally, what historical developments have fostered a world where national competition comes before collective action, even for obviously global problems like pandemics? Even supposedly non-violent competition may have violent consequences.

The Covid crisis has been full of competition. Many countries report their health statistics on a more granular, sub-national level: provinces in Canada, individual states or even counties in the US and Germany. Yet, national statistics have dominated in the global discourse. Perhaps to many readers of the *Financial Times*, it seemed natural to play around with graphs and compare Sweden to Switzerland to Senegal. This edited volume, though, highlights the complex competition that lies behind such purportedly "natural" units of comparison. Ramy Youssef reminds us that status competition is "a historically contingent social form." It is not a natural phenomenon that millions of people should pore obsessively over data dashboards and graphs showing the success of one country over another. The power of the frame of competition requires explanation. Indeed, the richest analysis of such phenomena arises from interdisciplinary engagement. So too, we can best understand how Covid-19 statistics have spurred national competition and, at times, obscured much more important effects by turning to history, epidemiology, sociology, and international relations.

There is a long history of why statistical representations of disease became the main mode of measuring disease and of making disease comparable across borders. Many scholars (Porter 1995; Speich Chassé 2013; Speich Chassé 2016; Jerven 2018) have examined the growing importance of numbers and statistics in modern economics and international institutions, while

Wernimont (2019) has explored the feminist media history of quantification, including mortality statistics. While health statistics had been gathered for centuries, the movement to standardize epidemiology accelerated in the interwar period under aegis of the League of Nations Health Office (LNHO). The epidemiologists and medical officials at the LNHO believed in collating, collecting, and communicating standardized statistics as the most effective method to prevent another pandemic like the Spanish flu. They thought that swiftly-delivered statistics of infectious diseases could enable public health officials to act more quickly to enact quarantines or other measures to prevent an epidemic. Although the LNHO also created medical exchanges and national health systems, its main focus lay on generating comparable statistical information. The LNHO formed the first international epidemiological intelligence system by pushing nations, empires, and territories to submit their data in standardized numerical formats that enabled comparison. By the late 1920s, the League's system encompassed two-thirds of the world's population.

The LNHO disseminated weekly bulletins of smallpox, cholera, and plague cases around the world. Such diseases were not necessarily the deadliest during that period. But they were the highest priority for empires that wished to smooth imperial trade and avoid the spread of disease from colonies back to Europe. The most powerful members within the League of Nations shaped how diseases should be understood—as individual cases counted by statistics—and they also decided which diseases would matter. The statistical mode took the focus away from examining how political, economic, and social conditions could exacerbate disease. This focus continued into the World Health Organization (Tworek 2019).

While much has changed in global public health since the 1920s, the focus on statistics has become even more pronounced. During Covid, it has been accompanied by an increasing reliance on comparative and competitive models. A ranking mania has pervaded much of the discourse around Covid. The US magazine *Foreign Policy* had created an index of Covid-19 performance by autumn 2020. In the Canadian province of British Columbia, public health officials created their original models around Covid-19 in March and April 2020 based upon comparison with a worst-case scenario (Italy) and best-case scenario (South Korea). It was seen as a moment of triumph when models no longer had to compare to any scenarios elsewhere, because the case count in British Columbia was so low. Declaring the end of competitive comparisons in modelling implied that British Columbia had outperformed any comparisons, possibly creating a complacency that contributed to an autumn surge of cases (though this was a very small surge compared to the rest of Europe and North America).

The case of British Columbia leads into broader questions about the competitive nature of comparisons. Such implicit and explicit comparison often made little sense on an empirical level. First, countries have classified cases in different ways. China does not count asymptomatic cases in its case count, even though these account for up to forty percent of all cases. Second, the United Kingdom only counts as Covid deaths those that occur within 28 days of a Covid-19 diagnosis. Such a decision would make little sense for many other diseases, such as cancer. It makes even less sense as some studies start to show that some Covid patients are re-admitted into hospital and may pass away after being readmitted. Third, some countries have later revised their statistics, which many speculated were manipulated from the start for political reasons. Russia was the most obvious example, adding hundreds of thousands of cases in late 2020. This indeed seemed a classic case of the suppressive impulse of statistical comparison: Russian officials wanted to highlight the swift development of their vaccine, Sputnik V, and to downplay the terrible conditions in Russian hospitals, rather than appear high in 'league tables' of Covid cases.

In other cases, a denial of international comparison offered a route to hold off the spotlight on poor policies. The rejection of comparisons also became a way of rejecting criticism. Many European governments dismissed New Zealand as an example of the successful suppression of Covid because it is an island nation. But Great Britain is an island too. Governance matters more than geography. In May 2020, as the UK's Covid deaths per capita seemed to be rising above other European countries, the UK government claimed that the country's statistics were not comparable with any other nation. To justify this assertion, politicians pointed to a *Guardian* article by statistician David Spiegelhalter. Yet Spiegelhalter had actually traced the complexities behind comparing international death statistics for technical reasons, including some that I have mentioned above. Spiegelhalter had to plead for the UK government to stop misinterpreting his article and weaponizing his explanations to cover for political errors (Taylor 2020).

Another obvious question of competitive comparison was to whom a nation compared itself. New Zealand has garnered enormous English-language media attention, as has Australia. So too has Taiwan, though sometimes less for its actual policies and preparedness than as a geopolitical anti-China stance. Alex Azar, Health and Human Services Secretary under former President Donald Trump, sought to increase cooperation with Taiwan over health but appeared not to promote any of the Taiwanese policies that had led to such impressive results, whether masks or significant public health institutional capacity. One group has used comparison with Taiwan, New Zealand, and Australia to advocate for a Zero Covid strategy in Canada (Global Canada 2020). Meanwhile, other effective responses have garnered significantly less media and scholarly attention, including Senegal and Uruguay. Suppression strategies that did not involve significantly increasing funding for public health or introducing paid sick leave have garnered far more attention than community-led or equity-driven strategies. Few in Europe or North America looked to Vietnam or Cuba for lessons, perhaps because these were not countries that they expected to manage the crisis effectively. Even non-comparison is politicized in the age of competitive ranking.

A further problem emerged from a focus on national-level statistics that obscured the differential and increasingly inequitable impact of Covid-19. In the United States, for example, policies exacerbated inequalities by failing to improve workplace safety for those who could not work from home such as people in meatpacking plants or Amazon warehouses (Okonkwo et al. 2020). Countries like Germany and provinces like Ontario did not make any effort to collect race-based data. In Toronto, civil society groups filled the gap. Racialized people comprised 79 percent of all Covid-19 cases up to November 30, 2020, although they only make up 52 percent of the city's population. The differences were even starker for some groups. South Asian or Indo-Caribbean residents of Toronto made up 27 percent of all Covid-19 cases, though they comprise just 13 percent of the population. Such data have emerged mainly because doctors and civil society have pushed for collecting more granular data. Only once such patterns emerge can public health act to prevent infection where it is actually spreading. Broad statistics and national comparisons could lead astray from the real problems at hand, which require "equity-driven policy" (Dosani 2021).

Statistical competition between nations has focused many Euro-American politicians on absolute numbers and pushed them towards more blanket measures, such as school closures or lockdowns. As one set of mathematicians and epidemiologists put it: "Focusing on high-level, broad policy decisions as singular causal determinants belies a complexity and heterogeneity of transmission dynamics to be considered if we are to move from 'flattening the curve' to turning it downward" (Baral et al. 2020). Without attention to smaller units of analysis, however, politicians cannot address the underlying structural conditions that facilitate the spread of Covid-19, such as homelessness, multi-generational households with no room for anyone to self-isolate, and precarious work conditions. Rather than one pandemic, as implied by national statistics, Covid-19 is actually "many microepidemics" with highly heterogenous effects that require much more specific interventions wherever possible (Mishra et al. 2020).

Such problems were compounded by data disappearance and the non-collection of certain types of data. The United States government under the Trump administration so abdicated its responsibility to collect basic statistics that *The Atlantic* magazine led a group of citizens to track the number of Covid tests and cases in the Covid-19 Tracking Project (2021). As Samanth Subramanian, one of the writers of a major project on data disappearance in the United States, put it (Huffington Post 2020), "precise, transparent data is crucial in the fight against a pandemic—yet through a combination of ineptness and active manipulation, the government has depleted and corrupted the key statistics that public health officials rely on to protect us." But problems with data collection are not unique to the United States. Many other countries, from Brazil to Tanzania, have seen politicians find ways to deny the state of the pandemic in their nation because they themselves had failed to create the testing infrastructure to understand the pandemic on the ground. Tanzania has not provided statistics on Covid-19 cases since April 2020. The politics behind such data collection long hid those really bearing the burden of the pandemic.

More broadly, these fights over statistics amongst epidemiologists, biostatisticians, journalists, politicians, and much of the public have obscured the qualitative aspects of this crisis. It is striking how few stories we know of the over two million individuals who have died. Even the incoming Biden administration's memorial service on January 19, 2021 featured forty illuminated columns in Washington, DC, each column representing 1,000 of the 400,000 Americans who had died at the time; the service did not mention any person by name nor tell their story. The lack of public mourning is a profound contrast to the many memorials to fallen soldiers, as well as the ritual of returning coffins in the United States. Civilian engagement with and understanding of deaths and violence during war has changed profoundly over time (Dudziak 2018). Perhaps the concealment of Covid-19 deaths dovetails with the now dehumanized drone warfare that has killed so many thousands. But the lack of stories remains a phenomenon to be explained. Some news organizations have filled that gap, including the *Guardian*, which has traced the deaths of over 1,300 healthcare workers in the United States. The Canadian Broadcasting Corporation (CBC) too has sometimes featured stories of those who have passed, often because the family wanted others to know the person's story. In the long run, though, the statistical mode inherited from the League of Nations has rendered other forms of suffering invisible.

Statistics have desensitized, making the pandemic more about a competition over cases than about mourning those who have passed away and finding public health solutions to prevent further cases. As Caroline Chen (Jaffe 2021), a ProPublica reporter put it,

> Sometimes when I'm looking at the charts, I have to remind myself what the numbers mean. It's become so easy after months and months of this to become numb. For example, even though the case count is finally starting to go down in Los Angeles County, and that *is* good news, it's not just a trend line. [...] Each person [...] was somebody's everything. I have to remember that, so I don't ever treat the numbers like just numbers in my reporting.

The absence of stories of suffering individuals further acts to obscure the disproportionate toll of the pandemic on racialized minorities in many European and American nations. Without stories to mobilize action, the statistics seem often to lead politicians away from the most effective solutions, including paid sick leave, rapid testing, and improved workplace safety for essential workers.

Ignoring stories has also had detrimental consequences for those who have suffered from what is currently colloquially called "Long Covid." Long Covid seems to compromise a wide range of symptoms from persistent fever to fatigue to skin issues to myocarditis. Yet, for many months, the individual stories of people who were suffering seemed to spread mainly on social media. The statistical focus on cases and deaths created a narrative binary of death and recovery. This binary elided the long-term effects of Covid-19. One UK doctor, Nisreen A. Alwan, suffered from fatigue and chest pain for months after Covid-19 symptoms (though she was never tested because there were so few tests in March 2020 when she developed symptoms). Like many others, her case was described as "mild," yet she continued to struggle with the post-viral aftermath. Thousands of people took to social media and formed support groups to document confounding, incapacitating, and long-lasting effects. "We are the unrecorded," lamented Alwan in July 2020. She pushed for more precise and nuanced definitions of Covid that do not simply divide between death, hospitalization, and mild cases before assuming a recovery within a few weeks. "Death is not the only thing to count in this pandemic, we must count lives changed," she pleaded (Alwan 2020). Nation competition has effaced a commitment to quality of life and to preventing chronic illness.

Perhaps ironically, many of the countries that have most effectively combatted the pandemic are those that spent least time obsessing over statistics. Instead, leaders spent more time creating rapport with their populations and conveying messages around civic responsibility and solidarity. In summer 2020, I worked with an interdisciplinary team to explore how nine jurisdictions (South Korea, Taiwan, Germany, Canada, Senegal, New Zealand, Norway, Sweden, Denmark) and two Canadian provinces (British Columbia and Ontario) had communicated around Covid-19 (Tworek et al. 2020). Amongst other findings, we point to the importance of values, emotions, and stories alongside scientific facts. We also show the culturally-situated ways of conveying values and emotions that have frequently resulted in much greater compliance with public health guidelines.

Examples were highly contextual and indeed, we pushed back against the idea that our report might pit countries against one another. Instead, we derived principles of effective communications that were implemented quite differently in different jurisdictions. In Taiwan, physical distancing was portrayed as an act of civic love. "The deeper the love," went one key government slogan, "the greater the distance you keep." The Health and Welfare Minister, Chen Shih-chung, has called for journalists and citizens alike to have empathy for other Taiwanese residents. "Have a heart!" Chen often urged the public. In British Columbia, meanwhile, chief medical officer Dr. Bonnie Henry conveyed statistics but has never given specific numbers as a guide for certain actions. Her mottos focused not on specific statistical values (like getting below 50 cases per 100,000 residents, as in Germany), but rather on asking people to work together, use layers of protection, be humble, and not shame those who did not seem to be following the rules. Henry frequently calls for empathy, noting that "we don't know everyone's story... we are all working hard to stay safe" (citations in Tworek et al. 2020).

Finally, vaccine delivery has become a new form of nation ranking and a serious source of competition. Media outlets like Bloomberg have created maps showing how many tens of millions have been vaccinated. Israel became the envy of much of the world for vaccinating its population so quickly, though most reports omitted that Palestinians have yet to benefit. Such fierce competition has consequences: in early January 2021, around 25 vaccines had been administered in low-income countries, while over 25 million people had received at least the first vaccine jab in high-income nations. Tobias Werron and Johannes Nagel's historical examination of "scarcity nationalism" could not be more apt for thinking about debates over vaccine deliveries in Europe and North America. Though writing about US ideologies of economic and naval power in the nineteenth century, so too in the twenty-first century has scarcity discourse become "a discursive mechanism, which links notions of scarcity to the imagining of competition." Rather than global collaboration under the World Health Organization's Covax scheme to deliver vaccines to the most vulnerable around the world, high-income countries compete to vaccinate their entire populations. Nation rankings and competition can cost lives.

Looking at Covid through the dynamics of competition illustrated in this volume can conceptualize our current crisis in new, interdisciplinary ways. While denaturalizing competition shows the strange cruelty of national comparison, other chapters also offer important reflections on who might use competition to frame economic recovery. Dieter Plehwe's chapter examines how "Economic Freedom Indices" created by the Canadian Fraser Institute and American Heritage Foundation became a "neoliberal policy tool." Such efforts and mindsets may shape the recovery to come. Plehwe's work alerts scholars and policymakers to be more critical of the "agenda-setting capacity of neoliberal think tanks."

Competition, particularly in rankings, seems here to stay. But scholars can offer vital interdisciplinary reflections on how and why competition emerged as well as how it affects diverse populations around the world. This volume poses vital questions: who is competing and for what? What discursive power does competition exert and how does that discursive power translate into policy? We might also end by asking: who is left out of competition, and whom does competition harm? These questions are all too real in times of Covid.

References

Alwan, Nisreen A. (2020): "What Exactly is Mild Covid-19?", The BMJ, July 28 (https://blogs.bmj.com/bmj/2020/07/28/nisreen-a-alwan-what-exactl y-is-mild-covid-19/).

Baral, S. D./Mishra, Sharmistha/Diouf, Daouda/Phanuphak, Nittaya/Dowdy, David (2020): "The Public Health Response to COVID-19: Balancing Precaution and Unintended Consequences." In: Annals of Epidemiology 46, pp. 12-13.

Brankovic, Jelena/Ringel, Leopold/Werron, Tobias (2018): "How Rankings Produce Competition: The Case of Global University Rankings." In: Zeitschrift für Soziologie 47/4, pp. 270-288.

Covid-19 Tracking Project (2021): "About Us." The COVID-19 Tracking Project at *The Atlantic* (https://covidtracking.com/about)

Dosani, N. (2021): Naheed Dosani on Twitter, Twitter, January 21 (https://twit ter.com/NaheedD/status/1352342126097551360).

Dudziak, Mary (2018): "'You Didn't See Him Lying ... Beside the Gravel Road in France': Death, Distance, and American War Politics." In: Diplomatic History 42/1, pp. 1-16.

Global Canada (2020): The TANZANC Model and Zero COVID Transmission: A Better Strategy for Canada?, Global Canada Discussion Paper (https://global-canada.org/wp-content/uploads/2020/11/The-Potenti al-For-Getting-to-Zero-in-Canada-Version-2.1.pdf).

Global Health Security Index (2019): Global Health Security Index: Building Collective Action and Accountability, Johns Hopkins University's Bloomberg School of Public Policy, Nuclear Threat Initiative, and the Economist Intelligence Unit (https://www.ghsindex.org/wp-content/upl oads/2020/04/2019-Global-Health-Security-Index.pdf).

Huffington Post (2020): "Data Disappeared," HuffPost Highline, undated (htt ps://highline.huffingtonpost.com/article/disappearing-data).

Jaffe, L. (2021): "'We've Let the Worst Happen': Reflecting on 400,000 Dead," ProPublica, January 23 (https://www.propublica.org/article/weve-let-the-worst-happen-reflecting-on-400-000-dead).

Jerven, M. (2018): "Beyond Precision: Embracing the Politics of Global Health Numbers." In: The Lancet 392/10146, pp. 468-469.

Milanovic, B. (2021): "Beware of Mashup Indexes: How Epidemic Predictors Got It All Wrong," globalinequality, January 22 (http://glineq.blogspot.co m/2021/01/beware-of-mashup-indexes-how-epidemic.html).

Mishra, S./Kwong, Jeffrey C./Chan, Adrienne K./Baral, Stefan D. (2020): "Understanding Heterogeneity to Inform the Public Health Response to COVID-19 in Canada." In: CMAJ 192/25, pp. E684-E685.

Okonkwo N. E./Aguwa U. T./Jang M. et al. (2020): "COVID-19 and the US response: accelerating health inequities." In: BMJ Evidence-Based Medicine, Online first, June 3.

Porter, Theodore M. (1995): Trust in Numbers: the Pursuit of Objectivity in Science and Public Life, Princeton: Princeton University Press.

Speich Chassé, Daniel (2016): "The Roots of the Millennium Development Goals: A Framework for Studying the History of Global Statistics." In: Historical Social Research/Historische Sozialforschung 41/2, pp. 218-237.

Speich Chassé, Daniel (2013): Die Erfindung des Bruttosozialprodukts. Globale Ungleichheit in der Wissensgeschichte der Ökonomie, Göttingen: Vandenhoeck & Ruprecht.

Steinmetz, Willibald (2019): "Introduction: Concepts and Practices of Comparison in Modern History." In: The Force of Comparison: A New Perspective on Modern European History and the Contemporary World, New York: Berghahn Books, 1-33.

Taylor, H. (2020): "Author of Guardian Article on Death Tolls Asks UK Government to Stop Using It," The Guardian, 6 May (https://www.theguardian.com/politics/2020/may/06/author-of-guardian-article-on-death-tolls-asks-government-to-stop-using-it).

Tworek, Heidi J. S. (2019): "Communicable Disease: Information, Health, and Globalization in the Interwar Period." In: The American Historical Review 124/3, pp. 813-842.

Tworek, Heidi J. S./Beacock, I./Ojo, E. (2020): "Democratic Health Communications during Covid-19: A RAPID Response," Centre for the Study of Democratic Institutions, University of British Columbia (https://democracy.arts.ubc.ca/2020/09/14/covid-19/).

Wernimonth, Jacqueline (2019): Numbered Lives: Life and Death in Quantum Media, Cambridge, MA: MIT Press.

Werron, Tobias (2015): "Why Do We Believe in Competition? A Historical-Sociological View of Competition as an Institutionalized Modern Imaginary." In: Distinktion: Journal of Social Theory 16/2, pp. 186-210.

About the Authors

Anatoly Boyashov is a post-doctoral researcher at the Research Training Group "World Politics" at Bielefeld University, Germany. Anatoly received his Ph.D. from Bielefeld University in 2020 (magna cum laude). Before research at Bielefeld University, Anatoly worked at the Center for Sociological and Internet Research in Saint Petersburg where he developed tools for the social network analysis of international organizations. Anatoly's publications cover thematic areas related to human rights, international organizations, the EU integration, and the Eurasian integration processes.

Katja Freistein is a Senior Researcher and Head of a research group Conceptions of World Order and Global Cooperation at the Centre for Global Cooperation Research. Her research is concerned with international organisations, development and global inequalities as well as discourse and narrative analysis. Recently, she co-edited a special issue with Global Society on "Institutionalising Inequalities Organising Global Stratification: How International Organisations (Re)Produce Inequalities in International Society" (with Caroline Fehl). She has published articles in journals such as Third World Quarterly, Journal of International Relations and Development, Journal of Comparative Policy Analysis, Review of International Studies, and Security Studies.

Dr. Didzis Kļaviņš is a Senior Researcher at the University of Latvia, Faculty of Social Sciences and Advanced Social and Political Research Institute (ASPRI). Didzis has obtained a Ph.D. in International Politics at the University of Latvia. He holds the Europaeum's M.A. in European History and Civilisation, jointly offered by Leiden University, Université Paris I—Panthéon-Sorbonne, and the University of Oxford. He has also studied at Uppsala University, the University of Oslo, and the University of Wisconsin-Eau Claire. He is the author and co-author of several publications focusing on changes in diplomacy and foreign policy. His research interests include: the transformation of diplomacy, innovations, artificial intelligence (AI) and diaspora diplomacy.

Yuliya Miadzvetskaya is a researcher at the Centre for IT & IP Law at the University of Leuven (KU Leuven). Prior to this, she worked as an academic assistant at the Department of European Legal Studies at the College of Europe, Bruges, and interned with the Legal Service of the European Parliament in Brussels. She holds an LLM in European Law from the College of Europe. Her research interests include (cyber)security, EU external relations, and EU Neighbourhood Policy.

Thomas Müller is a postdoctoral researcher at Bielefeld University. His research interests centre on hierarchies, the politics of comparison and quantification in world politics. In his PhD thesis, he traced the history of the allocation of special rights and duties to the group of great powers. In the context of the Collaborative Research Centre 1288 "Practices of Comparing", he currently studies the production and political uses of statistics in global security politics as well as the evolution of narratives about the changing international distribution of power. His most recent articles have been published in the Review of International Studies, in Global Society and in the European Journal of International Security..

Madeleine Myatt is a research fellow for cybersecurity and cyber norms in the DGAP's Technology & Global Affairs Program. As a member of the RTG "World Politics", she is pursuing her PhD on cybersecurity and public private partnerships and has worked as a research associate and lecturer for public policy & political sociology at Bielefeld University from 2016-2020. She has been involved in research projects on cyber diplomacy, right wing populism and digitalization; published and conducted research on cybersecurity strategies, cybersecurity cultures, public private partnerships, cyber intelligence, and hybrid warfare. She serves as academic expert at the European Centre of Excellence for Countering Hybrid Threats since November 2019.

Johannes Nagel is a doctoral researcher in History, currently associated with the Research Training Group 2225 "World Politics" and the Collaborative Research Center 1288 "Practices of Comparing" at Bielefeld University. His current interests are U.S. politics, global military history and the international relations of the long nineteenth century.

Dieter Plehwe is a senior fellow at the Center for Civil Society Research of the Berlin Social Science Research Center and lecturer at the University of Kassel, Department of Political Science. His research interests are in the field of transformation and varieties of capitalism, regional integration in North America and Western Europe, neoliberalism studies and policy related expertise, think tanks and lobbying. He is a general editor of Critical Policy Studies. He recently co-edited Market Civilizations (Zone Books 2021), The changing politics and policy of austerity (Policy Press 2021), Nine Lives of Neoliberalism (Verso 2020), and Liberalism and the Welfare State (Oxford University Press2017).

Daniela Russ is a postdoctoral researcher at the University of Toronto and the University of Guelph, Canada. Trained as a historical sociologist in Berlin, New York, and Bielefeld, she is currently working on her first book, *Working Nature: Steam, Power, and the Making of the Energy Economy (1830-1980)*. Her research interests lie in historical epistemology, energy history, and the critical theory of nature.

James Stafford is a postdoctoral researcher at the Research Training Group "World Politics" at Bielefeld University. A historian of Ireland, Britain and Europe since 1750, his first book, *The Case of Ireland: Commerce, Empire and the European Order 1776-1848*, is forthcoming with Cambridge University Press. He completed his PhD in History at Cambridge University in 2016, and worked as a Lecturer in Modern History at St. Hugh's College, Oxford, before coming to Bielefeld in 2017.

Thomas Turnbull is a research scholar at the Max Planck Institute for the History of Science, Berlin. Trained as an historian and geographer, his current research interests have been oriented toward the history of energy, the history of geographic thought, river history, and histories of and histories in the Anthropocene. Most recently, in 2019, he was involved in an interdisciplinary research project which took the Mississippi watershed as its object of inquiry, during which he explored the use of canoeing as an energy historical research method. He is currently collaborating with Daniela Russ in the collation and editing of a compendium of energy historical texts with a global and culturally thick purview.

Dr. Heidi Tworek is Associate Professor of International History and Public Policy at the University of British Columbia, Vancouver. She is the author and co-editor of three books, including the multi-award-winning News from Germany: The Competition to Control World Communication, 1900-1945 (Harvard University Press, 2019). She has published over 30 book chapters and journal articles on media history, the history of capitalism, infrastructure, and digital policy. One of her current projects examines the history and policy of health communications.

Tobias Werron is a professor of sociological theory at the Faculty of Sociology at Bielefeld University. His main empirical research interests focus on competition, nationalism and globalization from a historical-sociological perspective. He is currently pursuing interdisciplinary collaboration on practices of theorizing in the humanities and social sciences and is conducting a research project on the history of rankings (together with Leopold Ringel). He is a board member of the Institute of World Society Studies (IW) and deputy speaker of the RTG World Politics.

Ramy Youssef is a fellow at Utrecht University and holds a research grant funded by the German Research Foundation (DFG). He studied political science at the University of Vienna, was a research assistant at the Bielefeld Graduate School in History and Sociology (BGHS) and at the Chair of Macrosociology at the University of Konstanz, where he completed his doctorate in sociology in 2019. His research interests include social theory, historical sociology, sociology of knowledge and political sociology with a focus on world politics and diplomacy.

Social Sciences

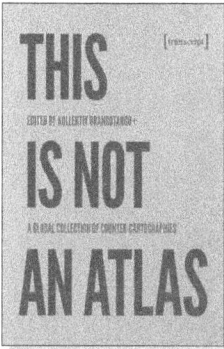

kollektiv orangotango+ (ed.)
This Is Not an Atlas
A Global Collection of Counter-Cartographies

2018, 352 p., hardcover, col. ill.
34,99 € (DE), 978-3-8376-4519-4
E-Book: free available, ISBN 978-3-8394-4519-8

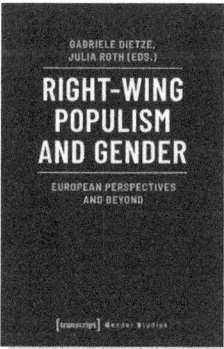

Gabriele Dietze, Julia Roth (eds.)
Right-Wing Populism and Gender
European Perspectives and Beyond

April 2020, 286 p., pb., ill.
35,00 € (DE), 978-3-8376-4980-2
E-Book: 34,99 € (DE), ISBN 978-3-8394-4980-6

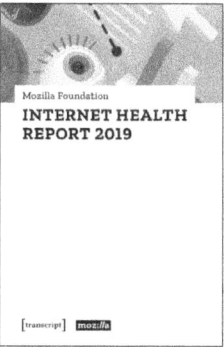

Mozilla Foundation
Internet Health Report 2019
2019, 118 p., pb., ill.
19,99 € (DE), 978-3-8376-4946-8
E-Book: free available, ISBN 978-3-8394-4946-2

**All print, e-book and open access versions of the titles in our list
are available in our online shop www.transcript-publishing.com**

Social Sciences

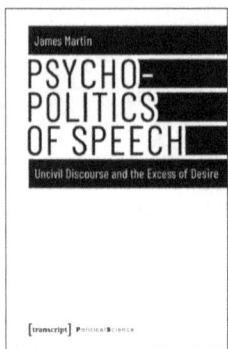

James Martin
Psychopolitics of Speech
Uncivil Discourse and the Excess of Desire

2019, 186 p., hardcover
79,99 € (DE), 978-3-8376-3919-3
E-Book:
PDF: 79,99 € (DE), ISBN 978-3-8394-3919-7

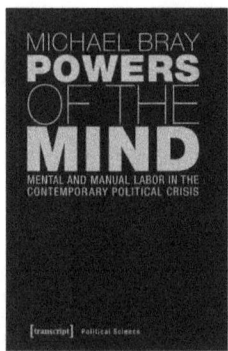

Michael Bray
Powers of the Mind
Mental and Manual Labor
in the Contemporary Political Crisis

2019, 208 p., hardcover
99,99 € (DE), 978-3-8376-4147-9
E-Book:
PDF: 99,99 € (DE), ISBN 978-3-8394-4147-3

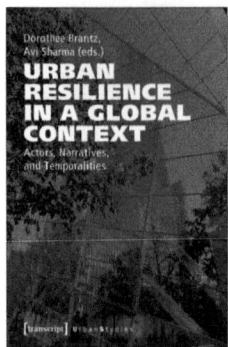

Dorothee Brantz, Avi Sharma (eds.)
Urban Resilience in a Global Context
Actors, Narratives, and Temporalities

October 2020, 224 p., pb.
30,00 € (DE), 978-3-8376-5018-1
E-Book: available as free open access publication
PDF: ISBN 978-3-8394-5018-5

**All print, e-book and open access versions of the titles in our list
are available in our online shop www.transcript-publishing.com**